Policies, Practices, and Protocols for International Commercial Arbitration

Basheer Ahmed Mohammed Khan
Supreme Court of India Bar Association, India

Kaushal Kishore
Supreme Court of India Bar Association, New Delhi, India

A volume in the Advances in Public Policy and Administration (APPA) Book Series

IGI Global
PUBLISHER of TIMELY KNOWLEDGE

Published in the United States of America by
IGI Global
Information Science Reference (an imprint of IGI Global)
701 E. Chocolate Avenue
Hershey PA, USA 17033
Tel: 717-533-8845
Fax: 717-533-8661
E-mail: cust@igi-global.com
Web site: http://www.igi-global.com

Library of Congress Cataloging-in-Publication Data

Names: Khan, M. Basheer Ahmed, author. | Kishore, Kaushal, author.
Title: Policies, practices, and protocols for international commercial arbitration / Mohammed Basheer Ahmed Khan and Kaushal Kishore.
Description: Hershey : Information Science Reference, 2023. | Includes bibliographical references and index. | Summary: "The policies, practices and protocols for International Commercial Arbitration have evolved into the current stage to fine tune the process of delivery of justice while the parties in dispute who have agreed to arbitrate using their own terms of contract and accepted procedures of arbitration in the context of the laws of the different countries where the commercial activities and the resultant contracts have been entered into. In this preface, an attempt has been made to discuss the various situations of international commercial arbitration culling out contexts from time immemorial to the current policies, practices, and protocols in the different regions of the world. It provides a brief description of the issues dealt with in this book through the various chapters"-- Provided by publisher.
Identifiers: LCCN 2023021797 (print) | LCCN 2023021798 (ebook) | ISBN 9781668440407 (hardcover) | ISBN 9781668440414 (paperback) | ISBN 9781668440421 (ebook)
Subjects: LCSH: International commercial arbitration. | Arbitration and award.
Classification: LCC K2400 .K43 2023 (print) | LCC K2400 (ebook) | DDC 341.5/22--dc23/eng/20230724
LC record available at https://lccn.loc.gov/2023021797
LC ebook record available at https://lccn.loc.gov/2023021798

British Cataloguing in Publication Data
A Cataloguing in Publication record for this book is available from the British Library.

All work contributed to this book is new, previously-unpublished material.
The views expressed in this book are those of the authors, but not necessarily of the publisher.

For electronic access to this publication, please contact: eresources@igi-global.com.

Advances in Public Policy and Administration (APPA) Book Series

ISSN:2475-6644
EISSN:2475-6652

MISSION

Proper management of the public sphere is necessary in order to maintain order in modern society. Research developments in the field of public policy and administration can assist in uncovering the latest tools, practices, and methodologies for governing societies around the world.

The **Advances in Public Policy and Administration (APPA) Book Series** aims to publish scholarly publications focused on topics pertaining to the governance of the public domain. APPA's focus on timely topics relating to government, public funding, politics, public safety, policy, and law enforcement is particularly relevant to academicians, government officials, and upper-level students seeking the most up-to-date research in their field.

COVERAGE

- Government
- Law Enforcement
- Political Economy
- Politics
- Public Administration
- Public Funding
- Public Policy
- Resource allocation
- Urban Planning

IGI Global is currently accepting manuscripts for publication within this series. To submit a proposal for a volume in this series, please contact our Acquisition Editors at Acquisitions@igi-global.com or visit: http://www.igi-global.com/publish/.

The Advances in Public Policy and Administration (APPA) Book Series (ISSN 2475-6644) is published by IGI Global, 701 E. Chocolate Avenue, Hershey, PA 17033-1240, USA, www.igi-global.com. This series is composed of titles available for purchase individually; each title is edited to be contextually exclusive from any other title within the series. For pricing and ordering information please visit http://www.igi-global.com/book-series/advances-public-policy-administration/97862. Postmaster: Send all address changes to above address.

Titles in this Series

For a list of additional titles in this series, please visit: http://www.igi-global.com/book-series/

Governmental Power Market-Ing in the VU-CHAOS World
Kittisak Jermsittiparsert (University of City Island, Cyprus) Srirath Gohwong (Universitas Muhammadiyah Sidenreng Rappang, Indonesia) Shayut Pavapanunkul (Universitas Muhammadiyah Sidenreng Rappang, Indonesia) and Nasaran Mahittichatkul (Universitas Muhammadiyah Sidenreng Rappang, Indonesia)
Information Science Reference • © 2023 • 296pp • H/C (ISBN: 9781668472804) • US $205.00

Financial Evaluation and Risk Management of Infrastructure Projects
Kleopatra Petroutsatou (Aristotle University of Thessaloniki, Greece) and Constantin Zopounidis (Technical University of Crete, Greece & Audencia Business School, Greece)
Information Science Reference • © 2023 • 300pp • H/C (ISBN: 9781668477861) • US $225.00

Historical and Political Analysis on Power Balances and Deglobalization
Emily Brynn Stacey (Rose State College, USA)
Information Science Reference • © 2023 • 253pp • H/C (ISBN: 9781668456330) • US $205.00

Juvenile Justice in African and Western Criminal Justice Systems
Simeon Peter Sungi (United States International University-Africa, Kenya) George Rugaimukamu Kakoti (Tennessee State University, USA) and Deneil D. Christian (Tennessee State University, USA)
Information Science Reference • © 2024 • 300pp • H/C (ISBN: 9781668493434) • US $215.00

Public Policy's Role in Achieving Sustainable Development Goals
Mahani Hamdan (Universiti Brunei Darussalam, Brunei) Muhammad Anshari (Universiti Brunei Darussalam, Brunei) Norainie Ahmad (Universiti Brunei Darussalam, Brunei) and Emil Ali (Universiti Brunei Darussalam, Brunei)
Information Science Reference • © 2023 • 370pp • H/C (ISBN: 9781668489031) • US $235.00

IGI Global
PUBLISHER of TIMELY KNOWLEDGE

701 East Chocolate Avenue, Hershey, PA 17033, USA
Tel: 717-533-8845 x100 • Fax: 717-533-8661
E-Mail: cust@igi-global.com • www.igi-global.com

Table of Contents

Detailed Table of Contents

In this chapter, the authors attempt to define the concepts of international commercial arbitration and alternative dispute resolutions precisely. International commercial arbitration is introduced briefly, along with the developing tendencies in alternative dispute resolution, the many international centers for commercial arbitration, and the many international enforcement issues that arise from these. In the context of Indian law, the Arbitration and Conciliation Act, 1996 (the Indian Act) defines international commercial arbitration as an arbitration involving a commercial relationship where one or both of the parties is a non-Indian citizen, non-resident, or non-Indian business entity. Questions about how the arbitration itself will go down are raised. Blackstone, a leading legal authority, makes it abundantly clear that arbitration refers to the decisions of one or more persons, with or without an umpire, on a specific matter in difference between the parties.

A number of factors are of critical importance in international commercial arbitration. The purpose of this chapter is to provide a narrative of the key terms used in commercial arbitration, a discussion of the different types of arbitration, and a brief description of international arbitration laws, as well as to emphasize the value of alternative dispute resolution and to define the concept and nature of the arbitration. International commercial arbitration has many facets, and reading about these problems can help gain deep insights into them. In terms of discussions, mediations, collaborative laws, and arbitration, alternative dispute resolution (ADR), sometimes known as external dispute resolution (EDR), is categorized into different forms. Laws governing the resolution of legal disputes fall under the purview of common law in some jurisdictions, such as the United Kingdom. The customs and practices of various nations give rise to distinct alternatives for resolving legal disputes.

The arbitration agreement must be paid extra care to carefully craft and draft to avoid future litigation of any kind. Several countries' laws and the United Nations CITRAL have given several provisions which need to be incorporated into the contractual arbitration agreement for it to be legally sound and executable, reflecting the evolution of arbitration as an alternative dispute redressal mechanism. Because of this, there are many facets of arbitration agreements that need to be discussed at length. These include the significance of arbitration agreements, the forms of arbitration agreements, their definitions, validity, foreign arbitration agreements to be executed in a domestic environment, the jurisdiction of the arbitral tribunal, the doctrine of Kompetenz-kompetenz, and international commercial arbitration agreements. The goal is to give readers the knowledge they need on these specific issues.

The United Nations (UN) is the organization in charge of overseeing international commercial arbitration and the organization that drafted the international trade laws (ITL). Because of the varied nature of national laws pertaining to international commercial arbitration, the United Nations has developed its own model laws to serve as a guide for the creation of nationally consistent laws governing international trade and commercial arbitration. Arbitration and agreement, definition and form of the arbitration agreement, substantive claim before the court, the arbitration agreement and interim measures by the court, number of arbitrators, and finality of an arbitration award are all topics that have been covered by the model laws. A brief analysis of the mandatory model law is presented hereunder.

There are a number of important aspects that must be met before the award can be considered final, including the following: jurisdiction of the arbitral award; the tribunal's independence and impartiality; the arbitral process; the autonomy of the parties and the arbitral award; grounds for setting aside the arbitral award; recognition and enforcement of foreign arbitral awards. The arbitration awards will need to be enforced because of the various articles of the UNCITRAL arbitration award and similar other laws of the countries. Even if the award is legally binding, the disputing parties can still take their case to court in the country where the relevant parts of the award were issued. The arbitral tribunal, for example, does not have any inherent jurisdiction. The arbitration agreement serves as the basis for the tribunal's authority. This chapter will attempt to cover the topic of such enforceability issues.

The legal framework for international arbitration agreements is established. Issues arising from any dispute will be examined within a legal framework, even though the arbitral awards are enshrined within the legally enforceable contracts of the parties. When comparing arbitration as an ADR method to other modes, the advantages and disadvantages of the resulting arbitration agreements are readily apparent. However, there are necessary conditions for the end result to be justifiable. Procedural laws play a significant role in ensuring this as well. For instance, the New York Convention and the established national arbitration statutes which apply in the case of individual countries specify and define the matters relating to the agreements, such as what constitutes an international commercial agreement by looking at each of the specific terms like "arbitration agreement," "international," "commercial," "disputes," "differences," etc. This chapter aims to discuss these terms contextually.

According to the rules of the arbitration court, any agreement, submission, or reference made or evidenced in writing with a duly signed or unsigned document shall be deemed to have been agreed in by the parties. The parties agree that the arbitration court's rules must also be taken into account. More in-depth discussions are required to shed light on such topics as the legal framework for international arbitral awards, the form and contents of international arbitral awards, the correction, interpretation, and supplementation of international arbitral awards, the annulment of international arbitral awards, the recognition and enforcement of international arbitral awards, and the application of preclusion, Lis Pendis, and Stare Decisis in international arbitration awards. The purpose of this chapter is to present these within the legal framework of specific arbitral courts, most notably the London Court of International Arbitration.

Arbitration is confidential in nature. The parties to a dispute must agree to keep the matter under wraps at all times. It should be noted that the UNCITRAL model law does not include a provision guaranteeing confidentiality in international commercial arbitration, which is a major reason why this is not guaranteed legally in many countries. However, countries like Scotland, New Zealand, Peru, and Australia have strict regulations governing the privacy of their citizens' personal information. The exact situation is unique in each country. Even though there is no express provision for confidentiality in UK statutes, case law has evolved to protect such information. As a result, it's important to examine and discuss the circumstances in various nations. This chapter will make an effort to shed light on the confidentiality clause per se, as well as the confidentiality of international arbitration.

Although the policies, practices, procedures, and protocols governing international commercial arbitration can vary from one country to the other, they all share a common goal: to facilitate the peaceful resolution of disputes between disputing parties without the need for drawn-out, expensive litigation. But policies shift, practices vary, and protocol requirements differ across nations. An effort to provide comprehensible discussions of these in a variety of national contexts is made in this chapter.

Various arbitration treaties have been established amongst different countries. Reading the arbitration agreements will help one to understand the importance given to different factors during the implementation of arbitration procedures. Some sample contracts from the Netherlands, the United Kingdom, Singapore, Hong Kong, the United States of America, India, and Japan have been briefly analyzed in general in this chapter. Furthermore, some attempts at making comparisons are made, with the resulting insights being highlighted.

The world of business has become small, interconnected, and driven by a desire for growth and profits. In all parts of the world, human desires and consumer appetites are demanding that the economy produce, distribute, and sell. The net result has been a rapid increase in commercial transactions: more negotiations, more contracts, more business obligations and, consequently, more disputes to be resolved. Most business disagreements, domestic or transnational, are resolved over the phone. Sometimes, a face-to-face meeting may be required; but negotiations are the main method of dispute resolution. Some intractable controversies survive. Whatever such methods may be called conciliation, mediation, med/arb, mini-trial, etc., they have created a new terminology for advocates and neutrals. From the foregoing discussions on identified issues, a concluding chapter attempts to provide the future of international commercial arbitration, the lessons from experiences, challenges to address and the summary and inferences.

Preface

BACKGROUND

Trade and Commerce are the salt of the earth. From time immemorial, human activities were centered on the exchange of goods and services among themselves so much so that one acquired the skills needed to produce tangible goods and intangible services to be exchanged with another for meeting with the requirements of life in the given context. Mostly, such exchanges used to be peaceful, adjustable and mutually satisfying and agreeable. But, in certain situations differences and disputes arose that made the entire deals obnoxious and destructive. In the early human life, there were only two ways of settlement of differences – one through muscle power and domination over the other and the second through the alternate dispute redressal involving mediation, negotiation, conciliation and arbitration. Most disputes used to be settled through one of these and where it failed, such disputes ended up with physical clashes and destruction for the conflicting parties. Mostly, in traditional societies, the disputes involved groups and communities, rather than individuals. Therefore, the traditional disputes resolution process normally adopted a communal approach unlike the individualistic approaches is in the western conceptualization. The emphasis was on reconciliation and reintegration of the disputing parties in the communities to which they belonged.

EVOLUTION OF ARBITRATION GLOBALLY

Globally, in a region-wise perusal of the emergence of conflicts and their settlement, a starting can be made with the study of the African region where the human settlements have taken place originally and the human movements have followed to other regions eventually. Observing from that angle, the major causes of conflict in the whole African continent can be seen, for instance, as about the ownership of land or personal relationships issues, properties of the families, honor, murder or poisoning and the fall outs from marriage relationships. Such conflicts were resolved after invoking the principles of equity and justice as practiced by the communities based on their customs and traditions. Thus, the jurisprudence of equity and justice as perceived in the societies were upheld. So, the role of peaceful settlement through negotiations and conciliations could be observed widely in the social systems of the African regions.

Arbitration in Asiatic Societies

In Asiatic societies, the geographical extant of China is wide and important. According to Neil J. Diamant, conflicts in China and other Asian nations are resolved through mediation rather than adjudication or appeals to political institutions. Archival sources in China and interviews with urban and rural officials exhibit that the preference for mediation in China and other Asian and even Western societies is largely correlated with region, class, and gender. So, it does not constitute a national pattern. Historical (19th century and Maoist China) and more contemporary materials show that mediation--to the extent that it was actually performed at the grassroots level--was but one method of resolving problems in China. There were other methods also which included "interpersonal violence, collective action, and even feigned suicide". It can be observed that a "disaggregated perspective on conflict resolution is a more accurate representation of China as it deepens market reforms and a more powerful way to predict China's capacity to manage the conflicts that follow such reforms" (Neil J. Diamant, 2000). Thus, it can be seen that in Asian countries, especially in China, the conflicts were sorted out through mediation over centuries. Adjudication or appeals to higher ups in the political institutions were few and far between. The Chinese have also used such methods like "Combining with personal goal pursuing". The important Chinese conflict resolution styles can be identified as "confrontation, severance, endurance, obey publicly/defy privately, and compromise".

Ancient Indian practices are equally important to observe, both in the past and the present. "Conflict resolution is predominantly an art whether it is in personal life or in a corporate setting. Ancient Indian texts have prescribed four step formulas to resolve any conflict. Each step to be applied consequently only when previous step fails" (Jwala Vedantam, 2015). These 4 steps can be detailed as below:

1. Sama (or Sowmya) (Polite Persuasion): Foremost attempt will be to explain in very polite way to persuade the disputants to settle on their own..
2. Bheda (or Differentiation): Second step is to differentiate the right and the wrong and elucidate the impact of continuing the disputes without any settlement.
3. Dana or Dam) (or remunerate): Where polite persuasion fails to find a solution, it is suggested to extend some pecuniary remunerations to arrive at resolution.
4. Danda (or Punishment): Painful punishment can also be considered for establishing justice if the other three methods do not help.

However, the same author writes as follows: "I have noticed at times during stressful situations I tend to skip step 1 (*Sama* -Persuasion) to 3 (*Dana* -Benefits) and end up with more stress for me and/or both parties end-up with emotional bruises. Most of the times when I am able to start from step 1 (*Sama* -Persuasion), issues are resolved within first 2 steps. I need to put into practice my personal patience and perseverance to be able to apply these steps in that given order." (Jwala Vedantam, 2015).

Different dispute resolution methods exist which are thousands of years old, dating from Confucian principles of promoting harmony and community, rather than individual, "justice,". The ancient civilization of China and then later other Asian countries, or African community, dispute resolution processes called "moots" (or in some countries *Ubuntu* or *gacaca),* which are mediation like processes in which community elders were involved. The elders listen to narratives of the dispute from the parties and either help negotiate a solution with the parties, or, more like arbitration, decide or command some remedy, with the goal of preserving community peace. These older forms of dispute resolution aimed at preventing future conflict and "escalation of the dispute beyond the parties, to restore the community to peaceful existence" (*Carrie Menkel-Meadow,2016).* Similar to this is the village panchayat of India, where Five Elders of the village sit and arbitrate or solve disputes. The practice of the good old days continues even today in many places in the rural villages in India. There are "Gram Nyayalayas" and "Khap Panchayat". They do use arbitration methods occasionally. The justice system which is outside the Indian constitution, however, is illegal.

Illegal justice system existed elsewhere in the world also. Continental Europe and in England of the west, during the middle ages saw the movement from "*trial by ordeal*" (putting disputing parties on a horse to joust, or dropping them into a fire or body of water to see if God would "protect" them and declare the innocent or non-wrongdoer) to *trial by evidence*. These were unscientific and superstitious ways of gathering evidence to prove the arguments in the disputes. The development of formal rules of evidence was designed to use rational forms of proof and judgment by "peers" (juries) about what had happened to cause the dispute. "Modern" justice "meant that judges or juries declared winners and losers (in both civil and criminal cases) so that the guilty would be punished or pay damages and the innocent would be vindicated by using the same rules of procedure and substantive rules of law to everyone ("equal justice under law")(Carrie Menkel-Meadow,2016). Similar practices of using the divine delivery of justice existed in very many other societies and communities in different parts of the world.

"Individual" justice, which in the late 20th century, caused many court systems to become very crowded (in countries like the US and Italy it could take as much as 5-10 years to get a hearing), and once there, the court and formal trial process became quite expensive, requiring the hiring of lawyers and other professionals (experts) and the paying of high fees (Carrie Menkel-Meadow,2016).

Arbitration in African Societies

In Africa, the dispute redressal mechanism in the context of a discussion on arbitration or any other quasi-judicial mechanism of dispute resolution has become more pertinent. African societies traditionally itself had institutional mechanisms as well as cultural sources to uphold the values of peace, tolerance, solidarity and respect for, and of, one another. These structures were responsible for "peace education, confidence-building, peacemaking, peace building, conflict monitoring, conflict prevention, conflict management, and conflict resolution" (Ayittey, George,2014). These mechanisms were effective in handling and managing conflicts among the people, because they reflected the socio-political orientation of the African people, addressing all the social, political and economic conflicts among a people who lived a communal way of life. It was customary as well as common practice for the people sitting down informally to discuss and agree on important issues. The traditional African system of government was inclusive and very transparent and open, where all people could participate in the decision-making process. While the West practiced majoritarian, or representative democracy Africans practiced participatory democracy, where decisions were taken by consensus at village meetings, "variously called *asetena kese* by the Ashanti, *ama-ala* by the Igbo, *guurti* by the Somali, *dare* by the Shona, *ndaba* by the Zulu or *kgotla* by the Tswana" (Ayittey, George, 2014).

"African traditional mechanisms of conflict prevention, management and resolution were largely effective and respected, and their decisions were binding on all parties, mainly because "the identity of an individual is linked to that of his or her family and these families are formed by the acceptance of marriage alliances" (Ademowo, Johnson (2015). Family was the most important agency in the conflict management process and the role of the chiefs, elders, family heads and others, to anticipate and resolve conflicts was considered most crucial. This is similar to some of the Asiatic countries and cultures also.

The major sources of conflict in Africa, as in some other Asiatic countries were land, chieftaincy, personal relationship issues, family property, honor, murder or poisoning, and matrimonial fall-outs. In resolving these kinds of conflicts, the principles of equity and justice, which is entrenched in African customs and traditions, were upheld. An example of Cameroon can be highlighted in this context to know how the African system operationalized in dispute resolution without formal judicial system by using the traditional indigenous systems. It is interesting to note that such concepts of equity and justice existed in all evolved human societies which were considered as essential part of social life. Nonetheless, the sources of conflict as observed in Africa in the yonder years can be observed as existing in the modern days too even in some of the advanced societies.

Another important example of the early arbitration mechanism was that of the Kom society. The Kom society of Cameroon in Africa had its own methods of dispute resolution. The traditional institutions, sites and objects have "a quasi-religious role" in the arbitration, mediation, conciliation and re-conciliation of conflicts at a micro and macro level in Kom society of Cameroon. The geographical location of Kom, its social and political history and cultural backgrounds are considered important in the dispute resolution of those societies.

Africa has several other traditional groups also. Kwifoyn was one such traditional group which had some specific characteristics. Kwifoyin was a very highly secretive and hierarchically organized traditional group. Membership of the inner circles of this group is closely limited. The society had an authority of impersonal kind, and the agencies of the authorities was not made accountable for the people. Thus, there was a schism between the authority and citizens. The pre-colonial African societies considered crime as an act that offended the authorities. The collective consciousness was not for accepting crime. Therefore, crime was considered an afront to the supernatural divine power. Divine power was mostly invoked to address the resolution of conflicts. The collective consciousness of the society was enshrined in the laws of public and private crimes of the African traditional groups. Another group was an all-male membership open to the whole clan. It was known as the Ntul Shrine. The Ntul shrine was the center of reconciliation, mediation and appeasement. It also offered a forum for arbitration. If ever one threatened the life of a neighbor or wounded, the conflicting two will be brought to the *Ntul* shrine, where the first attempt will be reconciliation. Moral and legal sanctions will be meted out as well, and the wounded party will be treated with medicines from the *Ntul* shrine. These can be compared to the modern-day arbitration procedures where confidentiality is woven into the arbitral procedures. The similarity between the most modern practices and the ancient practices in some of the societies as in the African region need to be underlined to gather insights into the evolutionary nature of this alternate dispute redressal system.

Another secret African society of men was the Chong Society and is a powerful organization at the village level. An individual may be authorized by the Fon to be in a Chong society. This society is empowered by *kwifoyn* to resolve conflicts and assist in the promotion of peace and harmony in the villages. It is thus tasked with tracking down and denouncing wrongdoers, whom it can reprimand and bring to justice, should they persist in wrong-doing. Commonly described by the Kom people as the embodiment of "power" or "authority", is a society of prestigious richer men, who are meant to maintain peace or disassociate themselves from all violence. The fundamental role of *Chong*, therefore, is the maintenance of peace in the community. It also played very ceremonial role and has been considered in the social sphere as a "high-life" or nobility of the elders. There also existed women's traditional societies, with *fimbuen* and *afaf* standing out as the parallel of the men's secret societies at the village level, performing similar roles in conflict resolution, and so constituting a women's council. While the main role of such councils is organizing bereavement, they also act as the representatives of women against injustices done to them. "A major criterion to belong is age, in addition to proof of having given birth, and a fee. Membership seats are distributed in the house according to established protocol, similar to a typical *Chong* house. *Anlu*, the women's cooperative evolved into an instrument of redress – a kind of female police force – with the women protecting womenfolk and equally punishing female crime, especially crime that bordered on the immoral" (The Kom Heritage Foundation, 2014). It is asserted that whoever puts into jeopardy the concrete realization of the common objectives or the achievement of the *bonum commune* creates a situation of conflict and becomes the enemy or the less friendly partner (Nkwi, Paul, 1987) This lends credence to the idea that in conflict resolution, the principles of equity and justice, which are entrenched in African customs and traditions, are upheld. In fact, in Kom traditional society, there is no award for winning an argument. As such, the end result of conflict resolution is to accommodate all parties involved in the conflict, through genuine collaboration by all, in the search for effective compromise. In doing so, unnecessary competition is avoided, because the ultimate aim of conflict resolution is amicable settlement by persuasion, mediation, adjudication, reconciliation, arbitration and negotiation, not necessarily reverting to the use of force or coercion at all cost, or at any cost. It can be specially noted that in a typical Kom traditional society, socialization is an important factor in conflict resolution. "Kom children are raised to consider that a quarrel or a fight with others is a quarrel or a fight between blood relations, and so it becomes imperative to avoid injury and harm, as well as avoiding situations of always trying to win at all cost. In Kom, this is a way of life, which is transmitted through myths, the use of proverbs, folktales, songs and idioms to children at a tender age, so that they may grow seeing human existence as unified and integrated" (Nkwi, Paul, 1987). It can also be observed that to inculcate this way of life, especially in a bid to establish truth, guilt and to discourage dishonest attitudes and evil actions, it was common practice in Kom traditional society to prevent, manage and resolve conflict through oath-taking, mostly at the shrine of a powerful deity, over an instrument that acted as a medium for contacting the deity. To avoid shame or even death, the consequences of oath-taking on falsehoods were made widely known. Therefore, the end of justice is already built in the social fabric through appropriate beliefs, practices and actions. It is interesting to find that to promote the virtues of peace, solidarity, harmonious living, respect for others and honesty, Kom traditional society instituted the celebration of festivals, during which these values were extolled in song. "Rituals and sacrifices were performed to the village deities and ancestors for peace, protection, good work, fertility, and so on. This culture of communal life created an ideal environment for conflict resolution, because it was also an opportunity for a mutual exchange of privileges, goods, favours and obligations, among others. Reciprocity equally fostered peaceful coexistence and, consequently, eliminated the likelihood of conflict and wars. Sanctions were imposed on families and individuals who contravened Kom customs and traditions. This was mainly to prevent stealing, willful murder, incest, abuse of elders, willful damage to property, lying, bearing false witness, poisoning and rape. It was also largely believed that deities could inflict sanctions through accidents, sickness, death, famine, poverty, misery, barrenness and loss of children, in addition to societal exile, ostracism, fines, compensation, restitution and the rendering of apology" (Nkwi, Paul, 1987).

Arbitration in Middle Eastern Societies

The early middle east civilizations like the Babylonian and Sumerian Civilizations also had their conflict resolutions in peaceful methods which are recorded from very early period itself. It is stated that "dispute resolution has been around for a very long time, certainly well before 'Time Immemorial". Solomon is said to have been the King of Israel during the tenth century BC. The famous judgment of Solomon, which shows the application of arbitration-mediation in ancient Israel can be easily reminded. "Two women came before the King, each claiming to be mother of the same baby. Solomon called for his sword and proposed to divide the infant in two and give half to each woman. The first woman, perhaps curiously, given the potentially gory consequences, agreed with the arbitrator's solution. But the second woman pleaded for the King not to kill the child and agreed instead to give up the baby to the first woman. Solomon then demonstrated his wisdom by determining that the second woman must be the child's true mother and awarded custody to her. Arbitration and mediation in ancient Greece can be traced back to the eighth century BC. Homer's epic poem, The Iliad, which tells the story of the Trojan War, contains the earliest substantial source of evidence of mediation and arbitration. King Agamemnon, the brother of Menelaus, King of Sparta, gathered the forces of Greece to rescue Menelaus' wife Helen, who had been carried off to Troy by Paris. In Book I, Homer records a dispute between Agamemnon, the commander of the Greeks, and the warrior Achilles over the return of the war-prize Chrysies to her father so as to appease Apollo and end the pestilence that had befallen"(The Winnie Whittaker Memorial Lecture, 2009).

Further, a perusal of the anthropological and sociological studies will throw ideas about how early humans may have resolved disputes without the use of fists, clubs, or spear-arrows. "Many of the following ways are quite different from the modern techniques of dispute resolution. Nevertheless, these modern techniques have come into existence because of these primitive ways. Hawaiian Highlanders of Polynesian ancestry used their own traditional system for an amicable resolution of disputes. It involved a family's coming together to discuss interpersonal problems under the guidance of a leader. The leader of the session is a person both sides revere and therefore, leads the session and has the role of a mediator.(Astha Dhawan, 2015). After hearing out both sides and attempting to get at the crux of the matter, the leader works to bring out a solution. China embraced Mediation quite early because of its conservative opinions about the resolution of disputes, which have originated from Confucian ethics. Confucius told that harmony should not be disrupted and adversarial proceedings were the antithesis of harmony. Given the emphasis on harmony, Chinese mediators have played quite a far-reaching role. Chinese mediators do more than solving and settling disputes, they also guide the parties on how to have a more harmonious relationship in the future. In the Western world, the story of ADR can be traced back to the ancient Greeks. One famous story of arbitration comes down through mythology. The procedure of arbitration set up by the Greeks was surprisingly formal. A lottery was used to choose an arbitrator for a given case. His foremost duty was to attempt to have an amicable settlement between the parties. If this didn't work out, then witnesses would be called and evidence was submitted in writing by the parties. Having said that, the parties often adopted various stratagems to postpone rulings or challenge the decision of the arbitrator. "An appeal would be brought before the Arbitrators, who would further refer the matter to the courts. In such an appeal, Demosthenes had once alleged that one Midias had used discourteous language towards Demosthenes. This outcome may seem like a setback at a very early age but also be seen as a self-policing mechanism. A traditional later upheld the board's censure of the arbitrator. The system, it seemed, had worked"(Astha Dhawan, 2015).

Arbitration in the European Context

Searching for the origin of the modern time arbitration, the picture emerges as of having started in 1794. According to the International Court of Justice, the modern history of international arbitration dates back from the Jay Treaty of 1794 between the United States of America and Great Britain. As per this treaty of Amity, Commerce and Navigation provided for the creation of three mixed commissions of American and British nationals. These commissions were expected to settle a number of issues between the two countries which could not be addressed through negotiations. This made possible for the restart of the process of arbitration. As a result, throughout the 19th century, the USA and the UK used the process of arbitration like other nations of the Europe and the Americas. The arbitration of the Alabama Claims of 1872 was the second phase of arbitration which was a decisive one. Treaty of Washington of 1871 between the United States and the United Kingdom facilitated arbitration claims of the breaches of neutrality during the American Civil War. a sharp growth in the practice of inserting in treaties clauses providing for recourse to arbitration in the event of a dispute between the parties. This also provided for the appropriate system for the disputes settlement through arbitration by establishing procedures, composition of the tribunals, the various rules to be followed the appropriate factors to be considered for the grant of award by the tribunal. It also provided for the suitable proposals for creating a permanent international tribunal for arbitration rather than having ad hoc tribunals which would sit for arbitration in every individual dispute.

A third phase of international arbitration started in 1899 at the initiative of Nicholas II, the Tsar of Russia. The most important issue at that time was that of peace and disarmament in Europe among the conflicts of the smaller European states. A convention called for the same aimed to create a permanent machinery for the arbitral tribunal to be styled as a Permanent Court of Arbitration. However, "Permanent court of Arbitration" was not the accurate mechanism for the facilitation of the law and practice of arbitration. As a result, in 1907 the Hague Peace Conference was held to improvise the arbitral proceedings which enabled countries like the USA, UK and Germany to submit proposals for a permanent court with duly qualified judges. Subsequently in 1913, because of the gift of Andrew Carnegie, a Peace Palace has been built which eventuality gave the opportunity for the development of international law. Some of the reputed cases decided through these international laws are the *Carthage* and *Manouba* cases (1913) concerning the seizure of vessels, and the *Timor Frontiers* (1914) and *Sovereignty over the Island of Palmas* (1928) cases. However, despite the fact that the above-mentioned cases are able to show that the disputes are addressed based on law and justice, they also had certain defects in terms of differing composition and the voluntary character. Eventually, a Permanent Court of International Justice (PCIJ) came into existence. International legal proceedings became a reality. As a result, the PCIJ became a permanently constituted body governed by its own Statute and Rules of Procedure, fixed beforehand and binding on parties having recourse to the Court unlike the arbitral tribunals. PCIJ had a permanent Registry which served as a channel of communication with governments and international bodies among other things. The proceedings of PCIJ were largely public and provision was made for the publication of the proceedings and verbatim recordings of the sittings and other documentary evidences. It is interesting to observe that much later the San Francisco Conference provided a degree of continuity particularly as the Statute of the PCIJ had itself been drawn up on the basis of past experience. It also worked reasonably well. The Charter of PCIJ, therefore, clearly stated that the Statute of the International Court of Justice was based upon that of the PCIJ. Thereafter, necessary steps were taken to transfer as much of the PCIJ's jurisdiction as possible to the International Court of Justice. Subsequently, the decision to create a new court (ICJ) necessarily led to the dissolution of its predecessor, PCIJ. So, PCIJ met last time in October 1945 and resolved to transfer all its archives and effects to the new International Court of Justice, which, like its predecessor, was to have its seat at the Peace Palace. All the judges of the PCIJ resigned on 31 January 1946, and the election of the first Members of the International Court of Justice took place on 6 February 1946. Of late, discussion is on the center stage about the history and possibilities of international arbitration. It is hoped that, eventually establishing this method of "settling disputes as a substitute for war with all its sacrifice of human life and energy, and the train of needless horrors which follows in its wake" can be avoided. While this is penned, the mad and senseless war between Ukraine and Russia is at its climax with many statements and pronouncements of the possibility of a World War III leading to armageddon as is talked loudly by the World Leaders. It is time that International Arbitration should seize of the situation and save the globe from destruction. The arbitration will have issues pertaining to all commercial, political, economic and other portents.

CONCLUSION

Regardless of the global civilizations, cultures and history, the dominant practices for settlement or resolutions of the conflicts and disputes were based on the fundamental understanding of bringing together the conflicting parties on to the settlement table before much damage is caused either to the individuals or the communities. Therefore, conciliation, negotiation, mediation, adjudication and arbitration were the time-tested methods to meet the ends of justice in an agreeable manner without losing time, resources or even the sentiments involved in bridging the gaps of perceptual differences or proximity of thoughts and understanding in a cooperative framework. While the ancient methodologies of arbitration were simpler, quicker or closer home, eventually the procedures of arbitration also have taken longer routes, greater resources and longer time periods though different legislations in different countries. Nevertheless, arbitration procedures are still considered simpler and quicker to reduce the winding judicial processes both for national and international commercial conflict resolutions. An effort is made in this book through the following chapters to bring together the different issues of international arbitrations dwelling upon the policies, practices and protocols of International Commercial Arbitration as known through various secondary sources, which are otherwise scattered and not placed sequentially in any other work. Therefore, this work bridges the gap in the arbitration literature as available in many published works currently available. In this book the attempt was to organize the work in eleven chapters. The first chapter gives the introduction with issues like International Commercial Arbitration and Alternate Dispute Resolutions discussed. Similarly, a brief history of International Commercial Arbitration, growing trends alternate disputes resolution, international centers of commercial arbitration and international enforcement are elaborated. In the second chapter such issues of international commercial arbitration such as concept and nature, disputes resolution in international trade, important terms used in commercial arbitration, types of arbitration and the international arbitration laws are explained. The third chapter is on arbitration agreement where the significance of arbitration agreement, forms of arbitration agreement, their definitions and validity, foreign arbitration agreements, jurisdiction of arbitral tribunal, doctrine of kompetenenz-Kompetenz, and international commercial arbitration are discussed separately. The UNICITRAL Model Laws are discussed in the fourth chapter with topics like UNCITRAL model laws on Arbitration, governing laws of arbitration, applicable laws and choice of laws, principles and judicial interventions, conflict rules, appointment of arbitrators and the Seat Theory of Choice of Law are dealt with in detail. Fifth chapter is on the enforcement of arbitral award. Jurisdiction of arbitral award, independence and impartiality of the tribunal, arbitral process, party autonomy and arbitral award, ground for setting aside arbitral award, recognition and enforcement of foreign arbitral awards are the topics of discussion. The international arbitral procedures are detailed in the sixth chapter where legal framework for international arbitral proceedings, selection, challenge and replacement of Arbitrators in International Arbitrations, rights and duties of international arbitrators, selection of arbitral seat in International arbitration, procedures in international arbitrations, disclosures, provisional reliefs, consolidation, joinder and intervention and choice of substantial law are the specific topics of elaborations. The seventh chapter is on International Arbitral Awards where issues like Legal Framework for International Arbitral Awards, Form and Contents of International Arbitral Awards, Correction, Interpretation and Supplementation of International Arbitral Awards, Annulment of International Arbitral Awards, Recognition and Enforcement of International Arbitral Awards, Preclusion, Lis Pendens and Stare Decisis in International Arbitration are discussed. Confidentiality is the eighth chapter. In this chapter, Confidentiality Clause, Confidentiality in International Arbitration, Legal representation in International Arbitration, Prominent International Arbitration Cases and Awards are the topics of discussion. Ninth chapter is on policies, practices and protocols where a review is attempted. Policies of International Commercial Arbitration, Practices of International Commercial Arbitration, Protocols of International Commercial Arbitration, and a Review of Issues are discussed. In the tenth chapter model agreements of Hague, UK, Singapore, USA, India, and Japan are provided. Observations from the comparative agreements are also presented for quick grasp of the issues. Lastly, the conclusion is given in the eleventh chapter where Future of International Commercial Arbitration, Lessons from Experiences, Challenges to address, Summary and Inferences are presented. The work provides the references and a select bibliography as well.

This book is the result of collation of several pieces of information that are available in the public domain and wherever material is quoted from previous work, the same is placed within inverted comas and the sources shown in brackets without any intent to own or plagiarise the previous literature. Special permission has been sought where the sources providers have mandated in their copy right. The information and matters discussed here are primarily for academic purposes and the same is not intended for any legal advice as the topics are concerning law. Where specific situations demand, the appropriate information may be obtained from the attorneys practising in the field. This is stated here as a disclaimer for alerting the users of the book.

Khan Basheer Ahmed Mohammed
Supreme Court of India Bar Association, New Delhi, India

Kaushal Kishore
Supreme Court of India Bar Association, New Delhi, India

REFERENCES

Ademowo, J. (2015). Conflict Management in Traditional African Society. Research Gate.

Ayittey, G. (2014). *African Solutions, African Problems, Real Meaning*. Research Gate.

Ademowo, J. (2015). *Conflict Management in Traditional African Society*. Research Gate.

Menkel-Meadow, C. (2016) *Is ODR ADR? Reflections of an ADR Founder.* From 15th ODR Conference, The Hague, The Netherlands.

Chiatoh, D. (2003). on the Afo-a-Kom Yahoo Chat. *Group*.

Diamant, N. J. (2000). Conflict and Conflict Resolution in China Beyond Mediation-Centered Approaches. *The Journal of Conflict Resolution*, *44*(4), 523–546. doi:10.1177/0022002700044004006

Nkwi, P. (1987). *Traditional Diplomacy: A Study of Inter-Chiefdom Relationships in the Western Grassfields, North West Province of Cameroon*. Yaoundé, Cameroon: Publication of the Department of Sociology, University of Yaoundé.

Nkwi, P., & Warnier, J.-P. (1982). *Elements for a History of the Western Grassfields*. SOPECAM.

The Kom Heritage Foundation. (2014). *A Short Cultural History of the Kom People*. Bamenda: Destiny Prints.

Vedantam, J. (2015). Four steps to conflict resolution from Ancient India. *Cloud Data Management, Analytics & Monetization*. Research Gate.

Westermann, W. L. (1907). Interstate Arbitration in Antiquity. The Classical Journal, 2(5). The Classical Association of the Middle West and South, Inc. (CAMWS)

Acknowledgment

No academic work can remain as standalone without the contributions from someone or the other. In a work like this, where most of the base materials are drawn from very many sources like the web sources, written books, periodicals, journals, law reporters, legal columns, reports of the courts, magazines etc. the prime acknowledgement and the resultant gratitude will be to the authors of the materials from whom we have drawn extensively. We take this opportunity to thank them profusely for the contributions made by the predecessors who gave us the materials and methods to work on and arrive at our inferences. Some of the previous literature is quoted and the references are mentioned. Even where the references could not be mentioned, the authors are grateful to such contributors from whom this work has drawn extensively, quoted or unquoted.

We take this opportunity to thank profusely Justice Dr. Karpagavinayagam, former Chief Justice of the High Court of Jharkhand for his incisive foreword for this work. He has favoured us with his love and affection through this foreword.

Every academic work requires quiet time from the hustle and bustle of day-to-day work. We acknowledge the kindness of all colleagues, clients and court staff who are affected by our engagement in this academic endeavor.

We are also thankful to the reviewers of this work, whose careful assessment, review and evaluation have added to the quality of the work. Our hats off to them for their timely help.

Our families have definitely lost the quality time which we would have otherwise spent with them. Our apologies to them as well as our heartfelt thanks for their cooperation to make this work happen.

No one, named here or otherwise is responsible for the blemishes in the work, that nevertheless remain and we alone are responsible for such lapses.

Chapter 1
International Commercial Arbitration and Alternate Dispute Resolution:
An Exordium

ABSTRACT

In this chapter, the authors attempt to define the concepts of international commercial arbitration and alternative dispute resolutions precisely. International commercial arbitration is introduced briefly, along with the developing tendencies in alternative dispute resolution, the many international centers for commercial arbitration, and the many international enforcement issues that arise from these. In the context of Indian law, the Arbitration and Conciliation Act, 1996 (the Indian Act) defines international commercial arbitration as an arbitration involving a commercial relationship where one or both of the parties is a non-Indian citizen, non-resident, or non-Indian business entity. Questions about how the arbitration itself will go down are raised. Blackstone, a leading legal authority, makes it abundantly clear that arbitration refers to the decisions of one or more persons, with or without an umpire, on a specific matter in difference between the parties.

DOI: 10.4018/978-1-6684-4040-7.ch001

BACKGROUND

According to one definition, international commercial arbitration (ICA) is "a process for private dispute resolution in which parties to a dispute from different countries decide to have their disputes settled through one or more arbitrators, without the involvement of the courts of a particular country." Moreover, the Indian legal system has further subdivided it asunder:

According to the Indian Arbitration and Conciliation Act of 1996 (the Indian Act), an "International Commercial Arbitration" is one "arising from a legal relationship which must be considered commercial where either of the parties is a foreign national or resident or is a foreign body" (Arbitration and Conciliation Act, 1996).

This chapter is aimed to achieve the following goals

1. To understand the features of international commercial arbitration (ICA) and alternate dispute resolution (ADR)
2. To understand the brief history of ICA in general
3. To introduce the growing trends of ADR
4. To enable recognition of the International Centres of Commercial Arbitration
5. To know some of the previous studies and to get a general view of the issues of enforcement

The methodology used for this study is analytical and descriptive and it is an analysis of material accessed from secondary published sources like journals, books, and the web resources

Arbitration as a mechanism of conflict resolution evolved over the millennia, and therefore, interest has been evinced to study the various aspects of arbitration from the earliest days. This necessitated a study on the history of arbitration. It can be noted that several pieces of literature exist on the history of arbitration. The attempt here is to provide a brief overview of the literature on the history of arbitration. Several of the studies reported are being documented for easy reference to the other researchers. The law of international commercial arbitration that came into existence in 1993 deals with international commercial arbitration and helps to settle commercial disputes in Russia (Ikko, Yoshida, 2009). While considering arbitration history, it is necessary to focus on and classify various situations where the arbitration has been satisfactory and where it failed (Earl, S. Wolaver, 1934). Commercial arbitration is expected to be a mechanism and means for settling disputes by referring them to a neutral person (Martin, Domke, 2023). In the context of commercial arbitration in India, the argument is that India can progress in the area of International Commercial Arbitration only if the law passed in the Parliament of India is followed and the interpretations of the courts are adhered to. (Shivam, Goel, 2015). Drawing a sketch of commercial arbitration, it is elaborated that a particular type and kind of arbitration has to be practiced in a particular commercial environment in a particular way (Arbitration Law, 2020). According to Walid Taha Akram, commercial arbitration is a mechanism specially established for the final determination which is binding based on contractual obligations with international content (Walid Taha Akram, 2016). In the seventeenth century, the agreement to arbitration was deemed to be a mandate which is revocable. This allowed a party to spoil all possible agreements if they are not suiting the interests of the party (Apurva Agarwal, 2022). Arbitration as an alternate mechanism for the resolution of disputes is a synonym for the different techniques which became popular in the 1990s (Borut Strazisar, 2018). Arbitration as a mechanism for reaching the end of justice was prevalent as early as civilization. It can be seen in the Roman Law and Greek Law of the sixth century (Meghas, 2021). International investment law and arbitration is a field that is highly evolving and rapid too. It needs a thorough perusal to comprehend firmly (Chin Lim et al, 2022). In the case of India, the history of arbitration law reveals that the Arbitration Act of 1940 had been under constant criticism. Therefore, to widen and include appropriate areas, the Arbitration and Conciliation Act of 1996 was passed in the Indian Parliament (Mondaq, 2016). In the case of Sri Lanka also, the Law and Practice of commercial arbitration were studied (Harsha Cabral, 2018).

Features of International Commercial Arbitration (ICA)

It is apt to mention the appropriate features of ICA which are as follows:

a. It will take time.
b. It will be strictly confidential.
c. It will not involve any public or governmental body.
d. There will be a point of contention.
e. An economic analysis of the disputed issue is required.
f. The tribunal will make a ruling based on the evidence and arguments put forth by the parties.
g. More than one nation's representatives will be attending.

h. One or both of the parties can be (in the case of the USA) a non-U.S. citizen, non-permanent resident, alien, or foreign organisation.
i. Disputes will be decided by one or more arbitrators.
j. There will be no involvement from any national court system.
k. This occurs outside of court, whereas litigation takes place in the court.
l. The arbitrator's decision is final and cannot be challenged in court except in exceptional circumstances.

International arbitration has been defined and the issues surrounding it have been studied by a number of different academic disciplines. There are a few studies of this kind that warrant a cursory examination.

PREVIOUS RESEARCH LITERATURE

The procedural aspects are the basis for any definition of international arbitration. The various conventions and laws pertaining to arbitration have given rise to the field of international arbitration, which encompasses all facets of the practise (Rubino-Sammartano, M 2014). Different types of international arbitration, such as commercial arbitration, investment arbitration, and arbitration between states, are just a few of the many implications of international arbitration (Born GB; 2003). The intricacies of domestic and international law, among others, make arbitration a difficult field to navigate, but this guide makes it all clear and understandable (Bantekas, I; 2015). In international arbitration, international treaties and developing legal norms play an increasingly important role. However, this issue has been barely discussed in commercial arbitration (Mayer, P; 1986). The rules of law, general principles, trade usages, alias lex mercatoria (Law Merchant), the limits of choice of the parties, and any other provisions of private international law unique to international arbitration must be observed (Poudrette, JF & Besson, S; 2007). International arbitration is a relatively new experiment that aims to reduce the likelihood of military conflict. Today, the term "international arbitration" refers to the process of trying to resolve a dispute on a global scale (Lord, EL; 1892). Current trends in international arbitration stem largely from investor-state and inter-state commercial disputes (Born, GB; 2015). When it comes to international commercial arbitration, there are often a number of unseen issues that can be categorised as soft power issues that are on the rise. The pliable influence of these corporations is a defining feature of international arbitration. According to (Alford, RP; 2003). It has been attempted to combine a theoretical and comparative analysis of the evidentiary and procedural stages of international arbitration with a practical one (Waincymer, J; 2012). International arbitration experts have shaped modern arbitration law through their own experiences, as well as through extensive writing and teaching (Gaillard, E; 2010).

Thus, commercial arbitration is a method of conflict resolution in which a neutral third party, an arbitrator, is chosen by the parties and then renders a decision based on the evidence and arguments presented to the arbitration tribunal. When all of these elements are present in a process, we have what is known as international commercial arbitration. ADR (Alternative Dispute Resolution) typically includes arbitration (ADR). Arbitration, as a concept, refers to the expedited resolution of a dispute between two parties without resorting to the formalities of a court's operating procedures. Arbitration, according to Blackstone's Law Dictionary, means: "The term "arbitration" refers to the process whereby a third party (or parties) is selected to investigate and make a binding decision on a dispute between disputing parties. The English court provided the following explanation of arbitration: "The term "arbitration" is used to describe the process by which a dispute between two parties is resolved through the efforts of a neutral third party, known as an "arbitrator." (Collins v. Collins, 28 LJ Ch 184; 53 ER 916 (1858). In contrast to litigation, which typically takes place inside a courtroom, arbitration is conducted outside of court, with judicial review of the arbitrator's decision being limited to exceptional circumstances. Therefore, "International commercial arbitration is an alternative method of resolving disputes between private parties arising out of commercial transactions conducted across national boundaries that allows the parties to avoid litigation in national courts," Of course, besides going to court, there are other ways to settle legal disagreements.

ORIGIN AND DEVELOPMENT OF MODERN SYSTEM OF ARBITRATION

Disputes that arose during the American Revolution were an early example of what would become known as arbitral disputes. The modern system of arbitration originated from the Jay Treaty of 1794. In an effort to resolve their differences, the United States and the United Kingdom agreed to form three separate commissions.

While modern commercial arbitration is a relatively new concept, it has its roots in international commercial arbitration practises developed in the Middle Ages to resolve the disputes that inevitably arise between merchants in the course of everyday trade. In the English-speaking world and elsewhere in Europe, this strategy was widely adopted. In the Mediterranean and along the Baltic Sea Trade routes, this was also a common way to deal with issues arising from commercial transactions. When formal courts were established, however, the popularity of arbitration quickly declined. The first international commercial arbitration was later enforced in England under the terms of the English Arbitration Act of 1889. In 1950, the English Parliament r-examined the 1889 Act and merged its provisions into the new English Arbitration Act. This Act eventually became the law of arbitration in all of the countries that were part of the British Commonwealth as a result of this. There was also a new law passed in the United States in 1925 called the Federal Arbitration Act. The International Chamber of Commerce, a sister organisation, was also founded to handle cross-border commercial disputes. The ICA, or International Court of Arbitration, is a remarkable arbitration body. ICA members come from over 142 different countries, and the organisation has handled over 25,000 arbitration cases. As the pace of international trade accelerated as a result of globalisation, liberalisation, and privatization's implementation everywhere, it became abundantly clear that disagreements would inevitably arise. A rise in consumer demand for a wide range of goods and services across national borders has contributed to the escalation of commercial conflicts. That's when arbitration really took off as a fantastic way to settle business-related disagreements. Establishment of courts like ICA in Europe led to an increase in the number of arbitral cases. To help facilitate international trade and investment, the judicial system has been actively working towards the resolution of commercial disputes since 1923. The ICA has many responsibilities, but one of its primary ones is to meet the requirements of the parties concerned. The ICA can easily adapt their offerings in response to changing needs and demands. It's important to keep in mind that the International Court of Arbitration is not a "real" court in the same sense that other judicial bodies are. As a result, the ICA cannot issue binding judgments in the many disputes that arise between its members. As an alternative, they provide judicial oversight and ultimately secure awards that can be enforced. The rules and regulations laid down by the International Chamber of Commerce are intended to be followed to a tee during the arbitration process. This is due to the fact that they have a realistic understanding of the many issues surrounding international trade and currency exchange. Over eighty legal professionals have been put in charge of ensuring that judicial supervision is carried out to the required level of excellence. Not only do the 142 member countries benefit, but so do an additional 85 or so.

The ICA's arbitration process employs a variety of techniques. Here are a few examples of these noteworthy procedures: I) Mediation; II) Expert Opinion; III) Arbitration; and IV) DOCDEX (Documentary Instruments Dispute Resolution Expertise)

Due to the delicate nature of the issues at hand, mediation must take place in a separate, private location. Through trials, the neutral arbitrator or adjudicator typically helps the disputing parties narrow their points of contention and identify areas where they can work together. As time goes on, this will aid in upholding arbitration rulings.

Second, knowledge and experience are essential, so this is a must. As a result, the ICA provides arbitrators with subject-matter expertise, as this is essential for evaluating the specific technical aspects at play in any given case.

Third, arbitration is a structured approach that can be adapted to the needs of international commercial arbitration. To the best of my knowledge, this is the main ICA method. Anywhere in the world, the ICA's arbitration decision must be followed.

Finally, the International Chamber of Commerce offers a service called Documentary Dispute Resolution Expertise (DOCDEX). Documentary aid, demand, and collection cases benefit from this. Invoking the ICC banking rules in international commercial disputes is a requirement, and this demand either guarantees or incorporates those rules.

There are numerous ADR mechanisms available. The following are examples of the TOP FIVE most typical types of ADR:

i. Mediation
ii. Arbitration.
iii. Non-Prejudiced Opinion.
iv. Conflict Resolution Meetings.
v. Local Conflict Resolution Initiative.

In this context, alternative dispute resolution refers to the following specific ones:

A. Mediation
B. Conciliations
C. Negotiation

D. Arbitration

Facilitation is a synonym for mediation. As a result of facilitation, the parties to the conflict are given the opportunity to determine the resolution themselves. The facilitator, also known as a mediator, is a neutral third party who has no stake in the outcome of the dispute.

A dispute can be resolved when the parties involved take charge of the discussion and work together to narrow the gaps in their understanding of the issues at stake. The facilitator or mediator takes careful and detailed notes on the points of agreement and disagreement and ultimately assists the parties in the conflict to reach consensus that can be crafted and drafted for signatures on the agreements.

It's fascinating to see how mediation can take many forms, depending on the parties involved and their perceptions of their shared ground and their divergent positions. So, the strategies for mediating the conflict will be developed. Common approaches include the following:

Face-to-Face Interactions

In this form of mediation, the disputing parties meet with each other individually. During mediation, the facilitator "shuttles" between the parties by requiring them to stay in separate rooms. After a period of back-and-forth, both sides present their proposed terms of settlement for consensus. An encouraging mediator is one who actively encourages a settlement by bringing the parties together to reach an agreement in a peaceful state of mind. It is evocative and, in this approach, the mediating facilitator evokes potential norms of settlement by mooting ideas and bringing parties together. The arbitrator makes the final decision instead of the disputing parties, making arbitration the most formal form of alternative dispute resolution. An arbitrator is a neutral third party who hears both sides of a dispute, considers their arguments, and renders a decision.

Conciliation

In the context of International Commercial Arbitration, conciliation is yet another alternative dispute resolution (ADR) option. A more amicable resolution can be reached through conciliation because it allows the disputing parties more time to ponder over issues and come to an agreement that will only be binding on them. In other proceedings, a decision is made by the presiding authority that is binding, but in conciliation, the parties come to a decision on their own. To reach a negotiated settlement, conciliation also involves convincing the disputing parties to sit down and talk things out. There are two prerequisites for conciliation of this type. Those things are:

Constant Confidence

Confidentiality

There is a proper way to carry out a conciliation, and it has been established that the following points have to be born in mind:

i. Beginning of Conciliation Efforts
ii. Statement for Submission to a Conciliator
iii. Procedures for Mediation and Conciliation
iv. The administrative framework for providing the required support
v. Determination of the scope and relevance
vi. A determination of the contractual nature of the situation
vii. Quantity and expertise of mediators
viii. The General Rules of Procedure should have the following:
    a. Free from bias, independent and objective
    b. True justice and fairness
    c. Confidentiality
    d. Publication of Data
    e. Parties' Cooperative Efforts with the Mediator
    f. Procedures and guidelines
    g. Convening Location
    h. Conferencing between the Parties and the Conciliator

The Conciliation Process should have:

i. Getting Started
ii. Statements to be submitted to the Mediator
iii. Procedures for reaching a conciliation agreement
iv. Help with administration
v. Settlement
vi. Compromise Resolution

Limitations on the Conciliator's Role

a. Conciliation Process Comes to a Close
b. Take the matter to court or arbitration if necessary.
c. Costs
d. Deposits

Given its low cost and quick turnaround time, the conciliation process is a preferable alternative dispute resolution mechanism. As a dispute resolution method, it is quick, easy, and useful for all involved. It is most useful in preventing favouritism and corruption. There should be fewer lawsuits filed overall, and parties who want to settle amicably should do so. In international commercial arbitration, it is referred to as an alternative dispute resolution method and is a useful tool.

Negotiation

An additional productive form of alternative dispute resolution is negotiation. The term "Alternative Dispute Resolution" (ADR) encompasses a broad category of conflict resolution techniques that can help parties in conflict reach a settlement without resorting to courtroom litigation. So, another way to end the international conflict is through negotiations. Negotiation is the process of resolving conflicts and achieving mutually agreeable outcomes without resorting to open conflict or argument. Both sides of a disagreement want the best possible outcome.

There are several steps to account for in any negotiation. To name a few:

a. Getting Ready
b. Sharing Data
c. Time for negotiation
d. Carrying it out
e. Conclusion

No matter how tempting it may be to try and wing it during negotiations, thorough preparation is always essential. In particular, the foundation of negotiation is the building of the highest possible faith. Given the centrality of bargaining, the ability to effectively communicate is obviously essential.

When two parties are at odds, negotiation allows them to talk it out and come to an agreement on how to move forward. In most cases, it requires some concessions on both sides. Conflicts are resolved through negotiation when both parties make concessions in order to reach an agreement. Organizations often feature negotiations between different levels of management, between different departments, between different teams, or between a team member and a manager. Interviewees and interviewers/HR managers engage in negotiations even before a position is accepted.

Therefore, certain abilities for the two or more parties who need to agree on a common logical solution are necessary when two interests have to locate a commonplace of agreement, whether in a dispute or discussion. Situations calling for negotiations arise frequently in organizations, including negotiating a salary increase with the HR manager after a promotion or after a substantial contribution over a period of time, negotiating a project deadline with the team lead or manager, negotiating a few days of leave or exemptions from work for a leisure holiday with the manager, negotiating with a potential customer the terms and conditions of the contract, etc.

Damage to the customer relationship can be expected in the absence of negotiation skills. To become an effective negotiator and to settle disputes in the workplace or the marketplace, it is necessary to develop soft skills known as "negotiation skills."

This set of abilities, however, is situationally and outcome-specific in the workplace. The willingness of one party to negotiate a solution does not guarantee that the other will be open to doing so. Such situations are common in the workplace and make negotiations challenging. In light of this, competence in this area of negotiation is essential.

Able to negotiate and the positive effects on finding other means of resolving conflicts.

Someone who acts as a mediator or facilitator in alternative dispute resolution (ADR) is a leader. In order to propel and accomplish the goal, leaders need to have strong negotiation skills. For the following to be accomplished, you'll need to use your negotiating skills:

An approach that prioritises the creation of goodwill and value in order to strengthen relationships. This helps to foster a lasting bond.

The best way to deliver a solution is one that lasts, one that resolves the conflicts permanently and out of context. A competent negotiator possesses these skills.

Future conflicts can be avoided to the greatest extent possible if the skilled negotiator is able to facilitate situations that lead to control of future conflicts.

Business success is the ultimate goal of any negotiation, and it is imperative that the right circumstances be created in order to achieve this goal through productive discussion and compromise. Alternate dispute resolution aims to facilitate the expansion of businesses by removing impediments to trade.

Skills Which are Relevant for Negotiators

The following are some of the relevant skills required for a successful negotiator:

Communicate and Convince

A failure to effectively communicate is often at the root of the problems that arise in interpersonal relationships. Therefore, the key ingredient for a successful negotiator is the appropriate comprehension and ability to communicate and allow the parties in conflict to get convinced. By effectively conveying the benefits of the negotiated agreement, the parties are more likely to reach a mutual decision to accept it.

Plan Strategically

A good negotiator will be prepared with a fallback plan and will strategically place arguments to help the parties understand the deal. Preparing thoroughly and methodically for the negotiation process is necessary.

Persuasion Ability

A strong ability to persuade the parties involved in the negotiation is essential for a successful facilitator and leader. It's impossible for the brain to process weak arguments. Successful negotiators need to have this skill in their toolkit.

Listening Attentively

A negotiator who listens attentively and analyses the situation before offering solutions. Consequently, one must be a listener negotiator to be a successful negotiator.

Problem Solving Psyche

An effective ADR negotiator will be able to identify the root causes of the dispute and devise creative solutions that take into account all of the relevant factors.

High Emotional Intelligence

Since the goal of the negotiation process is to resolve disputes outside of court, the negotiator needs high levels of emotional intelligence, so that they can stay level-headed during heated exchanges and still come away with a good understanding of the parties' feelings. The success of the alternative redress system will be aided by creating such conditions.

Methods Used for Negotiating Effectively

One side or the other, or even both, may feel they came out on top when a dispute is finally resolved. This is because of how the parties involved in the alternative dispute redressal system actually feel about the results of the procedure. There are, therefore, a few options, such as:

Fixing a Deal

Bargaining is called "haggling" when it's done with the specific goal of "haggling" something away from the other party. Since neither side is willing to budge, the negotiation grinds to a. There should be the ability to reach a deal and settle.

Clearance Transaction

Clearance Bargaining is a method of negotiation aimed at finalising a deal in which both parties feel they have achieved a satisfactory outcome. Both parties' goals can now be met, ending the conflict.

Soft Bargaining

One negotiating tactic is called "soft bargaining," and its goal is to get the other side to agree to your terms by suggesting creative solutions to the more contentious issues at hand.

Ways for improving negotiation skills

1. Recognize the benefits and drawbacks of the conflict and be mentally prepared to accept the outcomes as a result of the negotiations.
2. As the terms of a settlement to the dispute take shape, the negotiator should cultivate a willingness to compromise.
3. There needs to be a firm deadline for reaching an agreement as negotiations cannot be dragged for long. An early deadline to halt negotiations on the deal should be planned for.
4. The parties involved in the dispute should be presented with multiple options for resolving the conflict, all of which are reasonable and do not require a leap of faith to implement. As a result, all involved parties will be better able to settle on the most economical outcome.
5. The negotiator needs to have a firm belief in the merits of the proposed solution and assert it with authority if it is to be accepted by the other party. As a result, this will have an impact on the conflicting parties and the reprimand will be swift and conclusive.
6. The negotiator needs to be able to accept the possibility of falling short and not take it personally if it does occur.
7. There will be room for improvement in all of the negotiating skills the negotiator acquires in order to compensate for any weaknesses. Evaluate the areas where falling short, and work to improve until the outstanding results are consistently achieved.
8. A rehearsal is useful and there is room for practise, and a negotiation scenario can be worked out with some role playing. This will be useful as an alternative dispute resolution process during negotiations.

Alternatives to Negotiation for ADRS

There are a few alternative dispute resolution methods available besides direct negotiations. They are asunder:

a. Evaluation by a Third Party Neutral. A third party is consulted by both parties to evaluate the merits of each side's case and present their findings
b. Judges may recommend or order the parties to participate in settlement conferences. A judge or arbitrator can be consulted by the parties to help them decide how to resolve their differences, taking into account each side's relative strengths and weaknesses.
c. A Community Dispute Resolution Approach: This is a common practice in the United States. A low-cost alternative to resolving conflicts can be provided by trained volunteers. Community Dispute Resolution Centers can be used as a referral source for cases from the courts.

ICA and the International Centres for Commercial Arbitration (ICCA)

The law-making bodies of different countries have passed the necessary statutes for arbitration. In Malaysia, for instance, arbitration was made possible by the country's 1952 Arbitration Act. No distinction was made in the Act of 1952 between domestic and foreign arbitrations; its provisions applied to both. This led to a change in the law in 2002 that defined "domestic" arbitration separately from "international" arbitration. Invoking domestic and international arbitration provisions is required by the 2005 Act. Unless the parties agreed in writing otherwise, Section 3 of the Act shall govern the domestic arbitrations. Despite the provisions, some courts, such as the Putrajaya Court, have allowed parties to choose whether to apply the law after 2005 or the law from before. Globalization, privatisation, and liberalisation in India began in 1991, ushering in a flurry of new international connections and the inevitable disputes that inevitably accompany them. It was necessary to make room for the arbitration system through Alternate Dispute Redressal because the traditional court system was already at capacity. As a result, the Parliament of India enacted some new rules. This trend in the law began with the 1996 Arbitration and Conciliation Act. A number of changes to the 1996 law were necessary, however, as a result of court cases brought about by the legislation in practise. Therefore, in 2015, 2018, and 2019, amendments were made to the Arbitration and Conciliation Act with the goal of reducing the judicial system's role in the arbitration process. Further, it aided institutionalisation by leading to the formation of the Arbitration Council of India.

Section 2(1)(f) of the Arbitration and Conciliation Act, 1996 defines International Commercial Arbitration as a means of resolving disputes involving legal issues arising out of commercial contracts or otherwise. These circumstances required that:

One of the people involved must be a foreign national who is not a citizen or permanent resident of India.

A corporation with no ties to India is an option.

There is no restriction on the type of institution that qualifies as "foreign," so long as it is not based on India's government.

Looking back at how international arbitration has progressed in the Middle East is possible. New arbitral institutions have been set up in both the Kingdom of Saudi Arabia and the United Arab Emirates. Legal bodies in the area's settling disputes were modernized and revised. Both Qatar and the UAE have recently enacted new arbitration laws and drafted rules to govern their use. The MENA region has seen some encouraging developments in the realm of arbitration, all with the goal of making its countries more appealing to users of international arbitration.

The purpose of enacting Law No.2 of 2017 was to create the Arbitration Act for use in civil and commercial disputes in Qatar. The UNCITRAL Model Law served as a basis for this law. It can be used for both current and future arbitrators. When the parties to an arbitration agree that Qatari law applies, the seat of the arbitration need not be in Qatar. No difference in legal status is necessary for the law to apply to the private or public sectors. The U.A.E.'s new policy favouring arbitration is very interesting to observe. In order to ensure that arbitrators are unbiased, article 257 was added to the UAE Penal Code. This makes it illegal for arbitrators to show bias. Beyond the United Arab Emirates, Dubai has taken steps to create an arbitration-friendly environment.

The African continent is actively promoting arbitration by establishing a plethora of infrastructure to facilitate the process. The Association for the Promotion of Arbitration in Africa (APAA), the International Court of Arbitration (ICC) sponsored by the International Chamber of Commerce, the Lagos Court of Arbitration in Nigeria, the Cairo Regional Centre for International Commercial Arbitration (CRCICA) operating in Egypt, and the London Court of International Arbitration-sponsored Mauritius International Arbitration Centre (LCIA-MIAC) in Mauritius all provide useful services to the African arbitration community. Arbitration is becoming more common in African disputes.

The year 2019 saw the first full-fledged implementation of International Centres for Commercial Arbitration. A neutral, specialised location for all forms of alternative dispute resolution (ADR)—including in-person, hybrid, and online—is what we call a "arbitration centre." As a result, the alternative dispute resolution processes can take place in settings that are both private and secure. The London International Arbitration Centre is one such prestigious venue for resolution of disputes.

Such arbitration facilities exist in other nations as well. The locations of such establishments are provided in the list below. This list does not include every major city on the planet, but it does highlight some of the most important ones. The UNCITRAL model rules and regulations are used to govern the day-to-day operations of these facilities. The authorities responsible for appointing arbitrators and conducting administrative arbitration proceedings are appointed as per these rules and regulations. The International Centres for Commercial Arbitrations (ICCA) are located in the following different countries, which are as provided hereunder in Table 1.

Several international centers and countries have not provided the required information to enlist them. Though the international authorities have called for the appropriate information from the countries about their International Commercial Arbitration Centers, several countries have not provided the information. This makes the updating of the information difficult. Therefore, Table 1 is adopted as available on the website of the United Nations Commission on International Trade Law in a redrawn format.

Foreign enforcement is a major concern in the field of international commercial arbitration. International arbitral awards are often cited by proponents of arbitration as being simple to recognize and implement. With reference to the regulations, arbitration's strongest argument is the rules and regulations governing the recognition and enforcement of judgments issued by courts in other countries. However, as the parties to an international arbitration grow in knowledge and sophistication, it is possible that enforcing international arbitral awards will prove more difficult than originally anticipated. The prevailing party in international arbitration may feel like its job is done once it obtains an award, but if the losing party does not voluntarily comply in its favor, the prevailing party will only be able to reap the benefits of the award once the losing party agrees to do so. If the award is not immediately enforced, the prevailing party may need to take additional steps to obtain the benefit. Without this, all of the effort put into obtaining the award through arbitration will be for naught, and the time and money spent on the process may end up being greater than what would have been spent on litigation in court.

The findings of this study show that most arbitral awards are voluntarily complied with, which is very encouraging. Eighty-four percent of the lawyers polled in a Queen Mary International Arbitration Survey on enforcement found consensus in the finding that 76% of arbitration awards are voluntarily enforced by the parties to the arbitration. As such, this bodes well for the reliability and effectiveness of international arbitration. However, complications can arise if the award is challenged or if its implementation is met with resistance. For the alternative dispute resolution system to succeed, it is important to comprehend such cases and address concerns related to enforcement.

There are two common approaches to putting an arbitration ruling into practice. It can be done in two ways: 1) informally, and 2) in the appropriate regional courts. It is in the best interest of all parties involved to try to use more informal channels of communication to persuade a party to comply with an award if that party refuses to do so voluntarily out of a sense of unfairness. Applying commercial, diplomatic, or reputational pressure are examples of informal channels for international commercial arbitral awards. It is more fruitful to try to negotiate a reduction in the losing party's payment obligations or to lobby the government of the country where the losing party resides. As a result, the award may be complied with more quickly and more effectively. For the informal approach to compliance agreements to be fruitful, both parties must be patient and strategic. In the event that these fewer formal means of communication fail to yield results, the situation becomes complex and costly, rendering any prior arbitration experience useless. Despite the emergent results, however, there is still a case for arbitration.

In the event of enforcement difficulties, the prevailing party must identify one or more jurisdictions that are amenable to arbitration and in which the non-prevailing party maintains assets that can be seized to satisfy the award. The process of tracking down and securing the assets alone is sure to be time-consuming and costly. Some shrewd businesses are taking advantage of legal systems with weaker controls and enforcement. In such cases, the party's assets are often hidden and difficult to attach in order to enforce the arbitral award. However, the local legal systems and the speed with which they can be activated may be jeopardized by the laws of the enforcement jurisdiction. Thus, the degree of enforcement may differ.

The recognition and enforcement of foreign arbitral awards in 1958 was signed in New York, so there is a glimmer of hope. 150 countries have signed a treaty recognizing and upholding each other's right to enforce arbitral decisions. If the awards are considered local judgments in the signatory states, the parties to the arbitration agreement are bound to uphold them. Even if both parties are from New York State signatories to the NYC agreement, that does not guarantee that the arbitration awards will be upheld in every court in every state. Generally, local courts will enforce awards unless a valid argument is presented. Potential defences include the incompetence of the parties or the unenforceability of the arbitration agreement. The other party was not properly notified of the appointment of the arbitrator or the arbitration, which is another possible justification. It is possible to challenge the award on the grounds that it relates to a matter that was never brought up in the arbitration. It may be argued that the tribunal's composition or the procedure it used in the arbitration were not in accordance with the parties' agreement or the law that was supposed to apply to the arbitration. This arbitration award may be challenged on the grounds that it is not final and binding, has been voided, or is currently on hold. There is a possibility that the dispute's subject matter cannot be settled using arbitration laws. It is possible that the public policy of the enforcing state would prevent the award from being enforced. The Indian laws governing arbitration include this provision. Parties that were unsuccessful in obtaining an arbitration award may use these as a legal argument even though their home countries are among the 150 that signed the NYC. To be sure, it has been noted that various regional courts interpret the laws in varying ways. New York City has diverged from the rest of the country by recognizing only its own courts. It may be difficult to enforce the arbitral award in the local courts of the seat(s) of arbitration. The arbitral award is usually not recognized by the English courts because it has been declared null and void at the seat of the award. Even though the English court had clear concerns about the validity of the Russian court's reasoning, in Nikolay Viktorovich Maximov v. Open Joint Stock Company of 2017, the English Commercial Court declined to enforce an award set aside at its seat in Russia. In contrast, France uses a different method. French courts, on the other hand, have taken a different stance, holding that some 'zombie' awards can still be enforced even if they were previously vacated at the seat. Case in point: the French Court of Cassation (Cour de Cassation) upholding an international award that had been voided at the arbitral seat in Switzerland (Société Hilmarton Ltd. v. Société Omnium de traitement et de valorisation (OTV)). The Swiss legal system also did not incorporate this system. Even though it had been put aside at the seat, it was still very much alive. American courts use similar reasoning when making decisions. The Egyptian courts recently overturned an earlier arbitral award in the case of Chromalloy Aero services v. Arab Republic of Egypt. According to the court's analysis, the lower court misapplied Egypt's substantive law. Despite being ignored, Egypt's administrative law served as the governing principle. Washington DC's district court rejected the appeal of the set-aside ruling from the Egyptian court. The arbitration tribunal's mistake of law was found to be the basis for the Egyptian court's motion to set aside, according to the US court. The US court ruled that the matter was not one that should be examined by US courts with enforcement jurisdiction. This demonstrates that the NYC rules are not enforced consistently. About half the states in the country have not ratified the NYC agreement, and this fact must be borne in mind. A sizable number of African, Middle Eastern, and Pacific Island nations are among them. Arbitral awards can be enforced in such countries through bilateral or multilateral agreements. Despite this, enforcement may still be possible without a direct enforcement treaty if a third party which is a signatory to the NYC agreement state can be invoked. Arrangements for the enforcement of arbitral awards should be made on both a bilateral and multilateral basis.

CONCLUSION

Global business arbitration has been around for quite some time. Settlement of disputes in the interest of the continued survival and better future of sapiens for a peaceful and harmonious living has come a long way over a very long period of time, from the days of early compromises of commercial exchanges to later formally installed systems and their evolution as the current institutions of arbitrations. The foregoing discussions cover topics such as the transportation of goods between different regions, the establishment of terms and conditions of exchange, the emergence of disputes as a result of commercial interactions and exchanges, the identification of areas of common interest, and the resolution of differences of opinion, the availability of alternative methods for resolving disputes, the establishment of centers for commercial arbitration around the world, and the enforcement of arbitral awards.

REFERENCES

Agarwal, A. (2022). *A brief history of commercial arbitrations.* Linkedin.
Akram, W. (2016). *Arbitration as an alternative method of settling international business disputes.* United States Documents. ; https://documents.pub/document/arbitration-as-an-alternative-method-of

Alford, R. P. (2003). *The American Influence on International Arbitration.* Ohio State Journal on Dispute Resolution, Hein Online.

Bantekas, I. (2015). *An introduction to international arbitration, Books.* Google. Com. doi:10.1017/CBO9781316275696

Born, G. B. (2015). *International arbitration: cases and materials, Books.* Google. Com.

Born, G. B. (2021). *International arbitration: law and practice, Books.* Google. Com.

Cabral, H. (2018); 'Law and Practice of Commercial Arbitration in Sri Lanka https://ft.lk/opinion/-Law-and-Practice-of-Commercial-Arbitration-in.ln

Collins v. Collins, (1858); 28 LJ Ch 184; 53 ER 916

Domke, M. (2023);Commercial arbitration law |Britannicahttps://www.britannica.com/topic/commercial-arbitration

Gaillard, (2010), Legal theory of international arbitration

Goel, S. (2015); International Commercial Arbitration, https://www.researchgate.net

Lim, C. (2022). International Commercial Arbitration. *LibGuides.* https://libguides.nus.edu.sg/commercialarbitration/books

Lord, E.L. (1892). *International Arbitration.* Sage.

Mann, F. A. (1967). *British Year Book of International Law, 1967, State contracts and international arbitration.* Hein Online.

Mayer, P. (1986). *Mandatory rules of law in international arbitration.* Arbitration International. academic.oup.com

Meghas. (2021). *International Commercial Arbitration - Legal Services India.* Legal Services in India. https://www.legalservicesindia.com/article/2196/International

Mondaq. (2016). *India: Evolution Of Arbitration In India.* MONDAQ. https://www.mondaq.com/india/arbitration-dispute-resolution

Poudrette, & Besson, S, (2007). *Comparative law of international arbitration.*

Strazisar, B. (2018), Alternative Dispute Resolution, https://www.researchgate.net

The History of International Commercial Arbitration - A Sketch. (2020). Abitraion Law. https://arbitrationlaw.com/library/history-international-commercial.

Wolaver, E. S. (1934). *The Historical Background of Commercial Arbitration*. UPenn.

Yoshida, I. (2009, September 1). History of International Commercial Arbitration and its Related System in Russia. *Arbitration International*, *25*(3), 365–402. doi:10.1093/arbitration/25.3.365

KEY TERMS AND DEFINITIONS

A Clearance Transaction: The procedure by which financial trades settle; that is, the correct and timely transfer of funds to the seller and securities to the buyer. Often with clearing, a specialized organization acts as the intermediary and assumes the role of tacit buyer and seller to reconcile orders between transacting parties. The clearing is necessary for the matching of all buy and sell orders in the market. It provides smoother and more efficient markets as parties can make transfers to the clearing corporation rather than to each individual party with whom they transact.

Alternate Dispute Resolution (ADR): ADR is a process of solving differences and conflicts among parties by working together. It is a substitute for the traditional litigation system and tries to solve disputes without the intervention of the courts.

Arbitration Law: In India, arbitration is governed by the Arbitration and Conciliation Act, 19of 96. This act governs the arbitral proceedings in India.

Arbitrator: An arbitrator is a person chosen to decide a dispute between two or more parties. The arbitrator's decision is usually binding on the parties.

International Commercial Arbitration: International commercial arbitration is an alternative method of resolving disputes between private parties arising out of commercial transactions conducted across national boundaries that allows the parties to avoid litigation in national courts.

Legal Relationship: A legal relationship is a relationship between two or more parties that is recognized and enforceable by law.

Soft Bargaining: A negotiation approach where negotiators treat participants as friends, seeking agreement at almost any cost, and offering concessions easily in the interests of preserving (or creating) a good relationship with the other side. This approach is in contrast to hard bargaining where parties are competitive.

Chapter 2
Issues in International Commercial Arbitration

ABSTRACT

A number of factors are of critical importance in international commercial arbitration. The purpose of this chapter is to provide a narrative of the key terms used in commercial arbitration, a discussion of the different types of arbitration, and a brief description of international arbitration laws, as well as to emphasize the value of alternative dispute resolution and to define the concept and nature of the arbitration. International commercial arbitration has many facets, and reading about these problems can help gain deep insights into them. In terms of discussions, mediations, collaborative laws, and arbitration, alternative dispute resolution (ADR), sometimes known as external dispute resolution (EDR), is categorized into different forms. Laws governing the resolution of legal disputes fall under the purview of common law in some jurisdictions, such as the United Kingdom. The customs and practices of various nations give rise to distinct alternatives for resolving legal disputes.

BACKGROUND

While conflicts are common, it is essential that they be resolved, redressed, or settled to allow society to function normally. While judicial systems have long been seen as the standard by which justice is to be achieved, other, external dispute-resolution mechanisms have become increasingly important

DOI: 10.4018/978-1-6684-4040-7.ch002

in recent decades. Therefore, it is crucial to talk about the value of EDRs (External Dispute Resolution) and ADRs (Alternate Dispute Resolution).

In alternative dispute resolution (ADR) or External Dispute Resolution (EDR), a neutral third party helps parties in conflict to work through their issues. As a rule, this option is more convenient and economical than going to court. Alternative dispute resolution (ADR) can be useful because it can reduce the amount of time spent on resolving a dispute from years to weeks or months if used properly.

There are many positive aspects of ADR/EDR procedures. They are adaptable, economical, and quick, and give the parties more say over the outcome.

Disputes can be settled more efficiently, and overburdened courts can rest easier knowing that they won't have to deal with as many cases as usual.

In this chapter, an attempt is made to achieve the following objectives:

1. To provide a narrative of the key terms used in arbitration
2. To discuss different types of arbitration
3. To analyze the different arbitration laws to gain deep insights into the concept and practices

For the purpose of achieving the above objectives, the methodology used is analytical and descriptive using the secondary sources as available in the published material as also the web sources.

PREVIOUS RESEARCH LITERATURE

Many experts in the field have studied ADR methods and published their findings in academic publications. Insightful and illuminating, the analysis provided by these scholars' points to avenues that can be pursued to achieve the goal of justice in a timely and economical fashion.

Many perspectives are taken into account when examining alternative dispute resolution. Whether or not ADR is a silver bullet is questioned. Some argue that ADR is no longer akin to religious fanaticism. It has been observed that in the last ten years, what is known as ADR has emerged as practices and activities with a strong resolve to take legal battles outside the court through these alternate mechanisms, despite the fact that some scholars view it as a trendy idea and others see it as an alternative to the inefficiencies and injustices of the traditional court system (Harry T. Edwards,1985).Though not without an ideology, ADR never had a unified theory to explain what it accomplishes and how it works (Lieberman & Henry, 1986). References to the works of Ian Ayres, Bruce Hay, Louis Kaplow, A. Mitchell Polinsky, and Kathryn Spier will lead one to a wealth of information on the many facets of alternative dispute redressal (Shavell, S., 1995). According to experts, the push for non-traditional dispute resolution mechanisms stems from the mistaken assumption that these mechanisms are more efficient and cost-effective than traditional judicial procedures (Mnookin; 1998). It has been brought to your attention that the history of both conventional court litigation proceedings and alternative dispute resolution methods is well documented and recorded (Brunet, E & Tul, L; 1987). Some researchers claim that the high price of traditional courts is to blame for the widespread adoption of alternative dispute redressal systems over the past few decades of proceedings (Cheung, SO;1999). One can trace the development of conflict resolution and risk management in the legal system (Hensler, DR & Penn, ST; 2003). Some groups have set up their own dispute resolution agencies to help settle disputes amongst themselves. The ADRs, on the other hand, have gained traction and proliferated in recent years (Stone, KVW; 2004). It is argued that the current system of alternative dispute resolution is reflected in the online world (Cona, FA & Buff, L; 1997). Effective and widespread use of mediation and other non-conventional dispute resolution strategies have been attempted (Stipanovich, TJ; 2004). Many people believe that increasing the number of judges and other court employees won't do much to improve dispute resolution, so they're looking into alternatives to the traditional court system (Rigby, KJ; 1983). To this end, legal analysts have recently put a premium on ADR, or alternative dispute resolution, which includes mechanisms like arbitration, mediation, and so on that avoid the formalities of a court case (Delgado, R, Dunn, et al ; 1985). As alternative dispute resolution (ADR) and legal ethics have evolved, so have the norms for how legal disagreements are resolved (Menkel-Meadow, C, 2018). An examination of the mediation process in the Sri Lankan construction industry through the lens of alternative dispute resolution (ADR) provided valuable insight into the methods employed in Sri Lanka (Illankoon, I, Tam, VWY, & Lee, KN; 2022). Legal dispute resolution is simply a framework for learning about possible resolution strategies besides going to court (Goss, J-Alta, 1995). There has been significant growth in the use of alternative dispute resolution (ADR) methods, which encompass dispute resolution processes outside of the court system (Islam, MZ, 2012). The research examined the literature on alternative dispute resolution (ADR) and the various approaches it takes to conflict resolution (Ridley-Duff,R &

Bennett,A; 2011). For this reason, the litigator's guidebook is useful. As forms of dispute resolution, litigation and trials are included in alternative dispute resolution formats as well. (Atlas,NF, & Trachte-Huber, 2000). When disagreements arise in the healthcare industry, there are ways to resolve them. However, it is also lamented that courts are often seen as the only option for resolving conflicts(Liang, BA; 1998). Arbitration, mediation, and other forms of alternative dispute resolution (ADR) are all methods of settling legal disagreements with the help of impartial third parties (Sherman EF; 1992). In the United States, mediators with the appropriate training are appointed when necessary. However, the national legal system is a major determinant of the ADRs (Holbrook, JR & Gray, LM; 1995). The administrator of the United States District Court for the District of Utah, for example, is a trained mediator who mediates disputes. Because of the nature of the legal system, for example, the city-state of Singapore, ADR is becoming popular(Teo, EAL & Aibinu, AA, 2007). It is reported that alternative dispute resolution (ADR) methods are becoming increasingly important and widely used in Singapore. It is argued that the legal system is not the only option for settling legal disagreements and the alternative dispute resolution regime in Ethiopia is also prominent as examined(Gowak & SM, 2008). Depending on the nature of the problem or issue, the legal system in Geneva's Art Law system may employ one of several alternative dispute resolution (ADR) procedures. The framework for these procedures was developed through mediation by a group of legal experts (Bandle, AL& Theurich,S, 2011). Alternative dispute resolution in schools, commercial disputes, and international trade disputes were all discussed in a study (Kaufman, IR, 1990). It looked into the reform for a system in the federal courts during times of crisis in disputes (Kramer, HS, 2016). In the United States, alternatives to traditional adjudication come in a variety of forms (Sabatino JM & Emory LJ ; 1998). Medical malpractice cases and the use of alternative dispute resolution strategies were discussed (Metzloff TB, 1992). Alternative dispute resolution methods are argued to play a significant and useful role in the adaptation process and should be used and encourage (Lide, EC; 1996).

DEFINITIONS AND CHARACTERISTICS OF ARBITRATION

When two or more parties dispute to an agreement, arbitration is useful as it entails submitting the dispute to a neutral third party who then issues a binding decision. This method of conflict resolution is known as alternative dispute resolution (ADR) because it allows the parties to settle their disagreement without going to a traditional judicial court. By mutual agreement, the parties may submit their dispute to a third party, or "arbitrator," who will then render a binding decision. Rather than taking their case to court, the parties can use this ADR mechanism to settle their disagreement informally. Because arbitrators are given the authority to rule on a case and issue an award, arbitration is considered a jurisdictional form of ADR. The arbitral tribunal's decision is final and binding on the parties regardless of whether they agree with it, unlike in the case of mediation and negotiations. Arbitration is unique because it is based on mutual agreement. The only way for an arbitrator to rule on a dispute is if both parties agree to do so. Arbitration clauses in contracts are common forms of pre-dispute agreement between parties. If a dispute arises, the parties can agree to take it to an arbitral tribunal for resolution.

Various Arbitration Forms

Domestic or international venues can be used for arbitration. When there are multiple parties involved from different countries or when there are significant international trade interests at stake, the arbitration is considered international. The applicable law to the arbitration agreement between the parties may cause this definition to change.

Arbitrations come in a variety of flavors, including commercial, construction, investor-State or investment (ISDS), and so on.

Institutional arbitrations and ad hoc arbitrations are two broad types of arbitration proceedings. Institutions like the ICC, SCC, ICSID, UNCITRAL (PCA), LCIA, SIAC, HKIAC, DIAC, JAMS, ICDR, OHADA (CCJA), and others oversee the majority of arbitration proceedings.

The following are some of the key benefits associated with ADRs.

Dispute resolution times are shortened as a result. The cost of resolving a dispute is reduced, making it more affordable. The parties are given more leeway in determining the governing law that will be used to resolve the dispute. They are at liberty to do so.

It is experienced that the citizens and the government agencies can reach a quick and amicable resolution to the conflicts that arise through ADR. ADR allows the citizens and the agency to work out a solution that satisfies both parties without resorting to a neutral third party like a Judge of the formal judicial system.

The term "alternative dispute resolution," also known as "external dispute resolution" (EDR), is commonly used to refer to a wide variety of processes and techniques that parties can use to settle disputes, with the assistance of a third party. They're employed when two parties have fundamental disagreements and are unable to resolve their differences through more amicable means. Alternative dispute resolution (ADR) methods, however, are gaining popularity as an alternative to the traditional court system.

Although many powerful interests and their supporters were initially opposed to alternative dispute resolution, this approach has since gained widespread support from the public and the legal community. The European Mediation Directive (2008) expressly considers so-called "compulsory" mediation, which means that attendance is mandatory but does not require settlement to be reached through mediation. Some courts now require parties to resort to ADR of some type, usually mediation, before permitting the parties' cases to be tried. The use of alternative dispute resolution (ADR) to settle disagreements that arise after a merger or acquisition is also on the rise.

The growing caseload of traditional courts, the belief that ADR imposes fewer costs than litigation, a preference for confidentiality, and the desire of some parties to have greater control over the selection of the individual or individuals who will decide their dispute all contribute to ADR's rising popularity. A number of the highest courts in certain countries (including England and Wales) are enthusiastic supporters of the use of mediation as an alternative dispute-resolution mechanism. This trend has also been observed in the United States, where many courts have increasingly advocated for the use of ADR since the 1990s. However, it is unclear whether litigants can properly identify and then use the ADR programs available to them, potentially limiting their efficacy.

Negotiation, mediation, collaborative law, and arbitration are the four main subcategories within the broader field of alternative dispute resolution (ADR). Conciliation, which is sometimes counted as the fifth type of ADR, can be thought of as a subset of mediation for the sake of convenience. Common law jurisdictions, such as the UK, can use ADR alongside pre-existing legal systems, such as Sharia courts.

Aspects of ADR customs can change from one culture to another. A main topic is warranted by the existence of essential similarities, and differences between countries or regions should be discussed on subsidiary pages.

There are two traditional varieties of alternative dispute resolution (ADR). First, alternatives to the traditional legal system for settling legal disputes. The second type consists of less formal approaches that hang off of formal judicial procedures. Aside from built-in channels like ombuds offices and mediation programs, there are also external channels that can be used. Whether the approach is a pendant or not, the underlying tools and skillsets are similar because they are all specialized forms of negotiation.

Formal and informal judicial bodies, as well as mediated settlement conferences, all fall under the umbrella term "alternative dispute resolution." Arbitration (binding, advisory, or non-binding) and private judges are the two most common types of formal tribunal ADR (either sitting alone, on panels or over summary jury trials). Mediation before a mediator or mediation panel appointed by the court is the traditional formal mediation process. The United States employs a mediation method called structured transformative mediation. The mail system is a formal operation. Traditional examples of informal approaches include social processes, referrals to non-formal authorities (like a respected member of a trade or social group), and intercession. Both the presence and absence of a formal structure for the application of the process are crucial differentiators between formal and informal processes.

Freeform negotiation, for instance, refers to the use of tools apart from any predetermined procedure. A labor arbitration negotiation takes place in a highly structured and formalized environment.

Any organization's ombuds office should be able to direct employees to any of their formal, informal, rights-based, or interest-based conflict management channels. Nonetheless, ombuds offices can provide a variety of informal solutions in part because they do not have the power to make decisions.

Even though "ADR" is frequently discussed these days, this spectrum is often disregarded. "ADR" typically refers to significant but infrequently used external conflict management options. Hundreds of cases per year find resolution through an organization's ombuds office, which typically provides a variety of internal resources. These choices consist of the following:

For example, by not taking sides and instead affirming the visitor's feelings while remaining objective, taking the time to hear someone out and offering feedback imparting knowledge by way of direct communication, such as that concerning policies and rules or the background of a problem, gaining access to crucial information, such as from individuals reporting illegal or inappropriate behaviour, issues are reframed, providing assistance in creating and assessing potential solutions, suggesting alternative contacts, such as "key people" within the relevant department, managers, and compliance offices, assisting people in solving their own problems by taking a straightforward approach, such as by helping them conduct their own research, write a letter detailing their concerns, or participate in a role-playing exercise providing shuttle diplomacy by, for instance, assisting staff and managers in formulating proposals that may settle a dispute, facilitating talks, providing internal mediation services, informally "investigating" a matter, instigating or providing training on a specific issue, discovering new ways to spread an existing policy, etc., are all examples of helping facilitate a generic approach to a specific problem. Further, there are ways of discovering "new issues" and sharing them with the rest of the company, recognizing recurring problems, and discussing them involved in systemic reform, such as by advocating for new policies or procedures to be implemented and the act of following up with a visitor or on a suggested system change. Yet another possibility for conflict resolution is a referral to a trusted co-worker which can be a quick and easy way to get people working through problems. The majority of interventions from co-workers are unofficial and informal. Some of the court-ordered mediation processes are just formal ADR, yet the semblance of the ADR process exists despite its legal force even after filing a lawsuit. It is then a mix of ADR and legalism which are voluntarily chosen by the parties due to circumstantial concerns.

Most of the time, the provider sets the ADR process's dividing lines rather than the customer. Depending on their specific requirements and the constraints of their situation, well-informed consumers may employ a wide variety of strategies.

It is also necessary to realize that resolving conflicts is a primary objective of every alternative dispute resolution (ADR) procedure and conflict resolution ensures the success of the ADR process/

The Characteristics of Different Categories of ADR

i. A neutral third party does not mediate or impose a resolution in a negotiation. All parties involved are free to walk away at any time. (Note - a third party such as a chaplain, organizational ombudsperson, social worker, or skilled friend may be coaching one or both of the parties behind the scenes, a process called "Helping People Help Themselves".
ii. A neutral third party, the mediator, helps the parties work through their differences and reach an agreement (and may even make a proposal for an agreement, which is called a "mediator's proposal"), but does not impose an agreement on them. What is more commonly known as mediation elsewhere (including in the United Kingdom) is called alternative dispute resolution (ADR) .

iii. Each side in a collaborative law or divorce case is represented by a solicitor who works to mediate a settlement according to agreed-upon parameters. Together, the parties' legal experts (who are familiar with the procedure) and their chosen experts come to a satisfactory resolution. The parties are not forced into a decision.

iv. The parties to an arbitration agreement are not required to participate unless they so choose; instead, neutral third-party acts as a private judge to impose a ruling. Arbitrations are commonplace because parties frequently stipulate in their contracts that any disagreements will be settled through an impartial third party. This provision is commonly referred to as a "Scott Avery Clause" and has come under increased judicial scrutiny in recent years, especially when applied to consumer agreements (such as credit card agreements). Parties can still appeal the results of arbitration to a court, but the standard of review is very high.

Some Additional ADR Methods, Other Than the Primary Methods

a. A case evaluator is a third party who is not part of either party's legal team and who is not bound by the outcome of the case but who can provide advice on the merits of each side's position and an estimate of how a judge or jury might rule. This procedure, known as "early neutral evaluation," occurs soon after a lawsuit has been filed in court. A third-party expert is brought into the case to provide an impartial assessment of the situation. The expert's opinion may encourage a settlement after helping the parties better understand the merits of their case.

b. The term "family group conference" refers to a gathering of people who are all related to each other through blood or marriage. Family members learn communication and problem-solving techniques at this meeting (or often a series of meetings) with the goal of ending abusive or harmful interactions within the family unit.

c. A neutral fact finder is a third party who is neither party to the dispute nor a member of the court who is asked to investigate a matter and report or testify as to their findings. For difficult disputes involving science or hard data, the impartial investigation process can be invaluable.

d. As agreed upon by the parties, expert determination is the process by which a disagreement or dispute is referred to a neutral third party who is then tasked with reaching a conclusion on the issue at hand. Unless the parties agree otherwise, the procedure will be held in the strictest confidence and its outcome will be binding.

e. When people at a business, government agency, or educational establishment have grievances, they can go to an "ombudsman," a neutral third party designated by the institution to handle the situation. An ombudsman is a neutral third party employed by a company or government agency to investigate complaints.

f. The term "alternative" is often used to refer to a form of dispute resolution that is not a court case. A company's customer service department may be involved in corporate dispute resolution when it responds to complaints about the company's products, mediates conflicts between customers and third-party vendors, or contributes to a system of enforcement based on the company's good name. As a slang term, it can be used as an alternative to physical force or to let a disagreement go away.

g. A systems approach has been discussed more frequently in recent years as a means of encouraging "appropriate" dispute resolution and providing a variety of options for people who are in conflict. It means that there are situations where filing a formal grievance, going to court, calling the police, talking to a compliance officer, or contacting the government's inspector general is the best course of action. In other cases, the parties to the conflict can resolve it themselves with the right amount of facilitation and guidance from an impartial third party (such as a mediator or arbitrator). So, "alternative" means something other than going to court to settle a dispute. To be "appropriate," dispute resolution must take into account all of the relevant, responsible means of resolving the conflict at hand.

h. The process of alternative dispute resolution (ADR) that takes place online is called "online dispute resolution" (ODR, which is mostly a buzzword and an attempt to create a distinctive product). It's important to remember, though, that government agencies may offer ODR services, which means they could end up as a part of the court case. And in cases like the UDRP and domain name disputes, they can be made available worldwide when domestic remedies fail to adequately address the concerns of the disputing parties. The "alternative" requirement of ADR may therefore be difficult to meet through ODR.

Alternate Dispute Resolution: Opportunities and Obstacles.

The Opportunities and obstacles of ADR can be discussed as follows:

Some of the Opportunities of ADR are:

1. Useful in cases involving multiple litigants
2. Consumer participation can reduce costs and, in many cases, is completely free
3. Settlement probability and duration
4. Adaptability to change
5. Authority over procedure rests with the parties
6. The forum selected by the parties
7. Solutions that make sense
8. It's possible to think about more things
9. The potential for future interest protection is shared
10. Confidentiality
11. Managing dangers
12. A solicitor is not needed unless it provides an alternative to the adversarial judicial system

The Obstacles of ADR can be mentioned as follows:

i. A standard has to be set
ii. Court orders are required.
iii. Orders in the interim are required
iv. An absence of evidentiary standards
v. It's necessary to enforce laws
vi. Because of a disparity in power, suspicions bordering on criminality can arise
vii. There can be legal complexities
viii. Evidence analysis or live testimony may be required.
ix. A need for professional testimony

For as long as there has been "people's mediation," the parties have stayed in touch throughout the entire session. Mediation's success rate was greatly increased by a recent innovation in which the parties are separated after (or sometimes before) a joint session and the rest of the process is conducted without the parties in the same area.

Trade guild masters or other powerful authorities used to arbitrate disputes. Commercial vendors of arbitrators are a recent development, and these individuals typically hold no significant social or political sway over the contending parties. That kind of person is much easier to come by, which is a big opportunity. However, the difficulty is that the parties' social networks are not utilized. In case senior guild officials arbitrated certain contracts, they would bring together a knowledgeable expert on the subject with a powerful figure whose patronage, goodwill, and opinion would be taken into account.

Country Specific Contexts of ADRs

It is interesting to furnish the situations of ADRs in some select country-specific contexts. Some such country-specific contexts are:

Canada

When it comes to alternative dispute resolution (ADR), Canada experienced something of a "cultural shift" in the '80s and '90s.

It was around this time that people started looking for alternatives to the adversarial process of traditional court proceedings in order to settle their legal disputes. Continued development over the succeeding decades led to ADR's current status as a mainstream method of conflict resolution. In its 2014 decision in Hryvnia v. Mauldin, the Supreme Court of Canada stated that "However, in the decades prior to this declaration, there had already been a number of experiments in ADR practices across the provinces. The challenge of providing meaningful access to justice is now the greatest threat to the rule of law in Canada today... [The] balance between procedure and access struck by our justice system must reflect modern reality and recognize that new models of adjudication can be fair and just."

On January 4, 1999, the Ontario Mandatory Mediation Program went into effect, marking the beginning of one of the country's earliest and most significant alternative dispute resolution (ADR) initiatives. The program initially ran in a subset of courts across Ontario and Ottawa, but it was later expanded to cover Windsor, Ontario's third-largest judicial area, in 2002.

There has been a call for alternative dispute resolution (ADR) to be considered alongside conventional litigation in other states as well. In Quebec, for instance, the New Code became effective in 2015, requiring litigants to explore alternative dispute resolution methods like mediation before bringing their cases to court. The New Code also formalized the mediator's role in court by specifying that, should the dispute go to trial, the mediator will remain neutral and will not testify on behalf of either party. An alternative dispute resolution (ADR) program in which a judge is appointed to act as a mediator between disputing parties who voluntarily pursue JADR was documented in a 2009 report from Manitoba.

Canada's bloated court system is often cited as an argument in favor of alternative dispute resolution practices there. While this is a compelling case for alternative dispute resolution everywhere, the situation is especially dire in Alberta. Alberta has the highest population to Superior Court Justices ratio (63,000:1) due to its rapidly expanding population. On the other hand, the national average of one Justice for every 35,000 Canadians is nearly half as high.

Certain private organizations and post-secondary institutions in Canada offer mediation training that can lead to certification as a mediator. In Canada, the ADR Institute of Canada (ADRIC) is the go-to place for training in alternative dispute resolution. Both the Qualified Mediation and the more advanced Chartered Mediation certificates are available through ADRIC. These can be learned at any of ADRIC's seven regional affiliates spread across the country of Canada. Some of these are:

i. Organization for Dispute Resolution in B.C. (ADR BC)
ii. In Ontario, we have the ADR Institute (ADRIO)
iii. Dispute Resolution in Saskatchewan (ADR SK)
iv. The Atlantic Institute for Conflict Avoidance and Resolution (ADRAI)
v. The Manitoba Chapter of the Association for Dispute Resolution (ADRIM)
vi. Alberta Institute of Conflict Resolution (ADRIA)
vii. Mediation and Arbitration Institute of Quebec (IMAQ)

Iceland

The efficacy of mediation in Iceland can be seen from the fact that the Njáls have an Icelandic story about a peacemaker who becomes so powerful that he challenges the existing order. Tragically, it all culminates in the murder and burning alive of Njal in his home by his enemies, the escape of a family friend, a brief war, and the eventual resolution of the conflict through the intermarrying of the two strongest survivors.

India

The Arbitration Act of 1940 established a framework for alternative dispute resolution in India, so the practice is not new. In order to comply with the UNCITRAL Model's harmonization requirements, the Arbitration and Conciliation Act of 1996 was passed into law. As part of efforts to modernize India's judicial system, Section 89 was added to the country's traditional civil law, the Code of Civil Procedure (CPC) of 1908. Disputes can be settled outside of court under CPC Section 89 (1). When the court determines that a settlement is possible and that its terms are likely to be acceptable to the parties, it may refer the matter to arbitration, conciliation, mediation, or judicial settlement.

The Indian judicial system is notoriously slow, so the country has put a premium on alternative dispute-resolution mechanisms. The Lok Adalat system established by the National Legal Services Authority Act, of 1987 is a distinctively Indian take on alternative dispute resolution, in contrast to the more Western-style Arbitration and Conciliation Act of 1996.

The Centre for Public Policy Research in Kochi, India, is a think tank that recently completed a study on the topic of commercial dispute resolution in southern India. Compared to its counterpart in Kerala, the Court-annexed Mediation Centre in Bangalore has a 64% success rate, according to the study. Another interesting fact is that among the three southern states (Karnataka, Tamil Nadu, and Kerala), Tamil Nadu is said to have the highest adoption of dispute resolution, while Kerala has the least.

THE LAWS MANDATING ARBITRATION AND MEDIATION SERVICES

To define the law relating to conciliation and for matters connected therewith or incidental thereto, and to consolidate and amend the law relating to domestic arbitration, international commercial arbitration, and enforcement of foreign arbitral awards.

Arbitration

Before a dispute can be resolved through arbitration, the parties must have entered into a legally binding Arbitration Agreement. A written agreement is required per Section 7. The arbitration agreement must either be included in the contract at issue or referenced by the parties to another signed document. Written correspondence, such as letters, telexes, or telegrams, provides a record of an agreement and can be used to infer the existence of an arbitration agreement. A written arbitration agreement is also considered to exist when one party alleges the existence of such an agreement in a statement of claim of defence and the other party does not deny it.

Any of the disputing parties may initiate the appointment of an arbitrator, and if the other party does not cooperate, the requesting party may petition the Chief Justice's office to appoint an arbitrator. A challenge to an arbitrator's appointment must be based on either a reasonable doubt in the arbitrator's impartiality or a lack of proper qualification of the arbitrator as required by the arbitration agreement. The Arbitration Tribunal shall consist of a single arbitrator or, if more than one is appointed, of all such arbitrators.

Judicial intervention is limited to temporary measures only during the arbitration process. The arbitration panel has authority within its own territory. Therefore, a challenge to the arbitration tribunal's jurisdiction must be made directly to the arbitration tribunal. A party has little recourse if the tribunal denies their request other than to appeal the award to a court. In order to have the award nullified, a party can use the procedures outlined in Section 34 to petition the principal civil court of original jurisdiction.

When the time for appealing to have an award overturned has passed or when an appeal to have an award overturned has been denied, the award becomes final and binding on the parties and is treated as a decree of the court.

Conciliation

Conciliation is a compromise-focused alternative to arbitration. No prior agreement is needed for this procedure to take place. A conciliator can be appointed by either party upon request. Although one conciliator is recommended, two or even three can be used. All conciliators must work together if there are more than one. A conciliation attempt will fail if one of the parties rejects the offer.

Each side may submit a statement to the mediator outlining the dispute's context and the specific issues at hand. A copy of the statement is forwarded by both parties. The conciliator can ask for more information, request a meeting, or talk to both sides orally or in writing. The conciliator may even consider the parties' proposed solutions to the dispute.

When the mediator determines that a compromise is possible, he will draught the terms of the settlement and send them to the parties for approval. When both parties sign a settlement agreement, it becomes legally binding.

In many ways, this method can be compared to mediation in the United States. Mediation, on the other hand, is a completely informal form of alternative dispute resolution in India, unlike conciliation.

Country Specific Contexts of ADRs

The Lok Adalat of India

Lok Adalat means "people's court" in its etymological form. Village elders have traditionally played an important role in mediating conflicts in India. The current system of Lok Adalat, which is influenced by Gandhian ideals, is an improvement. For the purpose of exercising whatever jurisdiction, they see fit, the State Authority, District Authority, Supreme Court Legal Services Committee, High Court Legal Services Committee, or Taluk Legal Services Committee will hold fictitious courts (called Lok Adalat) on a regular basis. These are typically presided over by a retired judge, concerned citizens, or lawyers. Offenses that cannot be compounded are outside of its purview.

Lok Adalat is much quicker than traditional lawsuits because the plaintiff is not required to pay the court fee and there are no strict procedural requirements (such as those outlined in the [Indian] Civil Procedure Code or the Indian Evidence Act). In contrast to traditional courts, parties here have the opportunity to communicate directly with the judge.

Disputes that are currently being heard in conventional courts may be moved to a Lok Adalat if all parties agree. If one of the parties files a petition with the court and the judge believes there is a chance the case can be resolved through negotiation after hearing from the other side, the case may be transferred to a Lok Adalat.

Lok Adalats emphasise cooperative problem solving. When negotiations fail, the case must be brought before a judge again. If, however, the parties are able to settle on an agreement, the award will be final and legally binding. A civil court has issued this order, and it must be obeyed. Since the award was reached through mutual agreement, it is final and cannot be challenged in court. This is true even under Article 226 of the Indian Constitution, which allows the parties to the dispute to file a Writ Petition with the High Courts.

Every Lok Adalat is considered a Civil Court, and its proceedings have the same weight as those of a regular court.

Pakistan

The following is a brief synopsis of the applicable laws (or provisions) governing the ADR:

Criminal Procedure Code, Title XXII, Chapter XXII, Year 1898 (summary trial provisions).

Act of 1940 Concerning Arbitration (Indian).

The Constitution of Pakistan, 1973, Articles 153 and 154 (Council of Common Interest)

Article 156 of the 1973 Pakistani Constitution (National Economic Council)

Article 160 of Pakistan's 1973 constitution (National Finance Commission)

Article 184 of Pakistan's 1973 constitution (Original Jurisdiction when federal or provincial governments are at dispute with one another)

Arbitration Act of 2011 (Resolving Investment Disputes Across Borders)

Act of 2011 Recognizing and Enforcing Foreign Arbitral Awards and Arbitration Agreements

Legal framework for alternate approaches to conflict resolution, 2017

5. Somalia's ADR (Alternative Dispute Resolution) system is a culturally and historically significant form of mediation and informal justice. It is a form of justice in which an impartial third party hears arguments on both sides of a dispute and then reaches a mutually agreeable resolution.

South and Central Africa

Mediating and settling disputes amicably were cornerstones of African legal systems prior to the colonial introduction of modern state law. The official legal system in many countries now includes these traditional mechanisms. Specialized tribunaux de conciliation in Benin hear cases involving a wide variety of civil law issues. The outcomes are reported to the trial court, which confirms a successful conciliation or assumes jurisdiction over the case. Other Francophone African countries have tribunals that function similarly.

The United Kingdom

For cases involving disagreements between taxpayers and Her Majesty's Revenue and Customs, ADR is strongly recommended in the United Kingdom.

The regulated industries of finance, telecommunications, and energy all have ADR providers. Many industries beyond the regulated ones have their own schemes that offer membership on a voluntary basis. Two sets of regulations enforcing the European Directive on alternative dispute resolution were introduced in Parliament in March and June of 2015.

Throughout a variety of industries in the United Kingdom, ADR is now commonplace. If a business is unable to resolve a consumer dispute, they must direct the customer to an approved alternative dispute resolution (ADR) scheme. This is the case in the telecommunications, energy, banking, and law industries. In the aviation industry, where PACT is run by the Civil Aviation Authority, there is a "quasi-compulsory" ADR landscape where airlines are required to direct passengers to an approved ADR scheme .[30]

The Alternative Dispute Resolution for Consumer Disputes (Competent Authorities and Information) Regulations 2015[31] were passed in the United Kingdom on October 1, 2015 to establish rules pertaining to ADR and to implement measures to increase the use and application of ADR.

The United States of America

The US Arbitration laws facilitate the integration of ADR into existing policies and programmes,

Assist activities in acquiring or developing local programmes that utilise ADR methods that are both effective and economical,

Advocate for and facilitate the use of ADR, and offer instruction in negotiation and ADR techniques,

Assist internal neutrals involved in alternative dispute resolution with legal advice

These help Duty Of Notification lawyers and other representatives with controversies that are amenable to ADR when in-house neutrals are not used.

Questions about alternative dispute resolution can be directed to the ADR Office. According to the Administrative Dispute Resolution Act of 1996, the Duty Of Notification lawyers must have a "Dispute Resolution Specialist," who is the Assistant General Counsel (ADR). Members of the office represent the Duty Of Notification lawyer's interests on a wide range of Departments of Defence and interagency working groups that advance ADR across the Federal Government in the United States of America.

Conversations With a Plan

Unlike more conventional forms of ADR, such as mediation, structured negotiation is not sparked by a formal legal complaint and focuses instead on finding a mutually agreeable resolution to the dispute through cooperation and a focus on solutions. Structured negotiation has been used to set up agreements that typically arise from would-be Americans with Disabilities Act (ADA) legal complaints. The process is often implemented in cases where one or more parties seek injunctive relief. In contrast, "drive-by lawsuits," in which a single attorney files a series of ADA-related lawsuits in public and then quickly and confidentially settles them all, can be seen as counterproductive to the fight for more accessible and inclusive business practises.

In 1999, the first legal agreement in the United States was settled using structured negotiation; as a result, Citibank agreed to install Talking ATMs. Since then, several other financial institutions, including Bank of America and Wells Fargo, have also settled on installing Talking ATMs. It was not until the 2000 Bank of America settlement, reached through structured negotiation, that the Web Content Accessibility Guidelines were mentioned in a U.S. legal document (WCAG). Since then, many organisations in the United States have used structured negotiation to reach agreements with people with disabilities regarding access to technology and protection of their rights. For example, a company in the US which provides transportation services in the USA and some cities of Canada formulated a new policy of arbitration. The Lyft's new policy on welcoming people who identify as members of the LGBTQ community is the result of a structured negotiation process initiated by the company in response to a civil rights resolution. However, the policy became controversial among some of the employees leading to court litigations.

Benefits of Arbitration Over Litigation

Compared to litigation, arbitration has many benefits. Arbitration's primary benefit is that it allows for a dispute resolution process that can be modified to fit the unique circumstances of each case. It is possible, for instance, for the parties to reach an agreement on the identity of the arbitrator or, at the very least, on the qualifications the arbitrator must meet. Since there is usually no need for an appeal in arbitration, the proceedings tend to be more cost-effective than litigation. What's more, the resulting arbitral award can be enforced in 154 countries, whereas a court judgment can only be enforced in the country where it was issued, thanks to the 1958 Convention on the Recognition and Enforcement of Foreign Arbitral Awards.

International Commercial Dispute Resolution

A primary function of the WTO is to mediate disagreements between trading partners. For there to be a dispute in the World Trade Organization (WTO), one of the member governments must allege that another government is in breach of an agreement or commitment made by the two governments. The World Trade Organization's dispute resolution system is highly utilised.

Causes of Disagreements in International Trade

Both domestic cases seeking redress under a country's own laws (with oversight provided by the relevant WTO Agreements) and international cases challenging a country's alleged failure to live up to its trade agreement obligations can be considered trade disputes.

Dispute Settlement by Corporate

A primary function of the WTO is to mediate disagreements between trading partners. When one government member alleges that another government member has breached an agreement or commitment made in the World Trade Organization, a dispute is the result. One of the most active international dispute settlement mechanisms is housed within the World Trade Organization (WTO).

Causes of Commercial Disputes

The adoption of a trade policy measure or the taking of some action by one country is interpreted by another member of the World Trade Organization (WTO) as a violation of the WTO agreements or as a failure to live up to obligations, and thus a dispute arises. If a third group of countries claims an interest in the case, they will be granted certain rights.

Summary of Important Considerations for Resolving International Trade Disputes

The following are the considerations for resolving international trade disputes

1. Legal Principles That Apply
2. Legal System: Jurisdiction and Venue
3. Dispute Resolution Forum
4. Process Law That May Be Used
5. Award Enforcement in International Arbitration and the Recognition of Foreign Judgments:
6. Relevant Legal Phrases for Business Arbitration
7. Sources of Arbitration Clauses

When a dispute arises between the parties to an agreement, the arbitration clause stipulates that the dispute will be resolved through arbitration rather than through the courts.

An International Dictionary of Arbitration

Many of the terms and expressions used in international arbitration disputes are defined in the international arbitration dictionary provided below.

Just like in any other niche field, international arbitration is full of specialized legal terms and jargon that is rarely necessary. Some examples of these terms are those used in the law, common phrases, common types of contracts, and major international conventions and rules. By providing definitions and explanations, our international arbitration dictionary hopes to remove some of the mystery surrounding this field.

Listed below, in alphabetical order, are the most frequently used terms in international arbitration. This helps in understanding the specific jargons in international arbitration.

AAA is an acronym for the American Arbitration Association.

In contrast to arbitrations conducted by established organizations like the ICC or the LCIA, ad hoc arbitrations are handled on an ad hoc basis.

ADR refers to the various processes, such as mediation, conciliation, and arbitration, through which parties to a legal dispute can reach a mutually agreeable settlement outside of the traditional court system.

A friendly compositeur is an arbitral tribunal that has been given the authority to make a decision based on equitable principles, such as fairness, rather than strictly on the law.

Agreement reached between disputing parties in an effort to resolve the situation amicably. It is common practice for parties to exhaust all other means of conflict resolution before resorting to arbitration.

Annulment, also known as setting-aside, is the rare and extraordinary action of a national court to declare an award null and void.

When referring to a respondent's response to a claimant's request for arbitration or notice of dispute, the term "Answer" is commonly used.

An anti-arbitration injunction is a court order requiring a party to suspend ongoing arbitration proceedings issued by a court in a different country.

An anti-suit injunction is a court order from an arbitral tribunal or a national court that compels a party to suspend litigation proceedings filed with a state court.

Authority to appoint arbitrators; this could be the PCA or another institution such as it.

Whether or not a dispute between parties can be resolved by an arbitral tribunal rather than a national court is known as "arbitrability."

Organizations like the LCIA, the ICC, and the PCA that facilitate the resolution of legal disputes through arbitration are examples of arbitral institutions. In contrast to arbitral tribunals, the institution does not decide the disputed issue's merits.

A group of neutral individuals who have been tasked with making a decision regarding a legal dispute. An arbitration tribunal can issue a final and binding award that can be enforced just like a judgement from a domestic court.

An arbitration clause is a provision in a contract that states the parties agree to resolve any disputes through arbitration before a neutral third party (or panel of neutral third parties). Arbitration institutions typically have sample arbitration agreements available.

An arbitrator is a neutral third party who, unlike a national judge, is brought in to make a decision about a legal dispute because of the parties' confidence in their knowledge and experience.

Construction companies typically create "as-built" documentation during the course of a project. The deviations from the original schedule and the adjustments made are highlighted.

During construction arbitrations, it is common practise to conduct an as-built vs. as-planned damage analysis, which involves contrasting the actual schedule with the original, planned schedule.

Award - A decision made by an arbitral tribunal that is final and binding on the parties. As-planned - As agreed upon in the contract or original agreement.

The arbitral proceedings can be bifurcated so that they focus on two separate issues, such as jurisdiction and liability, or liability and quantum, respectively.

The term "Bilateral Investment Treaty" is used to describe an agreement between two states that guarantees investors certain rights in the event of expropriation of their investment, including compensation, compensation for damages, and the right to prompt and adequate relief.

The Bill of Quantities is a detailed list of all the resources and materials that will be used in a building project. The BIT is an agreement between two countries that encourages investment between them.

For a build-only contract, the contractor is responsible for carrying out the employer's plans without making any changes to them.

The "Calvo doctrine" is a principle in international law that states the courts of the country in which an investment takes place have jurisdiction over any subsequent disputes that may arise. Multiple Latin American constitutions explicitly uphold this principle.

Arbitrator who presides over a hearing; also known as "Chair" or "President"; is typically selected by the two other arbitrators or by the appointing authority.

A challenge of an arbitrator is a request to have that arbitrator removed from office, while a challenge of an award is a request to have that award reviewed by a national court. Award challenges are limited by national arbitration laws to very specific circumstances.

An example of a type of arbitration known as "chess-clock arbitration" is a hearing in which each side is given the same amount of time to make their case. The use of chess clocks guarantees an even playing field in terms of time.

Arbitration Commission of the China International Economic Tribunal (CIETAC).

A claimant is the party who requests arbitration.

Another arbitrator, not the chairman, appointed by one of the parties to the dispute.

Conciliation is a type of ADR in which a neutral Conciliator (third party) is appointed to hear both sides of a dispute and then write a non-binding document suggesting how to resolve the dispute. Conciliation is a lot like mediation, but it's more formalised.

Approving an arbitrator selected by one or both parties in the ICC arbitration system.

Awards reached by mutual agreement between the parties are called "consent awards."

Temporary orders of a conservatoire nature issued by a competent authority against a party prior to the rendering of a final decision, such as the attachment of assets in danger of being depleted.

The term "consolidation" refers to the process by which multiple arbitrations based on different contracts are merged into a single arbitration for practical purposes.

Contracting in construction on a "cost plus" basis means that the contractor will be paid for the actual cost of the work and materials, plus a fee.

Fees and expenses of the arbitral institution, fees and expenses of the arbitrators, and legal fees and expenses are all included in the cost of arbitration

A costs submission is a memorial detailing the expenses incurred by a party during the arbitration process for which they are seeking reimbursement. This is typically filed after all other procedural steps have been completed.

During international arbitration, a counterclaim is a claim filed by a party that was originally named as a defendant.

The critical path of a construction project is the sequence of activities that must occur in order for the project to be completed by the scheduled completion date.

When one party causes another party financial harm, that party may be held liable for damages

When one party fails to appear before the arbitral tribunal, the other arbitrators will make a decision in their absence.

Disclosure/Discovery – In accordance with this principle of common law, each party to a dispute is required to produce all documents that are relevant to the matter at hand. In contrast to common law jurisdictions, it is typically more restricted in international arbitration.

In order to calculate a project's worth, the time value of money is factored into a formula known as the "discounted cash flow."

The Treaty on the Energy Charter.

An emergency arbitrator is a person who is appointed in accordance with the rules of a particular arbitral institution to issue interim decisions before an arbitral tribunal is formally formed.

Quick action - An emergency arbitrator's rulings issued before a full tribunal can be formed

A contractual "escalation clause" mandates that parties exhaust all other means of resolving their dispute before resorting to arbitration.

Damages can be calculated using an estimated cost formula, which factors in the anticipated costs.

During an evidentiary hearing, witnesses for both sides testify in front of a judge or jury and give oral testimony.

Decisions are made ex aequo et bono when they are fair and reasonable, rather than based solely on legal considerations.

The Latin word "exequatur" means "to execute" or "to abide." An order that a party must comply with an arbitral award, issued by a state court such as the national courts of France.

Disputes between investors and states often revolve around the issue of expropriation, which is when a government takes private property without compensation.

In international investment disputes, a common standard of protection demanded of host countries is that they treat foreign investors fairly and equitably.

Fédération des Ingénieurs Conseils (FIDIC) is an international organisation of consulting engineers who work together to create uniform contracts for use in the international building industry.

Terms and Conditions for Design-Build and Turnkey Projects from the FIDIC Orange Book.

The FIDIC Red Book specifies the terms and conditions of contracts for civil engineering and construction projects.

EPC (Engineering Procurement and Construction) Turnkey Projects are governed by the terms and conditions outlined in the FIDIC Silver Book.

Final award - The last decision made by an arbitral tribunal on all elements of the dispute; FIDIC Yellow Book - Conditions of Contract for Electrical and Mechanical Works including Erection on Site. A partial award, such as one on jurisdiction, may come before this.

A forum is a court or tribunal from the Latin language.

Using a guaranteed maximum price (GMP) pricing strategy, the contractor is guaranteed to receive no more than the predetermined price.

Arbitral tribunal hearing where parties and/or witnesses are heard.

"Hong Kong International Arbitration Center" (HKIAC).

The International Bar Association (IBA) has issued guidelines to help prevent conflicts of interest in international arbitration. These guidelines are not legally binding, but they are widely followed by practitioners.

Evidence, including document production, is often organised according to the International Bar Association's (IBA) Rules on the Taking of Evidence in International Arbitration, which are not binding but are widely used by practitioners.

Organization for Uniform Domain Names (ICANN).

Worldwide Organization of Business Representatives.

Arbitrations initiated on or after January 1, 2012 must be conducted in accordance with the most up-to-date version of the ICC Rules (International Chamber of Commerce Rules).

The International Centre for Dispute Resolution.

Most investor-State disputes are settled at ICSID, the International Centre for Settlement of Investment Disputes.

Arbitration proceedings managed by an arbitral institution, such as the ICC, are referred to as "institutional arbitration.

Measures taken temporarily; equivalent to "conservative" measures. Temporary judicial orders issued against a party before a final award or judgement is rendered.

This is called a "joinder," which means that a new party has been brought into the arbitration process.

The term "jurisdiction" refers to the authority's right and power to make a decision about something. It is the agreement of the parties that gives the arbitral tribunal its jurisdiction in arbitration.

When a party asserts that a certain body lacks the authority to rule on a certain matter, they are making a jurisdictional objection.

Many national arbitration statutes uphold the legal doctrine of Kompetenz-kompetenz, which states that an arbitral tribunal has the authority to determine whether it has jurisdiction over a dispute.

London Court of International Arbitration (LCIA).

London Court of International Arbitration's (LCIA) arbitration rules

The applicable law for the proceedings of the arbitration, also known as the "Lex arbitri" (Latin for "law of the arbitrators").

The Latin phrase "lex fori" designates the law that will be used at the location where the arbitration will take place.

Commercial law, or lex mercatoria in Latin, refers to the body of rules and conventions developed through trade.

An amount of money that has already been decided upon in the event of a breach of contract is known as "liquidated damages."

Mediation is the most common form of ADR, and it entails appointing a neutral third party (the mediator) to help parties better communicate with one another in order to come to a settlement agreement. The settlement agreement, once signed, has the same legal force and effect as any other contract.

Most Favoured Nation (MFN)

The United Nations Commission on International Trade Law (UNCITRAL) created a "Model Law" (arbitration rules) that many countries have adopted as their own.

When it comes to investment, the host country is obligated to treat all countries equally under the terms of the "most favoured nation clause" of bilateral investment agreements. A most favoured nation clause allows other trading countries to take advantage of a host country's favourable terms for a trading partner, such as a reduced tax on a particular type of products.

Cases involving claims from multiple contracts are referred to as "multi-contract arbitration."

Arbitration involving three or more parties is known as multi-party arbitration and is increasingly used in the business world.

For example, a multi-tiered dispute resolution clause may require the parties to make good faith efforts to resolve their dispute through alternative dispute resolution methods before initiating arbitration.

The term "net book value" is used to refer to an item's value after depreciation and amortisation have been subtracted from the initial purchase price.

There are 148 countries that recognise and honour arbitral awards thanks to the 1958 New York Convention on the Recognition and Enforcement of Foreign Arbitral Awards.

An award that only addresses some of the disputed issues (such as jurisdiction) is called a "partial award."

In arbitration, a party can choose to have one of its own members serve as an arbitrator.

A pathological arbitration clause is one that has been poorly drafted to the point where its validity and, by extension, the availability of arbitration, are in doubt.

The acronym for the Permanent Court of Arbitration.

A party may withhold evidence (such as documents) under the legal principle of privilege.

Procedures are the rules and regulations that govern how an arbitration tribunal will carry out the proceedings.

Arbitral tribunal's directives regarding the procedure of the hearing.

Quantum - The amount of money that the losing party must pay.

Damages can be determined by applying the principle of "quantum meruit," a Latin phrase that literally translates to "the amount it deserves," which is based on what is fair under the given conditions.

Awards that are recognised by a state court are recognised as final and binding by that court.

Redaction is when parts of a document are removed for privacy reasons.

The Redfern Schedule is a commonly used document request management tool amongst parties and arbitral tribunals.

For a new decision, a national court can remit an award back to the arbitral tribunal.

Against a counterclaim filed by a Respondent, a claimant may file a rebuttal.

The phrase "Request for Arbitration" means "Notice of Arbitration." Sending a written demand for arbitration to the appropriate arbitral body.

The other party to the arbitration proceedings initiated by the claimant.

AKA: The Swedish Chamber of Commerce in Stockholm.

Some arbitration organisations provide a service called "scrutiny of awards" in which they examine an award closely before deciding whether or not to send it to the parties involved.

To try and reach a mutually agreeable resolution, one party may make an offer to the other party in the form of a sealed offer.

A legal principle known as "severability" states that an arbitration clause is severable from the underlying contract. This means that even if the contract is found to be invalid, the arbitration clause will be enforced.

The International Arbitration Center (SIAC) in Singapore.

Single-member tribunal is an arbitration panel with only one judge.

The initial documentation submitted by a claimant is called a "Statement of Claim."

Statement of Defence – Respondent's initial set of submissions in response to claimant's statement of claim.

When a respondent files a Statement of Rejoinder in response to a Statement of Reply filed by a claimant, the respondent is making new arguments.

Claimant's supplementary submissions in response to the defendant's statement of defence.

Relevant contract law or tort law, for example, are examples of substantive law that may be applicable to the merits of a dispute.

The Terms of Reference is a central part of ICC arbitration, as it lays out the roles and responsibilities of the arbitral tribunal and provides context for the dispute at hand.

The method of figuring out how much money should be paid out in damages. Everything that has been spent is factored in, regardless of whether or not it was the claimant's fault.

Separation of the arbitration process into three parts to address distinct issues, such as jurisdiction, liability, and costs, is called a trifurcation.

A truncated tribunal is one in which some of the arbitrators have been replaced, resigned, or passed away since their initial appointment.

A turnkey contract is a type of construction agreement in which the client has no further responsibilities once the work has been completed (hence the term "turn the key").

UNCITRAL stands for the United Nations Commission on International Trade Law.

A model arbitration law developed by the United Nations Commission on International Trade Law (UNCITRAL) in 1985. Many different countries' arbitration laws are based on it. Changes to the Model Law were last made in 2006.

The World Intellectual Property Organization, or WIPO for short.

Adjudication on a global scale.

Dispute resolution in international business.

Arbitration on a "As Needed" Basis.

Rapid Arbitration.

The use of an Institutional Arbitrator

Variety in Arbitration

A variety of arbitral forms

Conducted within the country. Both parties in a domestic arbitration must be Indian nationals, and the arbitration itself must take place in India. ...

Concluding legal disputes on a global scale through arbitration. ...

Dispute resolution in international business.

Arbitration on a "as-needed" basis.

Swift Arbitration.

Resolution through Established Institutions.

A BRIEF HISTORICAL SKETCH OF ARBITRATION

The arbitration was practiced from the very ancient days in different countries. For the sake of developing insights into the current and modern practices of arbitration, it would be helpful to have a brief historical sketch of arbitration.

Authors have debated whether or not the first arbitrator, King Solomon, actually used a procedure similar to the current one when he settled a dispute between two women who claimed to be the mother of a baby boy.

Similarly, in 337 BC, another powerful figure, Philip the Second, used arbitration to peacefully resolve a territorial dispute. The term "compromissum" was used in Roman law to describe methods of conflict resolution that ultimately resulted in an agreement between the disputing parties. Thus, we can see that there were numerous instances of arbitration that actually occurred in the ancient era and can be seen as a forerunner for the laws we have today.

By passing the Arbitration Act in 1899, India officially recognised and acknowledged the practise of arbitration, though it was limited to the three major cities of the time: Bombay, Madras, and Calcutta. Both Schedule II and the rest of Section 89 of the Code of Civil Procedure, 1908 were updated to reflect the expansion of the provisions. While the public may not have benefited as much as was hoped from arbitration, it was necessary to pass the Arbitration Act in 1940 in response to economic reforms in the country. The provisions of the previous Act and the Code of Civil Procedure have been wiped from existence.

Although the Act serves as a consolidation of pre-existing laws, prior to its passage no specific procedure existed for the enforcement of foreign awards. The fact that it only applied within national borders meant that it failed to accomplish its intended goal. According to a 1981 ruling by Justice D.A. Desai, Guru Nanak Foundation v. Rattan Singh, the Act has been poorly implemented and is therefore ineffective. He detailed how judges had been forced to find an alternative forum for dispute resolution due to the lengthy, costly, and inefficient judicial process; however, judges have harshly criticised the forum's operation.

With the hope of providing swift resolution to disputes, the Arbitration and Conciliation Act of 1996 was passed. It was the UNCITRAL Model Law on International Commercial Arbitration that served as the legal basis for the Act's coverage of international arbitration. However, the Act was criticised due to its prohibitively high costs, the lack of a set time period for making an arbitral award, and the court's interference beyond a reasonable limit that ran counter to the Act's spirit.

After that, several changes were made by passing the Arbitration and Conciliation (Amendment) Act, 2015 in 2015. The Arbitration and Conciliation (Amendment) Act, 2019 was passed after the committee's recommendations, which had been overseen by Justice B.N. Srikrishna, were taken into account. The Arbitration Council of India was set up to foster ADR in the country, to strengthen the existing arbitration in India, and to assess the efficacy of the country's arbitral institutions and arbitrators.

As of November 4, 2020, two major changes to the Arbitration and Conciliation (Amendment) Ordinance, 2020 are in effect. To begin, if a court finds probable cause to believe that either the contract or agreement upon which the award is based was obtained through fraud or undue influence, it may immediately enjoin the award's enforcement. Second, the Eighth Schedule of the aforementioned Act was removed after extensive review and debate removed the qualifications and experience required for approval of an arbitrator.

The Meaning of Arbitration

One way to avoid going to court to settle a disagreement is through alternative dispute resolution, which goes by other names, such as appropriate dispute resolution or amicable dispute resolution. Alternative dispute resolution (ADR) is used to settle legal disputes outside of the court system in an expedient and cooperative manner. One of the most well-known types of alternative dispute resolution is arbitration.

It is frequently employed in cases involving issues of a financial nature. In the event of a disagreement, the contracting parties may submit the matter to arbitration if they have included such a provision. To withdraw from arbitration unilaterally is not an option, unlike mediation, which both parties can do in a court of law. As a means of ensuring that neither party is given an unfair advantage, the parties are free to determine the location of any proceedings, the language used, and the law that will be applied.

A Variety of Arbitral Forms

When a dispute arises, rather than going to court, it is resolved by an arbitration panel. The dispute is settled by the tribunal, whose decision is final and not subject to appeal by either party. Legal procedures are unnecessary for the efficient resolution of disputes. Arbitration can take on a number of different forms, each of which is determined by the applicable law.

Confidential Settlements at Home

Both parties in a domestic arbitration must be Indian nationals, and the arbitration itself must take place in India. It is unclear what constitutes "domestic arbitration" under the Arbitration and Conciliation Act of 1996. From a cursory reading of Section 2(2), we can infer that domestic arbitration refers to situations in which the parties had previously agreed to resolve any disputes that may arise in India through arbitration. The proceedings must take place in the country's home jurisdiction and apply that jurisdiction's procedural and substantive law instead of those of India.

Adjudication on a Global Scale

International arbitration, as the name suggests, takes place in a country other than the one in which the parties to the dispute are located. This may be due to a clause in the parties' agreement or to the fact that the dispute was sparked by an international factor. It would depend on the specifics of the case as to whether foreign law or Indian law would apply.

Commercial Dispute Resolution on a Global Scale

According to Section 2(1)(f), international commercial arbitration is arbitration that occurs because of a dispute arising from a commercial contract where either one of the parties resides in a foreign country or is a foreign national, or where the core management committee of an association, company, or body of individuals is controlled by foreign individuals.

Having a foreign party involved triggers Part I of the Act, which means it falls under the purview of international commercial arbitration under Indian law. It would not, however, apply if the site of the international commercial arbitration was somewhere other than India. Due to the Company Incorporation Amendment Act of 2015, companies are no longer subject to ICA. In TDM Infrastructure Pvt. Ltd. v. Union of India, the Supreme Court examined the reach of Section 2 (1) (f) (iii). Contrary to UE Development India Pvt. Ltd., is controlled by a foreign entity, it would still be treated as an Indian company because it was formed in India. The definition of "foreign body corporate" would thus not apply to a company that has Indian nationality and has been registered in India, even if its ownership is held by a foreign entity.

Three additional forms of arbitration, all of which are based on the established procedure and rules, have been recognised in India.

Consensual Arbitration

When disputing parties agree to submit their dispute to arbitration on an ad hoc basis, this is called an ad hoc arbitration. Due to its low cost and well-developed infrastructure, it has become the preferred method of arbitration in India. In an informal arbitration, no arbitral institution's rules are followed and the proceedings are handled privately. The rules and procedure for the dispute resolution are up to the parties' mutual agreement. Commercial disputes on a global scale or at home can both benefit from this method of dispute resolution. Due to the fact that most disputes are settled in accordance with the law of the place where the arbitration will take place, the jurisdiction is crucial. If the parties have decided to keep the seat in India, for instance, then the Arbitration and Conciliation Act will not apply to the resolution of any disputes that may arise. The Act also allows for the arbitral tribunal or the parties to seek assistance from a suitable institution or individuals if necessary. In the event that the parties cannot agree on the number of arbitrators, the Chief Justice of a Supreme Court or the Chief Justice of a High Court shall appoint one arbitrator to serve on the tribunal.

Accelerated Arbitration

When traditional forms of arbitration are too slow or cumbersome to resolve a dispute, parties may turn to fast-track arbitration as a viable alternative. The primary purpose of arbitration is to quickly and efficiently settle a dispute, and this method does not necessitate any time-consuming procedures. Fast-track arbitration proceedings are required to be completed within six months under the terms of the Act. Unlike in other types of arbitration, the arbitrator relies solely on the written submission, and there is no need for more than one arbitrator to resolve the dispute.

Arbitration in a Formal Institution

To conduct an Institutional Arbitration, the contracting parties must agree to use an arbitral institution. The institution's governing body or the parties themselves can choose an arbitrator or panel of arbitrators. The Act's Part I allows for the selection of an arbitrator to resolve a narrow dispute between the parties.

When the parties fail to agree upon an arbitrator, the institution will choose one or more individuals who have the required knowledge and background for the case. However, the institution will provide a list of potential arbitrators for the parties to select from if they opt to make their own appointment.

As a result of a standardised procedure and an effective dispute resolution mechanism, it is widely used by businesses around the world. The International Court of Paris, the National Arbitration Forum in the United States, the Singapore International Arbitration Centre, and the Chartered Institute of Arbitrators in the United Kingdom are all notable arbitration centres.

The parties in the 2009 case M/S Nandan Biomatrix Limited vs. D 1 Oils Limited agreed to submit any disputes related to the contract to binding institutional arbitration. The highest court in the land looked into the agreement to see if it was legally binding and whether or not the lack of a certain institution rendered it so. It was decided that the agreement between the parties was legal because the parties had intended to resolve their disputes through institutional arbitration.

India's arbitration system has many benefits.

Both parties must agree to arbitrate in order for it to proceed, and a provision for arbitration must be included in the contract.

Parties' ability to choose their own forum, language, and governing law ensures a level playing pitch and prevents any unfair advantage for either side.

All communications between the parties during the arbitration process and following the announcement of the arbitrator's decision shall be treated as confidential.

Since neither party has to pay a disproportionate share of the costs, arbitration is often chosen by disputing parties instead of going through the more time-consuming and expensive court process.

Simple and informal procedure — neither party needs to hire a barrister to represent their interests, and the outcome can be modified to meet the needs of all parties involved. Since everyone is relaxed and at ease, it should be simpler for the parties to come to an agreement.

Parties have the option of choosing their own arbitrator or collaborating with the institution to have one appointed who has experience in the subject matter at hand.

Domestic arbitration must issue its award within a year of the final day of the pleadings, and international arbitration must issue its award within six months of the last day of the pleadings. However, no strict deadlines are imposed on the resolution of internal commercial disputes. As a result, the recognition is bestowed without undue delay.

Any arbitration award is final and binding on the parties involved because it can be enforced in court.

Ability to influence outcome through direct participation in decision-making process gives parties a strong position of control. This is a peaceful solution to the problem.

Arbitration Rules Around the World

There are different rules for governing the arbitration agreement. Therefore, a question arises as to which law should govern arbitration.

In international arbitration, the body of national rules known as the lex arbitri (also known as the "procedural law" of the arbitration, the "curial law," or the "loi de l'arbitrage") establishes the general framework for the proceedings.

Lex Arbitri

The term "Lex Fori," meaning "Law of the Court," refers to the law of the jurisdiction in which the proceeding is brought, while "Lex Arbitri," meaning "Law of the Place of Arbitration

The principle of "lex loci contractus"

Lex loci contractus is the Latin phrase for "law of the place where the contract is made" when two jurisdictions are at odds with one another.

Delocalization in Arbitration

Delocalization, in its simplest form, is the process by which international arbitration is released from the lex loci arbitri (procedural law of the place of arbitration), allowing it to "float" free of national jurisdiction regardless of the location of the arbitration.

Locus Regit Actum

The laws that must be followed in an international arbitration can vary widely. There are several sets of rules that may come into play during an arbitration, including the law governing the arbitration itself (Section A), the law applicable to the merits of the dispute (Section B), the law applicable to the arbitration agreement (Section C), the law governing the capacity of the parties to arbitrate (Section D), and the law of the place(s) of enforcement of an arbitral award (Section D) (Section E). Each of these laws may be the law of a different State in an international arbitration case.

Arbitration Law (or "Lex Arbitri")

The lex arbitri (or "procedural law" of the arbitration, "curial law," or "loi de l'arbitrage") refers to the body of national rules that establishes the general framework for the conduct of an international arbitration. This is typically the law of the jurisdiction hosting the arbitration.

Significant issues are governed by the lex arbitri, such as the grounds for challenging arbitrators, the procedure for annulling arbitration awards, the allocation of competence to decide jurisdictional challenges between domestic courts and arbitral tribunals, judicial assistance in relation to the constitution of the arbitral tribunal, judicial assistance in ordering evidence-taking, and interlocutory judicial review (if permitted) of procedural rulings of the arbitral t.

In most cases, however, the lex arbitri does not lay out the specific rules that must be followed during an arbitration. The specifics of an arbitration proceeding will be set by the arbitration agreement, the applicable institutional rules (such as the 2021 ICC Rules) or ad hoc rules (such as the 2013 UNCITRAL Arbitration Rules), and the tribunal's procedural orders.

Each nation has its own lex arbitri, which is a part of domestic law and can be found either as a part of the Code of Civil Procedure (as in France and Germany) or as a separate piece of legislation (as in England; see also our commentary on the 1996 English Arbitration Act). Here you can find a summary of the majority of laws governing arbitration in the United States.

See the status of the UNCITRAL Model Law on International Commercial Arbitration from 1985 and its 2006 revision here. This law has been adopted as lex arbitri by 84 states and 117 jurisdictions. Because of this, there is now a much-appreciated level of uniformity among the various domestic lex arbitri, which increases legal certainty and promotes the use of international arbitration by commercial parties for the resolution of disputes.

The Law That Will Be Used to Decide the Substantive Issues of the Dispute ("Lex Contractus")

Lex contractus, also known as the "governing law of the contract," is the substantive law that governs the merits of the dispute between the parties. The main agreement's existence, validity, and interpretation are all subject to the lex contractus. Depending on the scope of the arbitration agreement, it also applies to claims that are not contractual in nature (such as tort claims).

In international arbitration, the parties often have wide latitude in deciding what law will apply to their agreement. It is not required that such law be the supreme law of a nation. Rules of law, such as trade usages, the 2016 UNIDROIT Principles of International Commercial Contracts, the lex mercatoria, or Sharia law, may be considered by the arbitrators if the parties give them that authority. If the arbitrators are given the authority to do so (e.g., Article 28(3) of the 2006 UNCITRAL Model Law), they may use their common sense and the spirit of justice to reach a decision without resorting to the law. It is also not uncommon for arbitral tribunals to rule on a dispute based primarily on matters of fact (as is the case in international construction arbitrations and construction dispute board proceedings), with only a cursory reference to the law.

To increase predictability and avoid the expense and wasted time of arguing over the applicable law should a dispute arise, it is essential for parties in contracts with an international element to include a governing law.

In the absence of a governing law clause, arbitrators (and courts) will be asked to determine the law that should be applied, which is typically the law with which the dispute has the closest connection (see also a discussion on the relevance of the Rome I and Rome II Regulations for determining the law applicable to the merits of an international arbitration).

Notably, many lex arbitri and applicable institutional rules authorise arbitrators to directly apply the law (or rules of law) they deem appropriate when determining the lex contractus (the so-called direct approach). Article 1511 of the French Code of Civil Procedure provides for this (for a brief discussion, see question 6), as do Articles 21(1) of the 2017 ICC Rules and 22(3) of the 2020 LCIA Rules. This also means that arbitrators, unlike national judges, are not required to take the traditional conflict-of-laws path (the so-called indirect approach), though they may in practise be guided by generally accepted conflict-of-laws rules.

In this regard, it is important to note that the commonly used terms lex fori (i.e., the law of the court where proceedings are brought) and lex causae (i.e., a foreign law chosen to be applied by the forum court) are not easily transposable to the international arbitration context. Due to the fact that arbitrators, unlike judges, do not serve as organs of any legal forum, any law is arguably "foreign" to them and they have no basis for applying it.

The Law That Will Be Used to Interpret the Arbitration Agreement

When parties agree to arbitrate, they typically do not state which law will apply. See also our recommendations for drafting an arbitration clause in 2021) for more on how this law affects the arbitration agreement's own enforceability, validity, and interpretation.

Not identifying the law applicable to the arbitration agreement can cause inconsistent outcomes in domestic courts if the seat of arbitration is located in a jurisdiction other than the law governing the contract. For example, in Kabab-Ji SAL (Lebanon) v. Kout Food Group (Kuwait)([2020] EWCA Civ 6), an English court (applying English law as the law governing the arbitration agreement) found that a party had not become an additional party to an arbitration agreement and refused recognition and enforcement of an arbitral award, while a French court ruling upon the same legal issue in Kabab-Ji SAL (Lebanon) v. Kout Food.

Almost no one today would argue that an arbitration clause is not an independent agreement from the main contract in which it is found (the so-called principle of autonomy or separability of the arbitration clause), which is why this problem arises. This means that the law applicable to the arbitration agreement may or may not be the law governing the main contract; however, in most cases, both the law of the seat and the law governing the main contract are taken into account.

Article V(1)(a) of the 1958 New York Convention on the Recognition and Enforcement of Foreign Arbitral Awards ("New York Convention") provides that the arbitration "agreement [needs to be] valid under the law to which the parties have subjected it or, failing any indication thereon, under the law of the country where the award was made," i.e., indisputably the law of the country where the arbitration took place absent an express or implied choice by the parties. Article 16(4) of the 2020 LCIA Rules states that "the law applicable to the Arbitration Agreement and the arbitration shall be the law applicable at the seat of the arbitration" (see also our commentary on the key changes introduced by the 2020 LCIA Rules here).

Relevant Arbitrability Law for the Parties

In this regard, the New York Convention provides additional guidance in Article V(1)(a), which establishes that "parties to the [arbitration] agreement [...] were, under the law applicable to them, under some incapacity" as a ground for refusing to recognize an award. Since corporations are the typical parties to international commercial arbitrations, the law of the state in which they were formed is typically considered "the law applicable to them."

The Law Applicable in the Jurisdiction Where the Award Is Being Enforced ("Lex Executionis")

An arbitral award that falls within the purview of the New York Convention may be enforced in almost any jurisdiction where the losing party has assets. As of today, 166 States are parties to the New York Convention, the most recent of which is Sierra Leone. However, the New York Convention only lays out the broad strokes for enforcement or the barest minimum that must be reached.

In this regard, it is important to keep in mind that the formal recognition and enforcement of an award, on the one hand, and the actual execution against the debtor's assets, on the other, are two separate and consecutive proceedings. In the former case, the New York Convention applies in conjunction with the national procedural law of the country where recognition is sought, while in the latter case, execution against the award debtor's assets is pursued exclusively under the national law of the country in question.

Creditors of an award need to be aware that in addition to the rules and procedures of the arbitral tribunal, the domestic enforcement rules and court procedures of the State in which the assets of the liable party are located will apply. In contrast to litigation, where a court decision may not be enforceable in a foreign jurisdiction, this approach may seem complex but has advantages.

CONCLUSION

A number of different legal systems may have an impact on international arbitration, as has been discussed. A party's choice of the seat of arbitration, the law which will govern the arbitration procedure ("lex arbitri"), the law governing the merits of a dispute ("lex contractus"), and ideally the law governing the arbitration agreement itself when the lex arbitri and lex contractus are different, is highly recommended to avoid any unnecessary conflicts. The discussions attempted in this chapter provided an introduction to the issues in international commercial arbitration, the objectives of the discussions attempted here, the research methodology adopted, an overview of research on alternative dispute resolution, the definitions and characteristics of arbitration, various international arbitration centers, a brief history of arbitration and the practices of commercial arbitration in certain country-specific situations. The chapter also narrates the various research attempts by scholars relating to international commercial arbitration.

REFERENCES

Bandle, AL, & Theurich, S, (2011). Alternative Dispute Resolution and Art-Law-A New Research Project of the Geneva Art-Law Centre. *Journal of International Commercial Law & Technology,* Hein Online.

Brunet, E. (1987). *Questioning the quality of alternate dispute resolution.* Tulsa Law Review, Hein Online.

Cheung, S.O. (1999). Critical factors affecting the use of alternative dispute resolution processes in construction. *International Journal of Project Management*, Elsevier.

Cona, F. A. (1997). *Application of Online Systems in Alternative Dispute Resolution.* Buffalo Law Review, Hein Online.

Delgado, R. (1985). Fairness and formality: Minimizing the risk of prejudice in alternative dispute resolution. *Wisconsin Law Review*, Hein Online.

Edwards, H.T. (1985). Alternative dispute resolution: Panacea or anathema. *Harvard Law Review.* Hein Online.

Goss. (1995). *An introduction to alternative dispute resolution.* Alberta Law Review, Hein Online.

Gowak, S.M. (2008). *Alternative dispute resolution in Ethiopia-a legal framework*. African Research Review.

Hensler, D. R. (2003). *Our courts, ourselves: how the alternative dispute resolution movement is re-shaping our legal system*. Penn State Law Review, Hein Online.

Holbrook, J.R., & Gray, L.M., (1995). *Annexed Alternative Dispute Resolution Contemporary Law*. Hein Online.

Illankoon, I. (2022). Causes of disputes, factors affecting dispute resolution and effective alternative dispute resolution for Sri Lankan construction industry. *International Journal, Taylor & Francis.*

Islam, M.Z. (2012). Provision of Alternative Dispute Resolution Process in Islam. *Journal of Business and Management.*

Kaufman, I. R. (1990). *Reform for a system in crisis: alternative dispute resolution in the federal courts*. Fordham Law Review, Hein Online.

Liang, B.A. (1998). Understanding and applying alternative dispute resolution methods in modern medical conflicts. *Journal of Legal Medicine*.

Lide, E. C. (1996). ADR and cyberspace: the role of alternative dispute resolution in online commerce, intellectual property and defamation. Ohio State Journal on Dispute Resolution.

Lieberman, J.K. & Henry, J.F. (1986). Lessons from the alternative dispute resolution movement. *The University of Chicago Law Review*.

Menkel-Meadow, C. (2018). Ethics in alternative dispute resolution: New issues, no answers from the adversary conception of lawyers' responsibilities, Mediation, taylorfrancis.com.

Metzloff, T. B. (1992). *Alternative dispute resolution strategies in medical malpractice*. Alaska Law Review, HeinOnline.

Mnookin, R. H. (1998). *Alternative dispute resolution.* CORE. core.ac.uk

Ridley-Duff, R, & Bennet, A, (2011). Towards mediation: developing a theoretical framework to understand alternative dispute resolution. *Industrial Relations Journal*.

Rigby, K. J. (1983). *Alternate Dispute Resolution, Los Angelas Law Review*. Hein Online.

Sabatino, J. M. (1998). *ADR as Litigation Lite: Procedural and Evidentiary Norms Embedded within Alternative Dispute Resolution*. Emory Law Journal, HeinOnline.

Shavell, S. (1995). Alternative dispute resolution: an economic analysis. *The Journal of Legal Studies*. journals.uchicago.edu

Sherman, E.F., (1992). Court-Mandated Alternative Dispute Resolution: What Form of Participation Should Be Required. *SMUL Review*.

Stipanovich, TJ, (2004). ADR and the "Vanishing Trial": the growth and impact of "Alternative Dispute Resolution." *Journal of Empirical Legal Studies*.

Stone, K. V. W. (2004). *Alternative Dispute Resolution*. SSRN. papers.ssrn.com

Teo, EAL, & Aibinu, AA, (2007). Legal framework for alternative dispute resolution: Examination of the Singapore national legal system for arbitration. *Journal of Professional Issues in Engineering*.

KEY TERMS AND DEFINITIONS

Ad hoc arbitrator: Ad hoc arbitration refers to arbitration that is not administered by an institution. The parties are responsible for all aspects of the arbitration, including selecting the arbitrators, determining the rules and procedures, and arranging for a hearing location.

Collaborative Law: Collaborative law is a legal process enabling couples who have decided to separate or end their marriage to work with their lawyers and, on occasion, other family professionals in order to avoid the uncertain outcome of court and to achieve a settlement that best meets the specific needs of both parties and their children without the underlying threat of litigation.

Conventional Court: This refers to the traditional court system where disputes are resolved through litigation.

Early Neutral Evaluation: Early Neutral Evaluation (ENE) is a form of alternative dispute resolution where an experienced evaluator assesses the strengths and weaknesses of each side's case and provides an evaluation of the likely outcome if the case were to go to trial. This can help parties reach a settlement or narrow the issues in dispute.

External Dispute Resolution: This refers to any means of settling disputes outside of the courtroom. It typically includes early neutral evaluation, negotiation, conciliation, mediation, and arbitration[1].

Freeform Negotiation: Freeform negotiation refers to a negotiation process that is not bound by any specific rules or procedures. The parties are free to negotiate in any manner they see fit.

Institutional Arbitrator: An institutional arbitration is one in which a specialized institution intervenes and takes on the role of administering the arbitration process. Each institution has its own set of rules which provide a framework for the arbitration, and its own form of administration to assist in the process[2].

Chapter 3
Arbitration Agreements

ABSTRACT

The arbitration agreement must be paid extra care to carefully craft and draft to avoid future litigation of any kind. Several countries' laws and the United Nations CITRAL have given several provisions which need to be incorporated into the contractual arbitration agreement for it to be legally sound and executable, reflecting the evolution of arbitration as an alternative dispute redressal mechanism. Because of this, there are many facets of arbitration agreements that need to be discussed at length. These include the significance of arbitration agreements, the forms of arbitration agreements, their definitions, validity, foreign arbitration agreements to be executed in a domestic environment, the jurisdiction of the arbitral tribunal, the doctrine of Kompetenz-kompetenz, and international commercial arbitration agreements. The goal is to give readers the knowledge they need on these specific issues.

BACKGROUND

An "arbitration agreement" is an agreement between two or more parties to have any and all disputes arising out of or in connection with a specified legal relationship (whether contractual or not) resolved through arbitration. Arbitration is the most formal alternative to going to court, and it has many advantages. A neutral third party hears both sides of the argument and then makes a ruling. Disputes can be arbitrated between private parties or between private and public entities. There's every chance that one has signed an arbitration agreement if ever one had purchased a cell phone or a credit

DOI: 10.4018/978-1-6684-4040-7.ch003

card and such agreements are ubiquitous. While taking up a job or purchase of consumer durable goods or similar contracts of any nature, arbitration agreements have become common now considering the ease of settling disputes or the need for the avoidance of conflicts right at the threshold. It is pertinent to note that the National Employment Lawyers Association, reports that approximately 36 million Americans worked for one of the 27% of U.S. businesses that required employees to sign arbitration agreements as of 2010. Arbitration agreements are such that well-known negotiators discuss unorthodox methods of resolving conflicts that can transform enemies into allies. An arbitration clause in a larger contract is that which states that the parties to the contract will resolve any legal disputes between them through binding arbitration. Although arbitration clauses are most frequently seen in consumer and employment contracts, they can be proposed as an addendum to any contract negotiation in which one or both parties wish to avoid the risk of a future lawsuit. Businesses often require customers and employees to sign an arbitration agreement to reduce costs and improve the efficiency of dispute resolution. It is often unknowingly entered into arbitration agreements because arbitration clauses are included in the "fine print" of lengthy standard contracts. In arbitration, a third-party neutral arbitrator acts as a judge and issues a binding ruling to settle the case. While many arbitrators are former judges, that doesn't mean they always adhere to the letter of the law. When compared to mediation, arbitration is actually a much more malleable process, with rules that can be negotiated.

This chapter aims to achieve the following objectives:

i. To discuss the significance of arbitration agreements
ii. To analyse the forms of arbitration agreements, their definitions, validity, and foreign arbitration agreements to be executed in a domestic environment
iii. To study the jurisdiction of the arbitral tribunal, the doctrine of Kompetenz-kompetenz, and international commercial arbitration agreements

The methodology used here is analytical and descriptive. It is a qualitative analysis of material available from secondary sources like published books, journals, articles and web sources.

PREVIOUS RESEARCH LITERATURE

It is important to note that it is an a priori condition to have an arbitration clause in every trade-related contract. It is reported that "most scholars agree that the scrutiny and debates" are conditions that will have ga reat effect on the trade agreement and its enforcement (Dewan, S.; 2018). The effects of arbitration agreements need special attention. Many businesses are using arbitral agreements in practice because those businesses benefit from these arbitral agreements (Ware, SJ; 2001). It may also be seen that there are arbitral agreements between one-shot players and repeat players. This is so long as there are schemes for the enforcement for the arbitral agreements (Cole, SR; 1995). While contracts have the arbitration agreements, a "properly-worded" agreement clause is essential. Studies have shown that the consumers lack the awareness of arbitration agreements and do not necessarily comprehend those agreements(Sovern, J, et al 2015). There can be situations where some of the parties to the contract do not agree to arbitrate by not including some of the claims from the scope of their arbitration agreement. In such cases, the courts have to enforce the privately negotiated arbitral agreements. (Carbonneau, TE, 2003). There are agreements which are of an adhesive nature. It will help the claims of the individuals as against the class action arbitral agreements(Ware,SJ;2006). The enforceability of the arbitral agreement is examined in depth in international commercial law (Tang, ZS, 2014). The international perspective to the laws governing international arbitration agreements are discussed including the historical application of the law of the judicial enforcement forum (Born, GB, 2014). The circumstances that obligates an arbitration agreement and the arbitral tribune to the arbitration agreement were also discussed (Sandrock, O; 1993). The myth and reality of arbitration agreements in Health Care have been investigated and reported (Rolph,E et.al.,1997). The questions relating to the comparative aspects of prorogation and arbitration agreements were studied (Pryles, M, 1976). It is argued that the governing law of the arbitration agreement is relevant as it affects the spread of arbitration agreement in the Russian country context (Day, W; 2021) The principal criticisms of mandatory arbitration agreements were perused. It was observed that the actions for waiver provisions in mandatory arbitration agreements is an effort to reduce their efficacy (Glover, JM; 2006). A contract was signed having an arbitration clause. The arbitration agreement allowed for judicial awards of substance and errors of law added to the set standards (Cullinan, T.; 1998). In a country context, the Peoples's

Republic of China has an incomplete arbitration system. Though it is an active player in the arbitration system, its arbitration agreement clause is an ad-hoc one(Zhang, T, 2013). Umpteen such investigations have taken place by scholars looking into the different aspects of the arbitration agreement and their operation within the context of contracts.

GENERAL RULES THAT APPLY TO ARBITRATION PROCEEDINGS

The parties mutually agree upon an arbitrator from a panel provided by the arbitration service (Jossey-Bass, 2005). Instead of a public courtroom, the arbitration takes place in a private conference room. After the arbitrator has laid out the rules of procedure, each side (or their attorneys) will make an opening statement. This is followed by the presentation of evidence and, if necessary, the testimony of witnesses by both sides. During this time, the arbitrator may ask questions to ensure one has a firm grasp on the issues at hand (for more on the benefits and drawbacks of arbitration and mediation as dispute resolution procedures.

At the end of the hearing, the parties present their closing arguments and, in some cases, submit post-hearing briefs. The arbitrator then issues a written decision or award, sometimes including an opinion, within the time frame agreed upon by the parties. The decision of the arbitrator is usually final and cannot be challenged in court.

Arbitration, as opposed to a court case, can save time, money, and energy. Arbitrated decisions are generally upheld and can be enforced by the courts. This means that the results of arbitrations are binding, allowing the parties to move on without the added scrutiny that comes with a court trial.

Furthermore, arbitration can issue more novel decisions than traditional courts. According to Cole and Blankley, the only remedy available in a lawsuit alleging wrongful termination is monetary damages. Instead of compensatory damages, an arbitrator might direct the company to bring an employee back to work.

Many companies that deal with customers and employees alike include mandatory arbitration clauses in their contracts. According to Cole and Blankley, parties who regularly engage in arbitrations in order to avoid litigation are referred to as “repeat players” in arbitration terminology. In contrast, one-time participants, like individual shoppers, are usually unfamiliar with the arbitration process.

One-time participants in consumer contract disputes may be at a disadvantage in arbitration because they lack the familiarity with the process and the resources to build a solid case. One would likely be at a disadvantage in arbitration proceedings if, for example, one had a payment dispute with a cell phone provider.

Because arbitration decisions typically favour companies over consumers, consumer advocates have fought the corporate practise of requiring consumers to sign arbitration agreements. Non-profit watchdog group Public Citizen looked at 19,000 cases of California mandatory arbitration handled in 2003 by arbitrators appointed by the for-profit National Arbitration Forum (NAF), and they found that businesses prevailed over consumers in 94% of those cases.

Arbitrations between organisations with unequal resources are more likely to result in an unfair decision than those between organisations with comparable resources, such as when a company and a labour union attempt to settle a collective bargaining agreement or when two companies argue over a possible patent infringement.

Agreement to a binding arbitration is advisable because arbitration is likely to be less expensive, quick, and fair if the parties voluntarily agree to arbitrate in the future, mutually determine the ground rules of arbitration, and agree to choose an impartial arbitrator together. But if anyone is pressured into signing an arbitration agreement, an attorney can help weigh the options and predict the future course of action..

Arbitration Agreements: Types, Terms, and Legal Effects

Arbitration's popularity has skyrocketed in the last few years. It has succeeded as a standalone dispute resolution mechanism because of the underlying principles of party autonomy and confidentiality. The arbitration agreement establishes a legally binding process that must be adhered to by both parties and the arbitral tribunal. Although arbitration has become a popular option for resolving disputes because of its commitment to party autonomy and confidentiality, its technicalities can be intimidating to those unfamiliar with the process.

It's important to keep in mind that the arbitration process does not officially begin until much later than when a lawsuit would normally begin. When parties enter into an arbitration agreement, the arbitration process begins regardless of the nature of the dispute. The arbitration proceedings at the time of the dispute are mandated by, guided by, and established by the arbitration agreement. That is to say, the law is meant to serve and follow the facts, and not the other way around. When parties agree to resolve disputes through arbitration, the arbitration clause becomes an essential part of the agreement and calls for a lot of planning and thought.

When a disagreement arises, it is too late to back out of an arbitration agreement. In the Indian context, the Supreme Court of India ruled in Ravi Prakash Goel v. Chandra Prakash Goel that parties who have entered into an arbitration agreement are precluded from litigating their dispute in a court of law without first attempting to resolve it through arbitration. Under Section 8 of the 1997 Act, the courts are required to refer the parties to arbitration when an applicable arbitration agreement is present.

Agreement to Arbitrate Templates

Section 7 of the 1997 Act stipulates that the parties to an arbitration must commit their agreement to writing. In addition, the parties have flexibility in crafting an arbitration agreement under Section 7, as outlined below.

An Individual Arbitration Agreement

In addition to, or in reference to, the operative agreement, the parties may enter into a separate arbitration agreement.

Arbitration Provisions

The parties may include an arbitration clause in the agreement's effective portion if it addresses the resolution of legal disputes arising from the contract. An agreement to arbitrate is presumed whenever an arbitration clause is present.

Referencing in Other Works

A contract's arbitration provision can be modelled after one in a pre-existing agreement. According to Section 7(5), if the referred contract is in writing and the reference is made with the intent to make that arbitration clause the part of the contract, then the document referenced shall also be construed as an arbitration agreement.

A general reference to the incorporation of a separate arbitration clause will not be tenable in law, according to the Indian Supreme Court's decision in M/s Elite Engineering and Construction (HYD.) Private Ltd. v. M/s Techtrans Construction India Private Ltd. Incorporation by reference must be obvious and the intent of the parties must be made clear.

Via Verbal Interaction

Section 7(b) of the 1996 Act states that if the parties exchange letters, telex, telegrams, or any other means of telecommunication that serves as a record of the agreement between the parties, then the parties can infer that they have entered into an arbitration agreement. In short, an agreement can be inferred from the parties' correspondence if there is a clear and unmistakable intent to have disputes resolved through arbitration.

Recently, at Galaxy Infra and Engineering Pvt. Ltd. v. Pravin Electricals Pvt. as a result of the parties' email back-and-forth, the Delhi High Court ruled that their draft agreement can be interpreted as an enforceable arbitration agreement in the case of Ltd v. Agarwal.

The court ruled in Pravinchandra Murarji Savla v. Meghji Murji Shah that the substance, rather than the form, of an agreement is what matters.

To add more legal weight, Section 7(c) of the 1996 Act and the presence of an arbitration agreement may be inferred from a party's "non-denial" of a statement of claims or allegations, as in Prasad v. Monnet Finance Ltd.

In spite of the fact that the 1996 Arbitration Act of India has opened the door to a plethora of potential forms for arbitration agreements, it is still best practise to include such a clause in a written contract.

Constructing a Workable Arbitration Agreement

The Supreme Court of India, in the cases of Jagdish Chander v. Ramesh Chander and K. K. Modi vs. K. When asked what makes an arbitration agreement legal. An arbitration agreement should adhere to a set of principles established by the Hon'ble Court. These guidelines should be kept in mind. Written confirmation of the arbitration agreement is required. If there is a disagreement between them in the future regarding the contract, they should have agreed to take it to a private tribunal.

The private tribunal should have the authority to make fair rulings on the disputes at hand, after affording each party an adequate opportunity to present their side of the argument.

It is essential that the parties agree to be legally bound by the arbitral tribunal's ruling.

It must be crystal clear that the parties intend to have their dispute heard by a private court.

The parties must reach a "consensus ad idem," or an agreement on the same terms.

It is clear from the use of the word "shall" that the parties intend to make arbitration a binding obligation rather than a mere option. For instance, phrases like "the parties may, if they so choose, refer their dispute to arbitration" or "in the event of any dispute, the parties may also agree to refer the same to arbitration" are not to be interpreted as requiring arbitration.

Nothing in the terms of the agreement shall be construed to preclude or limit any of the foregoing requirements. A provision allowing the tribunal to rule on a claim without hearing opposing counsel is one such provision.

Although it is always preferable to draft clear and unambiguous clauses, an arbitration agreement may be considered a valid arbitration agreement if the basic attributes of a valid arbitration agreement (as aforementioned) are present therein, even if the words "arbitration", "arbitration tribunal", and/ or "the arbitrator" are not mentioned.

It should be stressed that the aforementioned is not an exhaustive list. When drafting arbitration agreements, it's important to think about how the parties might handle potential complications that could arise. Some such mechanisms are listed below.

Instances of Arbitration

Important consideration must be given to the composition of the arbitrator tribunal. Sometimes, the issues surrounding the contract are too complex to be resolved by a single arbitrator. It's also possible that the parties would like to use their right to nominate an arbitrator in some circumstances.

As per the Indian Arbitration Act of 1940, the number of arbitrators can be decided upon by the parties involved. When tribunals consisting of an odd number of arbitrators were appointed, the award was frequently delayed for an unreasonable amount of time due to disagreements among the arbitrators. In light of this, the 1996 Act amended Section 10 to permit the parties to appoint an arbitral tribunal with any number of members they saw fit, provided that the number of members was divisible by 3. Appointing more than one arbitrator can be costly for the parties and make it hard to find a mutually agreeable time and place, so typically only one or a maximum of three arbitrators are chosen.

Appointment Methods

Section 11 of the 1996 Act of India, it grants the parties the authority to develop and agree upon an appointment procedure on their own. In the event the parties are unable to agree on a procedure, the court will appoint the sole arbitrator, and in the case of a three-person arbitration panel, each party will appoint one arbitrator, and the two arbitrators will then select a presiding arbitrator.

In India, it has been common practise since the 1940 Act to grant exclusive authority to appoint an arbitrator to one party. More and more cases have arisen since the 246th Report of the Law Commission of India and the subsequent amendments in 2015 and 2019 where the unilateral appointment was struck down by the courts to uphold the principle of party autonomy. When the Supreme Court ruled in Perkins Eastman Architects DPC &Anr v. HSCC (India) Ltd, all parties involved, agreed that the arbitrator could not be appointed unilaterally. So, it's important to avoid giving exclusive appointment rights to one party in the arbitration clause.

Discussion Language

Language barriers are a common source of frustration during the resolution of any kind of dispute, whether it involves domestic or international parties. If this happens, the cost of the translation could skyrocket, causing even more financial strain on the involved parties. So, it's always a good idea to decide on the language of the arbitration proceedings ahead of time.

Private or Official Dispute Resolution

The parties to an arbitration agreement must mutually agree upon the type of arbitration to be used, either ad hoc or institutional. The procedure and modalities for an ad hoc arbitration are determined by the parties involved. An institution with expertise in arbitration procedures is chosen to oversee the arbitration and choose the arbitrator. The Delhi International Arbitration Centre (DIAC), the Nani Palkhivala International Arbitration Centre, and the Mumbai Centre for International Arbitration are just a few of India's many arbitration institutes (MCIA). More freedom and lower expenses are provided by the ad hoc system. In contrast, the institutional arbitration model provides a tried-and-true protocol, back-end support, and impartial experts as part of the arbitration process.

Institutional arbitration is less common than ad hoc arbitration in India. By passing the Arbitration and Conciliation Amendment Act of 2019, the government has attempted to encourage arbitral institutions to become efficient hubs for both domestic and international arbitration.

Position and Site

Before the decision in Bharat Aluminium Company v. Kaiser Aluminium Technical Services, Inc., the terms "seat" and "venue" were used interchangeably, but neither term is defined in the 1996 Act (Balco). The Supreme Court's decision in Balco established that a court's jurisdiction depends on both the location of the cause of action and its "seat," or the location where the arbitration itself takes place. Consequently, the courts in London will have jurisdiction over the arbitration, and Part 1 of the 1996 Act will not apply if the arbitration is seated there.

The Balco decision was watered down by a provision added to Section 2 of the Arbitration and Conciliation Act, 2015 (A.C.A.). The stipulation states that the provisions of Section 9, Section 27, and Section 37(1)(a) and 37(3) shall also apply to international commercial arbitrations even if the place of arbitration is located outside of India unless the parties agree otherwise.

In the wake of the Balco decision, questions arose about how to define "venue" or "place" in the context of an arbitration. The Supreme Court of India, in the case UOI v. Hardy Exploration and Production (India) Inc., defined "venue" to mean only the location of the arbitration hearings and "seat" to mean the location where the arbitrators actually sit to make decisions. This means that even if the seat of the arbitration is in India, the venue may be located elsewhere, and Part 1 of the 1996 Act would still apply.

Subsequently, in BGS-SGS SOMA-JV v. NHPC Ltd., a three-judge bench of the Hon'ble Supreme Court decided a domestic arbitration case and held that if an arbitration agreement specifies a venue but does not specify the seat or the rules governing the tribunal, the place of the venue will be interpreted as the seat of the arbitration. That's why the venue itself will have jurisdiction over the arbitration if a seat and a governing law aren't specified.

From the Indian Supreme Court's revolving door of rulings on this issue, it can be inferred that the seat and venue controversy centres on the arbitration's law of the arbitral court. The law of curial is the law that will govern the arbitration and the rights of the parties involved. As a result, the location of Competence-competence is a concept included in Section 16 of the Arbitration and Conciliation Act. It has two sides: first, it shows that the courts are reluctant to decide the issue before the tribunal has decided it; second, it shows that the tribunal can decide on its jurisdiction even without judicial backing. To what extent, if at all, can arbitral tribunal decisions be challenged in court, and what effect that would have on the binding effect of those decisions, are questions that necessitate further discussion.

In a case: "Union of India vs. M/s. When considering the case of East Coast Boat Builders & Engineers Ltd., the Hon'ble Delhi High Court noted that it was obvious from the scheme of the act that the legislature did not grant appeal against the order under Section 16(5) where the arbitral tribunal decides to reject a plea that it has no jurisdiction. According to the terms of this agreement, the arbitral tribunal shall move forward with the arbitration proceedings and render an award without unnecessary delay or interference from the court in its role as supervisor. In the case of Group Housing Society Ltd. (Regd.) vs. Ram Sharma and Associates, the Hon'ble Delhi High Court ruled that the arbitral process must continue and the award must be declared if a plea under Section 16(5) of the Arbitration and Conciliation Act is denied by the Arbitral Tribunal. In the meantime, the aggrieved party must wait until the award is announced, and there is no remedy against such order.

An appeal and trial are possible under Section 37(2) of the Arbitration and Conciliation Act if the tribunal decides to hear a claim that it lacks jurisdiction or is acting outside the scope of its authority. In Pharmaceutical Products of India Ltd. vs. Tata Finance Ltd., the Hon'ble Bombay High Court stated its view that if an arbitration tribunal rejects a party's challenge to its jurisdiction, the tribunal is authorised to continue with the arbitration proceedings and issue an award under Section16(5) of the Arbitration and Conciliation Act. To contest an arbitral award, a procedure is provided for in Section 16(5). An award can only be contested in accordance with Section 34. Whereas, under Section 37(2) of the Arbitration and Conciliation Act, an appeal can be filed against a decision by the Arbitral Tribunal accepting a party's plea that it lacks jurisdiction.

As a result, it is crystal clear that an order related to jurisdiction made by the Arbitral Tribunal that rejects a party's claim that it lacks jurisdiction cannot be appealed under Section 37(2) of the Arbitration and Conciliation Act, while an order accepting a party's claim that it lacks jurisdiction is appealable under Section 37(2).

An arbitration agreement may not always be made in a separate document. Instead, it is a part of the parties' contract, and either it or the contract itself is invalid because of this clause. In such a scenario, the validity of the agreement and the arbitration provision will be questioned.

While the Hon'ble Supreme Court ruled in the case of Jawaharlal Burman vs. Union of India that there is a difference between a contract and its part of arbitration agreement, the situation at hand necessitates a challenge to the contract itself, which includes the arbitration agreement. There is an arbitration clause that is valid if and only if a contract has been concluded, and there is no arbitration clause that is valid if no contract has been concluded. The Court further recognised that in a substantial number of instances, the arbitration agreement is an integral part of the overarching contract, and that challenging the validity or even existence of one would entail challenging the validity or existence of others.

Specifically for Waverly Jute Mills Co. Ltd. The Supreme Court of India, in the case of Raymon and Co. (India) Ltd. v. The Hon'ble Supreme Court, held that an arbitration agreement could cover a dispute over the contract's validity as well as any dispute over a claim made under the contract. To be valid and enforceable, such an agreement must stand on its own, unrelated to the contested contract.

According to the Hon'ble Apex Court of India's ruling in Jaikishan Dass Mull vs. Luchhiminarain Kanoria & Co., there can be no lingering doubt that an arbitration clause must also expire along with an invalid and unenforceable contract. LC Simon became known as Viscount Simon. Another key takeaway from Heyman vs. Darwins Ltd. is that an arbitration clause is rendered ineffective if one party to the contract claims that it is null and void from the outset. If the contract is found to be invalid as a whole, the arbitration clause within it will be null and void.

After the passing of 1996's The Arbitration and Conciliation Act, however, the situation changed. And Section 16 (1) of this Act declares that the arbitration clause, even if inserted in a contract, shall be considered as independent from the remaining of the contract, and a determination made by the Arbitral Tribunal regarding the invalidity of the contract shall not require ipso jure invalidation of the arbitration clause.

The Supreme Court stated in the case of Olympus Superstructures vs. Meena Vijay Khaitan that arbitral tribunals are now authorised under subsection (1) of Section 16 of the Act to look and reconsider on their own jurisdiction, which includes deciding on any objection related to the validity or even existence of the arbitration agreement and for such purpose, the arbitration clause which is a part of the contract and any decision by the arbitral tribunal. If the arbitral tribunal rules that the main contract is invalid, that does not mean that the arbitration clause is also null and void by operation of law, as stated in clause (b) of Section 16(1).

Arbitral Tribunal Loses Authority to Make Jurisdictional Rulings

A party may request that the Chief Justice or his designee take action under Section 11(6) of the Act if a mediator fails to act as required under the appointment procedure, the parties fail to reach an agreement as expected of the mediators, or a person or institution fails to carry out a duty vested in him under the procedure.

The resolution made by the Chief Justice or his designee under Section 11(4), Section 11(5), or Section 11(6) is final, as stated in Section 11(7). The Supreme Court's inability to re-examine its own jurisdiction after the Chief Justice has already made a decision on the matter is demonstrated thereby.

When Konkan Railway Corporation Ltd. faced off against Rani Construction Pvt. Ltd., the court ruled that the Arbitral Tribunal would not have been properly constituted and therefore be without jurisdiction in a case where the chief justice or any person designated by him may have nominated the arbitrator but the thirty-day period had not yet expired. If that happens, the injured party can ask the arbitration panel to rule on its own authority to hear the case (as Section 16 allows and declares it can do).

An order issued under Section 11 of the Act is considered an administrative order, as was determined by the Hon'ble Supreme Court in the case Sundaram Finance Ltd. vs. NEPC India Ltd. If this is the case, then no avenue of recourse under Article 136(1) of the Constitution exists. Because the Court in this case was unwilling to interfere with the independence of the arbitration process, it had previously declared that the Chief Justice's duties were purely administrative, effectively preventing the Chief Justice from ruling on issues like the arbitration agreement's validity or existence.

It is not possible to interpret Section 16 of the Act as allowing the Arbitral tribunal to ignore a ruling made by a court or the Chief Justice if that ruling was made before the Arbitral tribunal was referred to. The arbitral tribunal cannot disregard the finality of a prior order passed before it entered upon the reference, as that finality is guaranteed by the statute that creates the arbitral tribunal itself.

The Arbitral Tribunal may not re-evaluate the issue of its jurisdiction if it has already been investigated for validity or presence of the arbitration provision by the Chief Justice or a person designated by him. In that scenario, it could not investigate the question of its jurisdiction.

The Courts With Authority to Make and Enforce Arbitration Decisions

In India, decrees are enforced in accordance with the Code of Civil Procedure, 1908 (CPC), while arbitral awards are enforced under both the Act and the CPC.

All questions of jurisdiction for the enforcement of the arbitral award were resolved in the case Sundaram Finance vs. Abdul Samad &Anr, decided by a two-Judge Bench of the Hon'ble Apex Court of India. There was no longer any room for doubt after the Supreme Court clarified that a court of competent jurisdiction can recognise and enforce an arbitral award made pursuant to the Arbitration and Conciliation Act, 1996 and that a transfer order can be obtained from any court. Undoubtedly, this was a seminal ruling that broadened the scope and authority of the arbitration panel.

ARBITRATION AWARD REVIEW PROCESS

Awards made in arbitration cannot be challenged in court on the grounds that the court lacks subject matter jurisdiction over the dispute. The highest court in the land has made it clear that an arbitrator's decision should be treated as if it were a judicial ruling made by the parties themselves. The Supreme Court ruled in a single case that a person's gut feeling can't be the deciding factor in whether or not an award is satisfactory. But this doesn't mean you can't challenge the outcome of the arbitration or that the arbitrator's decision is final.

For the smooth and timely progress of a case, the law provides for certain remedies. Modification, remission, and setting aside of an arbitration award were the three remedies provided for in the now-defunct Arbitration and

Conciliation Act of 1940 Act; these remedies were expanded upon and reorganised in the Arbitration and Conciliation Act of 1996. The Tribunal and the parties now have the responsibility of determining the appropriate remedy for any mistakes.

In the event of an appeal, the award will be sent back to the arbitral tribunal so that it can be corrected, and the award will then be set aside as a result of the setting aside remedy.

Some of the reasons why an arbitral award might be overturned are outlined in Section 34. These include, among other things, the following: an invalid agreement; inconsistency; inefficiency on the part of one of the parties; lack of competence in the subject matter of the arbitration process and the arbitral award; conflict with public policy; inconsistency in the appointment of the arbitrators; etc.

According to the 1996 Act, a court cannot reverse an arbitral award on the basis of a different interpretation of the evidence or a different interpretation of the law. The Supreme Court's ruling in Brijendra Nath vs. Mayank established that estoppel bars further challenges to an arbitral award if the parties take action in reliance on it while the application challenging its validity is pending.

The original purpose of the arbitration process was to help people stay out of court altogether. The British government was the main source of its spread throughout India. The purpose of India's Arbitration Act of 1940 was to establish formal rules for the country's arbitration process. A later law, the 1996 Arbitration and Conciliation Act, made some changes to this one. Legislative authority is not available to an arbitral tribunal. Based on the specific circumstances at hand, the tribunal will determine its own jurisdiction. Jurisdictional scope for the arbitral tribunal is largely established by the terms of the arbitration agreement. Awards made in arbitration cannot be challenged in court on the grounds that the court lacks subject matter jurisdiction over the dispute. Any decision made by the Chief Justice, or his designee, in accordance with Sections 11(4), 11(5), or 11(6) shall be final and binding for all purposes. The Supreme Court's inability to re-examine its own jurisdiction after the Chief Justice has already made a decision on the matter is demonstrated thereby.

"Competence Doctrine" (Kompetenz-Kompetenz)

According to the principle of kompetenz-kompetenz, an arbitral tribunal is authorised and has the ability to make decisions regarding its own jurisdiction, including the determination of all jurisdictional issues and the existence or validity of an arbitration agreement.

The Indian Supreme Court has stated, "The issue of limitation is not to be examined at the Section 11 stage," reiterating the "competency" principle.

A court's discretion in appointing an arbitrator under Section 11 of the Arbitration and Conciliation Act, 1996 (Act) is subject to interpretation and change. Since the text of the section itself did not provide much clarity as to the issues that may be examined in permitting or rejecting an application under Section 11 prior to the Arbitration and Conciliation (Amendment) Act, 2015 (2015 Amendment), the law in this regard had evolved only through case laws.

The Supreme Court's seven-judge constitution bench in SBP & Co. v. Patel Engineering Ltd. provided a definition of the authority granted by Section 11.

In addition, it was determined that, at the pre-reference stage, the court would examine all threshold issues regarding jurisdiction, the existence of the agreement, whether the claim was a dead one; a time-barred claim sought to be resurrected; or whether the parties had concluded the transaction by recording satisfaction of their mutual rights and obligations, and received the final payment without objection, under Section 11.

The Supreme Court's interpretation, which allows the court appointing an arbitrator to decide preliminary jurisdictional issues, undermines the effect and importance of the kompetenz-kompetenz principle encapsulated in Section 16 of the Act. Accordingly, the law commission in its 246th report had recommended that the scope of judicial intervention under Section 11 must be statutorily restricted to an examination as to the existence of the arbitration agreement alone,2 which was duly incorporated by the insertion of Section 11(6A), by way of the 2015 Amendment.

According to the doctrine of kompetenz-kompetenz, an arbitral tribunal has the authority and the ability to rule on its own jurisdiction, including deciding all issues related to jurisdiction and the existence or validity of an arbitration agreement. The idea behind this doctrine is to limit the court's involvement as little as possible so that the arbitral process is not halted in its tracks over a frivolous preliminaries objection brought up by one of the parties.

By superseding all contrary precedent, Section 11(6A) of the Act makes it abundantly clear that when deciding an application under Section 11 of the Act, a court must focus solely on whether or not an arbitration agreement exists. Therefore, it is imperative that the arbitral tribunal be given complete discretion over the issue of jurisdiction. A later in a case, Duro Felguera S.A., upheld both the original provision and the revised version, as well as the kompetenz-kompetenz principle. lawsuit against Gangavaram Port Pvt. Ltd.

The issue of jurisdiction and the statute of limitations is at hand. The Supreme Court of India clarified in the 1996 case of Pandurang Dhoni Chougule v. Maruti Hari Jadhav5 that a plea of limitation is a plea of law that concerns the jurisdiction of the court which tries the proceedings, and that a ruling in favour of the party raising the plea would oust the jurisdiction of the court.4 It is well-settled that "jurisdiction" is a word of many hues, and it takes colour depending on the The Supreme Court upheld this decision in the case of Indian Farmers Fertilizer Co-operative Ltd. v. Bhadra Products.

In light of this, the Supreme Court wasted no time in clarifying the law when it recently considered the issue of rejecting an application under Section 11 on the ground that the claim is barred by limitation in Uttarakhand Purv Sainik Kalyan Nigam Ltd. v. Northern Coal Field Ltd. The Supreme Court determined that the issue of limitation must be left for determination by the arbitrator in light of the law set out in Section 11(6A) and Section 16 of the Act, as well as the legislative policy to restrict judicial intervention at the pre-reference stage.

The Supreme Court elaborated by stating that there are exceptions to the komeptenz-kompetenz doctrine and situations in which a court may intervene at the Section 11 stage itself. If an application for appointment of an arbitrator is filed under Section 11 of the Act, the court may refuse to do so only if it determines that the arbitration agreement was obtained through fraud or deception; if the parties have not concluded an agreement to arbitrate in accordance with Section 7 of the Indian Contract Act, 1872; if the agreement to arbitrate has not been memorialised in writing; or if the disputes at hand are not within the scope of the arbitration agreement.

While this restatement of the kompetenz-kompetenz principle and the intent of Section 11(6A) is much needed and most welcome, it should not be forgotten that the Arbitration and Conciliation (Amendment) Act, 2019 (2019 Amendment) seeks to remove Section 11(6A) altogether8 while transferring the power of appointing arbitrators to designated arbitral institutions9. This could have some absurd consequences. It is possible that parties will be forced to waste time and money on pointless and avoidable arbitrations if even this preliminary determination as to the existence of an arbitration agreement is not made at the pre-reference stage. It is important to note, however, that the Arbitration Council of India is free to include provisions similar to Section 11(6A) in the rules and regulations that it will create to govern the arbitral institutions or panels that have been designated. This issue may be revisited once the 2019 Amendment's Section 3 is notified and new regulations are implemented by the Arbitration Council of India.

UNCITRAL's Model Law and Arbitration Rules for International Commercial Disputes Both Codify the Principle of Kompetenz-Kompetenz

"[t]he arbitral tribunal shall have the power to rule on its own jurisdiction, including any objections to the existence or validity of the arbitration agreement," as stated in both Article 16(1) of the Model Law and Article 23(1) of the Arbitration Rules.

The principle of kompetenz-kompetenz is not explicitly addressed in American arbitration law, but courts have consistently recognised such power where the parties have granted it to the tribunal. The legal doctrine of "kompetenz-kompetenz" holds that a court or arbitral tribunal may have jurisdiction over the question of whether or not it has the authority to rule on a particular matter because it has the "competence" to do so. Originating in Germany's Federal Constitutional Court, kompetenz-kompetenz has since become a significant legal principle in the context of international arbitration.

Arbitration of International Business Disputes

The Arbitration and Conciliation Act of 1996 as it applies to International Commercial Disputes

Disputes that arise between private parties out of international commercial transactions can be arbitrated instead of litigated in national courts through international commercial arbitration.

The Possible Outcomes of Arbitration

In arbitration, what are the three possible outcomes?

There are three ways in which parties can initiate arbitration proceedings: through the court system, through a written contract, or through mutual agreement.

An Evaluation of the international commercial arbitration system

To avoid having to go to court over a civil dispute, many people now turn to a process called alternative dispute resolution. Alternative dispute resolution can be accomplished through one of three recognized processes: arbitration, conciliation, or mediation. Alternative dispute resolution, or arbitration, is a process by which disagreements between parties can be settled through the mediation of a third party. Since there are so many cases pending in court, hearings, and rulings take longer than they should. People spend a lot of time and money going through the court system in an attempt to get justice, but the system is so backed up that they rarely get a decision in a timely manner, and even if they do, it's usually not sufficient to justify the initial investment.

The justice system is instrumental in resolving conflicts and promoting social harmony. It is the right of anyone whose liberties have been violated to seek redress in a court of law. Long waiting periods for results cause some to be wary. So, this sort of issue is what inspired the development of alternative dispute resolution.

Various Methods of Conflict Settlement

In ADR, the parties work together to find a solution to their dispute rather than going to court. Basically, it's meant to take the place of the standard court system. Alternative dispute resolution is a method of resolving legal disagreements that avoids the use of courts. For the purpose of hearing both sides and facilitating a mutually agreeable resolution, a third party is always appointed in this procedure. A total of four different forms of ADR are practised in India. The Lok Adalat, which encompasses Arbitration, Discussion, and Conciliation. The Arbitration and Conciliation Act of 1996, the Legal Services Authority Act of 1987, and Section 89 of the Civil Procedure Code are all examples of laws that recognise the validity of alternative dispute resolutions.

There is a significant savings in both time and money when using alternative dispute resolution methods. People avoid the expense and inconvenience of going to trial by using these means to settle their differences out of court. As a result, their connection is strengthened. To ease the workload of the Indian Judiciary, the field of alternative dispute resolution has emerged as a viable option for litigants.

The Role of Arbitration in Modern Society

Traditional Indian dispute resolution methods include arbitration and conciliation. An explosion in international trade and commerce has resulted from the industrial revolution. In order to maintain economic momentum and avoid protracted court trials, the parties to a dispute often turn to arbitration as a means of resolving their differences. During the time of monarchies, territorial and commercial disputes were typically settled through arbitration.

Panchayats are community meetings held in rural areas to settle disagreements between local residents. In this context, the Panchas acts as an authoritative arbitrator. An increase in the need for legal provisions can be traced to the proliferation of associations fostered by cross-border trade and bilateral commercial ties. The development of ADR was a boon to commerce on both the domestic and international levels, as it provided an alternative to the traditional court system. The parties to a dispute can use a neutral third party to help them reach a decision and a resolution.

On August 22, 1996, India passed the Arbitration and Conciliation Act, which went into effect the following year. The main reason for passing the Arbitration and Conciliation Act was so that international and domestic businesses could continue to operate in an atmosphere of hostility. It was passed to help the judicial system shoulder less responsibility and to lessen the court's already light load. Disputes between parties can be settled through arbitration by presenting them to a neutral third party. The name for this neutral third party is "arbitrator." In an effort to lessen the time and resources spent in court, some choose to use arbitration as a means of resolving legal disputes. When the arbitration process is complete, the arbitrator's decision will be final and binding on both parties.

A hearing is held by the arbitrator, who has been appointed by the parties or by a statutory body, to determine the basis for the dispute between them. As adjudication is the primary goal of arbitration, there is no room for negotiation. Once the arbitrator has determined the basis for the dispute and heard both sides, they will then impose their impartial and fair decision.

An arbitration agreement is necessary for the arbitration procedure to take place. When two people enter into a contract, they often agree to use an arbitration clause if a disagreement ever arises over the terms of that agreement. This clause states that the dispute must be settled through the use of a neutral third party, rather than through the courts. Both Section 2(1)(b) and Section 7 of the Arbitration and Conciliation Act define "arbitration agreement." In 2020, legislators introduced the Arbitration and Conciliation (Amendment) Ordinance to make changes to the original Act and Ordinance. The focus of this ordinance was on the accreditation of arbitrators as well as the court's power to immediately halt the enforcement of arbitral awards if it finds evidence of fraud or corruption.

Arbitration for Economic Disputes on a Global Scale

Disputes that arise between international parties under internal commercial agreements can be expedited through international commercial arbitration.

International commercial arbitration is defined in Section 2(1)(f) of the Arbitration and Conciliation Act as disputes arising out of a legal relationship in which one of the parties is not a citizen, resident, or habitual resident of India. Trade disputes between companies in different countries are increasingly being resolved through international commercial arbitration.

Similarly, to domestic arbitration, the process for initiating international commercial arbitration is the same. In the case of TDM Infrastructure Pvt., the Supreme Court clarified the scope of Section 2(1)(f) of the Arbitration and Conciliation Act. Inc. v. UE Development India Pvt. Ltd. According to the court's ruling, a company that is registered in both India and abroad is considered to be an Indian corporation for the purposes of this law. As with domestic arbitration, an impartial third party, or "arbitrator," is used in international arbitration. By respecting each other's cultural and linguistic backgrounds and working together, the parties to international commercial arbitration are more likely to find a mutually agreeable resolution to their dispute at a lower cost and without damaging their relationship. As a means of resolving international disputes, international arbitration is sometimes referred to as a "hybrid form" because it permits the use of both the Code of Civil Law Procedure (1908) and the Common Law Procedure. Contracts involving multiple parties typically include an arbitration clause as a means of resolving legal disputes between the parties without resorting to litigation.

For example, the ICC's model arbitration clause states succinctly: "All disputes arising out of or in connection with the present contract shall be finally settled under the rules of arbitration of the International Chamber of Commerce by one or more arbitrators appointed by the said rules."

International Commercial Arbitration: 3.6(a) Procedure

When carrying out the procedures of international commercial arbitration, there are a number of steps that must be taken. How to do it is detailed below.

Pre-Arbitration Notice

One party must serve notice of arbitration on the other party seeking to refer the dispute to arbitration before any arbitration proceedings can begin. The arbitration process officially begins once the respondent has received the notice of arbitration. The two most important parts of this notice are:

The arbitral award is not the final word on the dispute at hand, but it does address issues that go beyond the scope of the original disagreement.

Nothing about the arbitral trials or the arbitral proceedings was in accordance with the parties' agreement.

A court may vacate an arbitration award if it determines the dispute involves issues that cannot be resolved through arbitration or if the award is in conflict with public policy.

An arbitration ruling from outside the country

Foreign awards are addressed in the section of the Act that includes the New York Convention Awards and the Geneva Convention Awards. Foreign arbitral awards are defined as disputes between the parties arising out of the legal relationships by the New York Convention. Section 44 of the Arbitration and Conciliation Act defines a foreign award. Section 53 of the Geneva Convention defines foreign awards as "differences between the parties arising out of commercial matters."

CONCLUSION

A reliable and stable dispute resolution process is essential for a rapidly developing economy to entice foreign investment. Since there is a significant backlog of cases in Indian courts, commercial players in India and elsewhere have developed a strong preference for settling disputes through arbitration.

Indian arbitration, despite being one of the original members of the New York Convention, has not always adhered to international best practices. However, a significant shift in perspective has occurred over the past five years. Indian courts and lawmakers have revised the country's arbitration laws to conform to global standards. Indian courts have been generally supportive of arbitration, and the years 2015, 2019, and 2021 saw the passage of amendment acts that could pave the way for the incorporation of international best practices into Indian arbitration law.

REFERENCES

Born, G. B. (2014). *The law governing international arbitration agreements: An international perspective*. Hein Online.

Carbonneau, T.E. (2003). The Exercise of Contract Freedom in the Making of Arbitration Agreement. *Vanderbilt Journal of Transnational Law*, Hein Online..

Cole, S. R. (1995). *Incentives and Arbitration: The Case Against Enforcement of Executory Arbitration Agreements Between Employers and Employees*. UMKC Law Review, Hein Online.

Cullinan, T. (1998). *Contracting for an Expanded Scope of Judicial Review in Arbitration Agreements, Vanderbilt Law*. Review, Hein Online.

Day, W. (2021). *Applicable Law and Arbitration Agreements*. Cambridge.

Glover, J. M. (2006). *Beyond Unconscionability: Class Action Waivers and Mandatory Arbitration Agreements*. Vanderbilt Law Review, Hein Online.

Jossey-Bass. (2005). Arbitration. The Handbook of Dispute Resolution. Research Gate.

Pryles, M. (1976). Comparative Aspects of Prorogation and Arbitration Agreements. *International & Comparative Law*. Cambridge Press.

Rolph, E. (1997). *Arbitration Agreements in Health Care: Myths and Reality*. Law and Contemporary Problems, Hein Online.

Sandrock, O. (1993). *Arbitration Agreements in Groups of Companies*. International Law, Hein Online.

Sovern, J. (2015). *Whimsy little contracts with unexpected consequences: An empirical analysis of consumer understanding of arbitration agreements*. Maryland Law Review, Hein Online.

Ware, S.J. (2001). Paying the Price of Process: Judicial Regulation of Consumer Arbitration Agreements. *Journal of Dispute Resolution*, Hein Online.

Ware, S. J. (2006). The Case for Enforcing Adhesive Arbitration Agreements-With Particular Consideration of Class Actions and Arbitration Fees. *Journal of American Arbitration*. papers.ssrn.com

Zhang, T. (2013). *Enforceability of ad hoc arbitration agreements in China: China's incomplete ad hoc arbitration system*. Cornell International Law Journal, Hein Online.

KEY TERMS AND DEFINITIONS

Arbitral Award: An arbitration award (or arbitral award) is a determination on the merits by an arbitration tribunal in an arbitration, and is analogous to a judgment in a court of law. It is referred to as an 'award' even where all of the claimant's claims fail (and thus no money needs to be paid by either party), or the award is of a non-monetary nature.

Arbitral Template: It is a document that outlines the procedures and rules that will be followed during an arbitration proceeding. It can include information on the selection of arbitrators, the language of the arbitration, and the format for presenting evidence.

Arbitral tribunal: It: is a panel of one or more unbiased adjudicators which is convened and sits to resolve a dispute by way of arbitration. The tribunal may consist of a sole arbitrator, or there may be two or more arbitrators, which might include either a chairman or an umpire. The parties to the arbitration are usually free to determine the number and composition of the arbitral tribunal

Competence doctrine: It refers to the principle that an arbitral tribunal has the power to determine its own jurisdiction. This means that it can decide whether it has the authority to hear and decide a dispute.

Discussion language: In arbitration refers to the language or languages that will be used during the arbitration proceedings. The language or languages of the arbitration can be agreed upon by the parties. Failing such agreement, the arbitral tribunal shall determine the language or languages to be used in the proceedings, taking into account the parties' due process rights

Prorogation: It refers to the extension or prolongation of a legal term or session. In the context of arbitration, it could refer to the extension of the term of an arbitral tribunal or the prolongation of an arbitration session.

Verbal Interpretation: It refers to the process of interpreting spoken language during an arbitration proceeding. This can be important when parties to the arbitration speak different languages.

Chapter 4
Mandatory Uncitral Model Laws:
An Anlysis

ABSTRACT

The United Nations (UN) is the organization in charge of overseeing international commercial arbitration and the organization that drafted the international trade laws (ITL). Because of the varied nature of national laws pertaining to international commercial arbitration, the United Nations has developed its own model laws to serve as a guide for the creation of nationally consistent laws governing international trade and commercial arbitration. Arbitration and agreement, definition and form of the arbitration agreement, substantive claim before the court, the arbitration agreement and interim measures by the court, number of arbitrators, and finality of an arbitration award are all topics that have been covered by the model laws. A brief analysis of the mandatory model law is presented hereunder.

BACKGROUND

International trade is an essential activity of humankind in a globalized environment to enhance trade and commerce and benefit from the comparative cost of production of goods and services as also making available the goods and services produced across the world. It improves the standard and quality of living across the globe. With the explosion of international trade, there

DOI: 10.4018/978-1-6684-4040-7.ch004

are always possibilities of international disputes arising. In the absence of an appropriate legal framework, the settlement of these conflicts will be extremely difficult and the pace of growth of trade will be affected adversely. The United Nations is the appropriate international forum to provide the legal framework and as such the UNCITRAL Model Laws were introduced to be used by all the nations for smoothening their international trade through settling international commercial conflicts with the help of arbitration

In this chapter, an attempt has been made to achieve the following objectives:

i. To understand the nature and features of the UNCITRAL Model Laws
ii. To gain insights from the previous scholarly works on UNCITRAL Model Laws
iii. To make an analysis of the Model Laws and
iv. To provide the judicial precedents of the Model Laws

The methodology used is descriptive and analytical. The secondary sources as available in printed material like books, journals, and articles have been accessed as also web sources are perused.

PREVIOUS RESEARCH LITERATURE

Many scholars have carried out studies of the model laws and their implementation as well as implication in different contexts. The scholarship available is substantial for an inquisitive reader of the developments in respect of UNCITRAL Model laws. It is important to pay attention to the fact that these laws are by and large indicative and not exhaustive. The major part of the laws directs the states to legislate their own laws who are keen to have arbitration as a method of dispute redressal in their countries. If there is any specific rule in the laws of the states which enact arbitral law in the pattern of the model law and if the rules are less restrictive and more flexible than the model laws, the laws of the land will prevail and not that of the model laws of the UN (Berends, AJ, 1998). It is argued that a clear comprehension of the elements of the model law framework is essential to understand the impact of the laws (Binder, P; 2019). A number of general principles for review of a model law on procurement was propounded. This is because of the legitimate differences in the regulatory policies (Arrowsmith, 2004) According to a third world point of view, for different reasons, the newly established independent states assert their sense of legal nationalism and accordingly deviations from the model laws have taken place (Somarajah, M; 1989) The structure and features of the model law was also discussed for the first time (Hoellering, MF, 1986). It is pointed out critically that the provisions of the UN law represent a lack of international enthusiasm for adopting the model law(Mohan, SC; 2012). But it is also appreciated that among the different model laws adopted over a long period of time, the most notable is the law on International Commercial Arbitration (Van Ginkel, E; 2004). It is also pointed out that the model law is a road to universalism (Mevorach, I; 2011). In a country context, in New Zealand, the government released a Cabinet Paper recommending the legislative changes required for the implementation of the UNCITRAL Model law(Clift, J; 2004). What is the situation when it comes to e-Commerce. In the USA President Clinton and Vice President Albert Gore, Jr., formulated a framework for global electronic commerce which was supportive of the provisions of the model laws(Overby AB,; 1999). While it comes to the question of implementation of the laws, the texts of the laws in some countries are very similar(Peterson, RK; 1993). "whether or not known to the parties from the outset, tends to suffer from a weakness which may be regarded as the main reason and justification" (Herrmann, G; 1985). It is reviewed to know the goals and structure of the model law once a jurisdiction enacts a law based on the model laws (Gabriel, HD; 2019) The model law was debated and perceived as a highly complex subject (Hunter,JMH; 1985). Yet, it is viewed that the model laws are highly potential for harmonization (McCormack, G & Wai Yee,W; 2018). It is further commented that the UNCITRAL Model laws have been a successful instrument and eulogised by stating that "probably even more successful than many of its drafters had expected (Bachand,F & Gelinas,F; 2013). However, despite the efforts to foster uniformity and harmonization, the model laws had to be revised(Bucy,DR;2010). Yet it is observed that the model laws would lack the flexibility inherent in the model law approach decreasing the likelihood of the aim of the laws to provide for the unification and harmonization of the national laws(McNerney,ME & Esplugues,CA;1986) In the case of German legal context, the German Arbitration Act is based on the provisions of the UNCITRAL model law .It was unavoidable and the model law had to be adopted because of the legal and institutional framework of Germany(Bockstiegel,KH; 1998) In the case of England, the model laws were a remarkable achievement as the legislation enacted was in the light of the model law (Dteyn, J; 1994).

INTERNATIONAL TRADE LAW OF THE UNITED NATIONS: A BRIEF REVIEW

When it comes to international trade law, the United Nations Commission on International Trade Law (UNCITRAL) is the main legal body of the United Nations. The United Nations General Assembly created it after realising that disparities in the national laws governing international trade were creating barriers to free trade. Thus, this commission was set up with the intention of actively contributing to the reduction or elimination of these obstacles. The UNCITRAL Model law was created to help states create their own domestic law and update their laws on arbitral procedure to reflect the unique characteristics and requirements of international commercial arbitration. It emphasises international agreement on the most important features of state-adopted international arbitration practises across regions, legal systems, and economic structures. The Model Law contains 8 chapters and 36 Articles, and it is intended to be incorporated into or used as a basis for the legislation of various countries in the area of arbitration.

Major Characteristics of Model Laws

The major characteristics of the model laws can be seen as under:

It establishes rules and provisions with the goal of standardising international commercial arbitration. The Model Law's Article 1 lays out the main thrust of international commercial arbitration, stating that an arbitration is considered international if the parties' places of business were in different States when the arbitration agreement was signed, or if one of the places is located outside of the state in which the party of the agreement has its place of business, or the site of the transaction(s) that constitute the commercial relationship, or the location where the events giving rise to the dispute took place. Alternately, the parties to the arbitration agreement may specify multiple locations for the dispute resolution process. It reflects the arbitral tribunal's make-up and the provision making the award enforceable. It would be enacted in a State if the seat of arbitration is located within its borders and if the arbitral award is enforceable in all jurisdictions. The 'party autonomy' principle, on the other hand, states that the disputing parties have the right to choose the governing law of the arbitration proceedings.

The court's involvement in the arbitration process is limited to the following issues: the appointment of arbitrators, the challenge and removal of an arbitrator, the jurisdiction of an arbitral tribunal, and the reversal of an arbitral award. Furthermore, the court can aid in documenting evidence, recognising arbitration agreements, and enforcing arbitration awards.

It emphasises the core elements of an arbitration agreement or clause that must be present if the parties to a dispute decide to use arbitration as a means of dispute resolution. The Model Law also specifies the nature of the provision and provides judicial recognition for it. It protects both the independence of the tribunal and the will of the parties by specifying the number of arbitrators, the manner of their appointment, and the steps to be taken during the arbitration process. It specifies the procedures to be followed in making the award, enforcing the award, and challenging the award. Consequently, the Model Law includes these crucial components to standardize the arbitration process on a global scale and alleviate some of the challenges associated with it.

Differences Between UNCITRAL Law and UNCITRAL Rules

The UNCITRAL Arbitration Rules (Rules) provide an all-encompassing set of procedures that parties must agree to in order to conduct arbitration proceedings arising out of commercial relationships. It also details procedures for the appointment of experts by the arbitral tribunals and addresses issues related to multi-party arbitration, joinder, liability, and the arbitration process itself. To that end, it includes provisions for the requirement of the reasonableness of costs and a review mechanism for arbitration proceedings. Importantly, the Rules are chosen by the parties themselves to govern the conduct of the arbitration and to resolve the dispute.

When it comes to domestic arbitration laws, however, the UNCITRAL Model Law provides a set of patterns that national governments can adopt.

The Preamble of the Act notes that the provisions of the Act are connected to and based on the UNCITRAL Model Law, showing that the Indian legislature gave the Model Law careful consideration when enacting the Act. Accordingly, the Act largely reflects the Model Law in its provisions. The following are some of the Act's features:

It has a definition clause very similar to the one in the Model Law and is applicable to both domestic and international commercial arbitration.

It requires that an arbitration agreement be in place before any arbitration proceedings can begin. Specific provisions for the arbitration agreement and for court intervention in the arbitration agreement in the event of a dysfunctional tribunal are spelled out.

The Model Law-like composition and jurisdiction of the arbitral tribunals are spelt out. It gives the tribunals the authority to make decisions within their purview and to issue binding awards with only limited judicial oversight.

It, like the Model Law, contains rules governing the procedure of arbitration hearings, with an emphasis on the independence of the arbitrators and the consent of the parties.

It details the processes for making the award official, enforcing it, and possibly overturning it. It is crucial because Section 34(2) of the Act specifies the conditions under which court intervention is permitted.

Furthermore, it has been observed that the most recent developments in arbitration as reflected in recent judicial decisions demonstrate the government's backing to make India a hub of institutional arbitration for both domestic and international disputes. Judicially, arbitration has gained support, as shown by decisions from India's highest courts.

The Model Law's Article 9 on arbitration agreements and interim court orders has been incorporated into Section 9 of the Act. According to the Model Law, a party can seek a court's protection from an interim measure of protection during arbitration proceedings. However, even after the arbitral award has been enforced, a party may still approach the courts to go further under the Indian Act, which gives the court authority beyond that granted by Article 9. In foreign-seated arbitrations, Section 9 of the Act states interim measures by the court, and it cannot be invoked after the institution of an arbitral tribunal when there is a speedy remedy available to the parties. The commendable addition of this provision under Section 9(3) of the Act by way of the Arbitration and Conciliation (Amendment) Act, 2015 is due to this act. The 246th Law Commission Report recommended, "to reduce the intervention of the judiciary concerning the grant of interim measures once the Arbitral Tribunal has been constituted." The 2015 amendment aims to ensure that all interim applications can be heard by the tribunal once it is given jurisdiction over the case. This change is consistent with the spirit of the 2006 version of the UNCITRAL Model Law. Therefore, the court has delegated primary authority to Indian tribunals.

It is worth noting, though, that the UNCITRAL Model Law on International Commercial Arbitration, 1985 (Model Law, 2006) is ambiguous on whether or not courts should be a backup option in cases where an arbitrator is unable to resolve a dispute. The idea that courts would only step in if the arbitral tribunal had failed to do its job was tabled for later consideration. The

Model Law's influence on the decision to take this course of action is thus not made explicit. Interestingly, the courts in India have shifted the primary power to the arbitral tribunal through its various judicial precedents, which is commendable only if it is effective. This rule is also applicable in cases involving arbitration in a non-U.S. venue.

JUDICIAL PRECEDENTS

Some judicial precedents from the model laws are worth noting. Because the term "commercial" is not defined in the Model Law, it is open to a wide range of interpretations and is subject to change depending on the outcome of a case. The term should be broadly construed as it constitutes the bulk of international trade everywhere. The Supreme Court of India defined "commercial" in R.M. Investments and Trading Co. v. Boeing Co. (1994) to encompass all "commercial relationships" that serve to bolster relationships of a "family, cultural, social, economic, or political nature." In this case, the court ruled that the contract for a consultancy service fall under the definition of "commercial" and, as such, is subject to the arbitration clause.

Article 7(1) of the Model Law should be read in conjunction with the original definition of arbitration, as the 2006 Amendment made no changes to this section. The binding nature of a "arbitration agreement" is one of its most prominent features. In Jagdish Chander v. Ramesh Chander & Ors. (2007), the Supreme Court ruled that an arbitration clause in an agreement must express the parties' "determination and obligation to go for arbitration," rather than simply leaving open the possibility of future arbitration. An arbitration agreement is not valid and binding if it is based on a possibility rather than an obligation. Article 9 of the Model Law establishes the principle of interim measures of protection that may be exercised from the courts of a given State and is not provided for the parties but to the courts of a given State. The Delhi High Court noted in Max India Ltd. v. General Binding Corporation (2009) that the parties had agreed to have any disputes over the agreement's ancillary matters resolved through arbitration in Singapore and in accordance with Singaporean court procedures. As a result, they have denied the party access to the Indian courts that might have provided emergency relief pending the outcome of an overseas arbitration.

Article 11 of the Model Law establishes the procedure for the appointment of arbitrators and articulates the principle of 'party autonomy,' which allows each party to an arbitration agreement to independently select their own arbitrator. The term "necessary measures" has not been defined, so in the case of Ministry of Railway New Delhi v. Patel Engineering Company Ltd. (2008), an Indian court determined that it means whatever is required to finish the job. When we talk about taking "necessary measures," we're referring to those actions that make practical sense in order to carry out the desired action.

CONCLUSION

Given the increasing use of arbitration to resolve disputes between foreign and domestic parties, it is only fair that arbitral tribunals be given authority to issue protective measures during the proceedings. Although the intent of the Indian law in this area is praiseworthy, the Model Law (2006) as amended was not fully clear document and hence, needs judicial clarifications from situation to situation.

REFERENCES

Arrowsmith, S, (2004). *Public procurement: An appraisal of the UNCITRAL model law as a global standard.* International & Comparative Law Quarterly, cambridge.org

Bachand, F, & Gélinas, F, (2013). *The UNCITRAL model law after twenty-five years: Global perspectives on international Commercial Arbitration.* UN.

Berends, A. J. (1998). *The UNCITRAL Model Law on cross-border insolvency: a comprehensive overview.* Tulsa Journal of International & Comparative Law, Hein Online.

Binder, P. (2019). *International commercial arbitration and mediation in UNCITRAL Model Law jurisdictions.* UN. books.google.com

Böckstiegel, K. H. (1998). *An introduction to the new German arbitration act based on the UNCITRAL model law.* Arbitration International.

Bucy, D. R. (2010). *How to best protect party rights: the future of interim relief in international commercial arbitration under the amended UNCLTRAL model law American University International Law Review.* Hein Online.

Cliff, J. (2004). UNCITRAL Model Law on Cross-Border Insolvency-A Legislative Framework to Facilitate Coordination and Cooperation in Cross-Border Insolvency. *eHein Online*.

Gabriel, H. D. (2019). *Uniform Law Review*. The UNCITRAL Model Law on Electronic Transferable Records. academic.oup.com

Herrmann, G. (1985). *The UNCITRAL Model Law–its background, salient features and purposes*. Arbitration international. academic.oup.com

Hollering, M. F. (1986). *The uncitral model law on international commercial arbitration, The International Lawyer*. JSTOR.

Hunter, J. M. H. (1985). *The UNCITRAL Model Law*. International Business Law, Hein Online.

McCormack, G & Wai Yee, W (2018). The UNCITRAL model law on cross-border insolvency comes of age: new times or new paradigms. *Texas International Law Journal*, Hein Online.

McNerney. (1986). ME & and CA Esplugues. International Commercial Arbitration: the UNCITRAL Model Law, Boston College of International and Comparative Law. Hein Online.

Mevorach, I. (2011). On the road to universalism: a comparative and empirical study of the UNCITRAL Model Law on Cross-Border Insolvency. *European Business Organization Law Review (EBOR)*.

Mohan, S. C. (2012). Cross-border Insolvency Problems: Is the UNCITRAL Model Law the Answer? [- Wiley Online Library]. *INSOL International Insolvency Review*, *21*(3), 2012. doi:10.1002/iir.1203

Overby, A. B. (1999). *Will Cyberlaw be uniform—an introduction to the uncitral model law on electronic commerce*. Tulsa Journal of International & Comparative Law, Hein Online.

Paterson, R. K. (1993). *International Arbitration: Implementing the UNCITRAL Model Law*. Hein Online.

Somarajah, M, (1989). *Journal of International Arbitration*. Hein Online.

Steyn, J. (1994). *England's Response to the UNCITRAL Model Law of Arbitration*. Arbitration International. academic.oup.com

Van Ginkel, E. (2004). *Journal of International Arbitration*. Hein Online.

KEY TERMS AND DEFINITIONS

Arbitration Rule: It is a rule that governs the conduct of arbitration proceedings. These rules can be set by the parties themselves or can be based on model rules such as the UNCITRAL Arbitration Rules.

International Trade: It refers to the exchange of goods, services, and capital between countries. It is governed by international trade laws and agreements between countries.

Judicial Precedents: They refer to past court decisions that serve as a guide for future cases with similar facts or legal issues.

Model Laws: They are non-binding legal texts that are developed by international organizations to serve as a guide for countries when developing their own national laws. An example is the **UNCITRAL Model Law on International Commercial Arbitration** which was developed by the United Nations Commission on International Trade Law (UNCITRAL) to provide a framework for countries to use when developing their own arbitration laws.

Necessary measures: They refer to actions that are required to be taken in order to achieve a specific goal or objective.

Party autonomy: It is a principle in arbitration that allows parties to have substantial control over the process used to resolve their conflicts.

Preamble: It is an introductory statement in a legal document that explains the purpose and intent of the document.

Chapter 5
Enforceability of Arbitration Decision

ABSTRACT

There are a number of important aspects that must be met before the award can be considered final, including the following: jurisdiction of the arbitral award; the tribunal's independence and impartiality; the arbitral process; the autonomy of the parties and the arbitral award; grounds for setting aside the arbitral award; recognition and enforcement of foreign arbitral awards. The arbitration awards will need to be enforced because of the various articles of the UNCITRAL arbitration award and similar other laws of the countries. Even if the award is legally binding, the disputing parties can still take their case to court in the country where the relevant parts of the award were issued. The arbitral tribunal, for example, does not have any inherent jurisdiction. The arbitration agreement serves as the basis for the tribunal's authority. This chapter will attempt to cover the topic of such enforceability issues.

BACKGROUND

In international commercial arbitration, there is an important and critical issue as of the enforcement of the arbitral award. If it is not for the enforcement, there is no necessity for the entire process of alternate dispute resolution like arbitration. However, enforcement of arbitral award is a major concern and question which need to be studied very meticulously.

DOI: 10.4018/978-1-6684-4040-7.ch005

An arbitral tribunal does not have any "inherent" jurisdiction. The agreement between the parties establishes the arbitral tribunal's authority to rule on the dispute at hand. No statute grants jurisdiction to an arbitral tribunal.

In accordance with the Indian Arbitration and Conciliation Act of 1996, in the case of India, there is a requirement of the composition and jurisdiction of the arbitral tribunal. An arbitrator or panel of arbitrators is defined as "an arbitrator or arbitrators appointed for determining a particular dispute or difference" in Rule 2 of these rules and in Section 2(d) of the Arbitration and Conciliation Act, 1996. Arbitration jurisdiction, in brief, made it clear that the courts of the seat of arbitration have jurisdiction to hear disputes related to the arbitration even if no part of the cause of action arises there.

It is aimed in this chapter to achieve the following objectives:

1. To examine the significance of the decision of arbitral awards
2. To review briefly the issues investigated in the scholarly discussion on the enforcement of arbitral decisions
3. To analyse the situation arising out of the enforcement of arbitral decisions

The methodology adopted for the achievement of the above objectives is analytical and descriptive. The secondary sources available in the published works as also web sources were studied and analysed.

PREVIOUS RESEARCH LITERATURE

The question of enforceability of the decision of arbitrators has several dimensions. The arbitration clause in the contract, the seat of arbitration, the competence of the arbitrators, the secular nature of the contract, the finality of the relief, the possibility of reaching any different arbitral decision, the effectiveness of the arbitral process, the different approaches possible for the arbitration, the annulment of the decision are some of the very critical issues that concern the enforceability of arbitration. Therefore, a wide variety of investigations have been made by erudite scholars on different aspects of enforceability of arbitration decision. Several researches of the scholars have been reported in scientific journals. The issues related to the possibility of enforcement by court following the decision of the court at a place of arbitration were perused. It was discussed about the possibility of reaching a different decision when the enforcement of vacated award at the seat of arbitration (Zafarovich, TS ; 2022) In the case of effectiveness of the arbitral process, it becomes pertinent to analyse the possibilities for the court for the enforcement of interim arbitral decisions(Kojovic,T, 2001). The question of the Mohammadan and Jewish legal decisions in the secular courts were studied. There were cases involving Beth Din precedent in the United States and it was decided that the enforceability of the arbitral decision would depend on the conditions under which the secular courts will consider the adjudications (Lee Ann Bambach, 2009). There should be a system of community enforcement of the arbitral award imposing obligations for customary prescriptions (Schachter, O; 1960). Lex Mercatoria or the Law Merchant is an important issue if the arbitral award ignores the law of the land or the legal practices of the mercantile community. The procedure for the arbitral enforcement should be as per the practices of the community (Rivkin, DW; 1993). A party seeking enforcement of an arbitration award has to follow the civil procedure law or else it will impede enforcement actions(Bersani,MD;1993).The judicial enforcement of arbitral awards in South Africa are those which affirmed the common law position to the enforcement(Baboolal-Frank,R; 2022). It is also debated whether a foreign award by the arbitrators will be interfered with by the judicial or state authorities(Mistelis,LA; 2013). Annulment of an arbitral award is a challenge in international commercial arbitration. The recognition and enforcement or the refusal there of by a State of a decision rendered abroad annulling an arbitral award has to be carefully considered(Gharavi,H & Liebscher,C; 2002). International commercial arbitration in the countries like the United States of America, Europe, South Africa, Middle East has such situation that enforcement of foreign arbitral award provide for arbitrability and public policy as the grounds for refusing the recognition and enforcement of foreign arbitral award(Anusomsena,V; 2012). An empirical study of the enforcement of arbitral awards in the Peoples Republic of china was carried out. There was a survey of 89 foreign and CIETAC arbitral award enforcement cases that were to be perused. However, the data was incomplete and several awards enforcement were pending (Peerenboom,R; 2001). The national courts refuse recognition and **enforcement** of an **arbitral award** if recognition and **enforcement** of the **award** would be contrary to the enforcing country's legal system. It has supported the concept of lex loci like in the case of lex mercatoria (Choi, S; 1995). The universal effect of a setting aside in the country of origin and the court with the final authority on the validity of an international arbitral award was perused (van den Berg,AJ; 2014). In the case of Germany, the arbitral award should not violate the public policy of the country failing which the enforceability will remain as a challenge (Kleinheisterkamp,J; 2009). While enforcing the arbitral award, it has to be justified that unless it is injurious to the public good of the country, enforcement is a must(Villiers,L;; 2011).

ENFORECEABILITY AS PER SOME LEGAL DECISIONS IN THE COURT

Enforceability of the arbitral decisions depend on the arbitral awards and the decisions of the legal environment of the countries. Sometimes the arbitral awards may be directly enforced especially when both the parties agree to the awards. In case of any further disputes, many issues of the arbitral agreement and the court decisions will come to the centre stage. These can be analysed from the point of view of the enactments of the countries where the arbitration has been carried out. The courts also step in when their powers are invoked by one or the other party. For example, Article 27 of the Comprehensive Act Regarding Arbitration and Conciliation Conducted in 1996 in India, the Court may be petitioned for assistance by the arbitral tribunal or by a party with the approval of the arbitral tribunal. Appropriate evidence needs to be submitted to the arbitral tribunal without intervening channels. In making an order under subsection (4), the Court may warrant the evidences in support of the petition. However, when the Arbitration Tribunal is in place, the Commercial Court lacks jurisdiction because an Arbitral Tribunal has already been established.. Once an Arbitral Tribunal has been established, the Court shall not hear any further arguments. In a case of Anand versus Sri Krishan, (August 18th, 2009), a filing under Section 9 was made with the court. The court and the arbitration panel both need to hear as arbitral tribunal is solely responsible for the reason that the breach of the arbitral tribunal's order is irremediable. The time of arbitral decision is also important. In an instant case of The Maharashtra State Power Board case against Datar Switchgear Ltd. filed on October 7, 2002, until the final decision of the Arbitral Tribunal was made. On September 27th, the Arbitral Tribunal issued its decision on the petition. However, it was held invalid because the Arbitral Tribunal lacked jurisdiction when it issued its ruling on September 27th, 2001. In another case in the high court of Bombay in LentjesEngergy (India) Pvt. Ltd. vs. Nirma Ltd. LLC on July 26, 2002, held that since the arbitration over these boilers was still ongoing, the court did not need to rule on the merits. It would be the same as the court making a decision on the facts at hand before the arbitration is decided. In the high court of Gujarat, on July 1,

2014, Silor Associates Sa filed a lawsuit against Bharat Heavy Electrical Ltd. Held that the Court may be petitioned for assistance by the arbitral tribunal or by a party with the approval of the arbitral tribunal. The arbitral tribunal may make a presumption of guilt against that party. In a case at the Supreme Court of India, on Nirmal Private Infrastructure, it contrasted with Aanant Developers Private Ltd. Of November 26, 2015. The arbitral tribunal issued an order on October 5, 2015, and it was directed that the order be enforced, in addition, to the Court Commissioner's report that the arbitral tribunal should have issued interim measures in favour of the petitioner. In a case of the High Court of Mumbai, Manbhupinder Singh Barinder vs. Neeraj Kumarpal Shah of on March 11, 2020, a former Supreme Court judge has been appointed as the new chairman of the arbitral tribunal.

The arbitrator has informed the parties in a letter dated April 26, 2019, that the arbitration panel has been properly convened. In a petition to the Gujarat high court, Arcelor Mittal Nippon Steel vs. Essar Bulk Terminal Ltd., it was resolved by the Arbitral Tribunal, which will also receive any pending applications. According to the petitioners' arguments, all applications must be decided by the Arbitral Tribunal, even if it is ineffective. The petitioner has argued the issues in detail. Mr. Thakore petitioned this Court in great detail.

The judiciary has an impartiality and independence. Overall, a system based on the rule of law is reflected in the independence and impartiality of its judiciary. In regards to the human right to a fair trial, the two principles together form "an absolute right that may suffer no exception," as stated by the United Nations Human Right Committee. On the one hand, the individual's right to have their case heard by a fair and impartial tribunal is a fundamental protection against being subjected to unfair or biased treatment. Adjudicators who are truly independent resist or reject any outside pressure or influence and are unbiased in their treatment of the disputing parties and the issues at hand.

Methods of Arbitration

By agreeing to submit their dispute to an arbitrator or panel of arbitrators for resolution, the parties loose the opportunity of approaching the public court and instead opt for a private, out-of-court dispute resolution process known as arbitration. As has been discussed in the previous chapters, the following is expected from the arbitration process. The American Arbitration Association breaks it down into five basic steps:

1. Documentation and kick-off.

2. The Appointment of Arbitrators.
3. First round of testimony.
4. Preparation and information sharing.
5. Opinions based on hearings.

However, it is possible to have appellant jurisdiction for arguments presented after the hearing. Stockton follows the arbitration laws established by the California Arbitration Act, which has been amended several times since its initial passage in 1961. The American Arbitration Association outlines the five main steps of the arbitration process to give you an idea of what to expect:

The process begins with the filing of a Demand for Arbitration by one of the parties. Choosing an arbitrator requires cooperation from both sides, as they must find someone who is impartial and qualified to handle their specific dispute. The parties meet for a preliminary hearing to talk about the meat of the case, share relevant information, and compile lists of potential witnesses. Preparedness and information sharing between parties, with arbitrators handling any complications that arise. The parties have the opportunity to present their case to the arbitrator through a series of hearings. After the hearing has concluded, the parties may submit additional evidence to the arbitrator. The arbitrator makes a ruling (the award) and the case is over. A mediator works with parties to help them find a common ground so they can reach a settlement, but does not evaluate or render judgements. This is the main difference between arbitration and mediation, which is much less formal than litigation but where the arbitrator's role is similar to that of a judge. A reputable Stockton arbitration lawyer with experience is a good choice when a contract or legal agreement calls for the use of arbitration to settle a dispute. One such agency that is noted for the work is Quinn & Kronlund, LLC which has been in business for decades and has successfully mediated or arbitrated thousands of cases.

Depending on the complexity of the case, the arbitration process can take anywhere from a few months to a year or more, with the hearing itself lasting anywhere from a few hours to a few weeks.

One arbitrator is chosen by each party, and if they can't settle on a unanimous choice for President of the Tribunal, that role is filled by the ICSID Secretary-General (or the Chairman of the ICSID Administrative Council). Independent Action of the Parties and the Decision of the Arbitrator is important.

It is discussed here about the situation when private arbitration rather than a national court system might be the best option for resolving a dispute between two parties. It begins by addressing a fundamental theoretical difficulty with arbitration, specifically, the question of how much of it is grounded in national law and how much can be attributed to international or transnational norms. The chapter continues with a discussion of the issue of which law applies to an arbitration agreement, drawing attention to the fact that courts and arbitral tribunals may take contrasting approaches. The next section then delves into the question of whether or not a court or arbitral tribunal should be making the final call on the legality and scope of an arbitration agreement. Distinctions between jurisdictional and admissibility concerns are made, and various understandings of the principle of "competence-competence" are discussed. The scope and effectiveness of arbitration agreements are then evaluated across four dimensions: how they are to be interpreted, the impact on third parties, the extent to which they are exclusive, and the availability of class arbitration. The limitations of the dispute types that can be submitted to arbitration are also discussed at length in this chapter. Different approaches to the issues discussed can be found among the various legal systems.

The need for a swift resolution of justice in today's society has led to an increase in the use of non-traditional dispute resolution mechanisms. When parties agree to submit their disputes to arbitration under the express conditions agreed upon by the parties, arbitration proceedings are now widely recognised as a fast and effective remedy for resolution of disputes. It is evident that the autonomy of the parties to an arbitration agreement is the driving force behind an arbitration proceeding. Arbitration law has long recognised the importance of this concept, which can be translated as "freedom to opt" or "parties at will." It is on the basis of this principle that arbitration laws in different countries are based. Arbitration agreements are completely subject to the terms and conditions agreed upon by the parties to them. The arbitration shall take place at such place as the parties may mutually agree upon, and shall be governed by such substantive and procedural laws as the parties may mutually agree upon. It is pertinent to understand that Article 19 of the UNCITRAL Model Law embodies the principle of 'party autonomy' by stating that parties are free to agree on the procedure to be followed by the arbitral tribunal in conducting the proceedings. Section 2(6) of the Arbitration and Conciliation Act, 1996 (the Act) contains explicit provisions stating that parties are free to authorise any person, including an institution, to determine the issue between the parties. Under subsection (2.8), the parties are free to establish their own ground rules. In addition, Section 19(2) states that the parties are free to determine the arbitration tribunal's rules of procedure through mutual agreement.

It is a well-established principle of party autonomy that parties are free to choose any of the conditions in the arbitration agreement to resolve their disputes regardless of any place, law, rules, and procedures to follow. It is the "brooding and guiding spirit" of the arbitration process.1 The law is set up so that the parties to an arbitration can choose both the procedural law and the substantive law.2 The arbitration agreement is the central element that reflects the autonomy of the parties.3 This includes the parties' ability to appoint and organise the arbitral tribunal, decide where the arbitration will take place, and so on. Since Indian courts previously ruled that arbitration must take place in India if both parties are Indian, this principle of party autonomy had previously been in the shadows in India.

When the question arose in 2008 before the highest court as to whether arbitration between two Indian subsidiaries of Malaysian companies would be international commercial arbitration or domestic arbitration7, the pendulum swung in favour of party autonomy. According to Section 28 of the Arbitration and Conciliation Act, the Indian court ruled that this particular arbitration would be treated as domestic and could proceed as planned. Contrary opinions held that Indian parties cannot contract out of Indian Law8, so this decision was not implemented.

Subsequently, in Centro trade Minerals and Metal v. Hindustan Copper9, the Supreme Court, sitting as a three-judge bench, reaffirmed the importance of party autonomy in arbitration. The court ruled that "party autonomy" is virtually the backbone that permits parties to adopt the foreign seat as the proper arbitration law. As a result of this widespread acknowledgement, arbitration is now able to clear the way for the exercise of party autonomy.

Furthermore, it was held in Bharat Aluminium Co. v. Kaiser Aluminium Technical Services10 that party autonomy is an essential and guiding element of arbitration, so arbitrators can choose to apply any of three laws to their entire agreement: (1) the appropriate law of agreement, (2) the appropriate law of the arbitration agreement, and (3) the appropriate law of the conduct of arbitration, also known as "curial law." The arbitration agreement may also specify the applicable substantive law, in addition to the applicable procedural law.

Moreover, in PASL Wind Solution v. GE Power Conversion11, the Supreme Court upheld the principle of party autonomy and held that two Indian parties could choose foreign seats of arbitration despite the fact that both parties are Indian. An additional benefit is that the arbitrator's foreign award will be enforceable under the Act's second section.

Using Section 17 of the Arbitration and Conciliation Act 1996, the hon'ble Supreme Court recently upheld the legality of an emergency award made in India. This case involved Amazon Investment Holdings LLC and Future Retail Limited and others. Both parties agreed that India would serve as the arbitration's seat and that the Singapore International Arbitration Center's (SIAC) rules would apply to the proceedings. The Amazon team contacted SIAC in hopes of receiving a quick award. A petition for enforcement of the emergency award thus granted was filed with and granted by a single judge of the Delhi High Court. Later, the Future Group successfully appealed to the division bench and had the execution stayed. Nonetheless, Amazon Group went all the way to the Supreme Court, which ultimately ruled in its favour for the reasons laid out below.

An emergency arbitrator's award is an order under Section 17(1) of the Act, and as such, it is enforceable in court under Section 17(2).

There would be no recourse under the Arbitration Act for a party that sought to enforce an emergency arbitrator's award pursuant to Section 17(2) of the Act.

Amazon v. Future, decided by India's highest court, ushers in a new era of arbitration in the country by placing a premium on the independence of the disputing parties. Specifically, the parties' election would allow an emergency arbitration award made in an arbitration with its seat in India to be enforced by Indian courts in the same manner as a court decree. Since such an emergency award would be final and not subject to appeal, the parties can rest assured that enforcing it will be easier and more reliable. This decision is a positive step forward because it brings the Indian arbitration industry in line with international norms for the recognition and enforcement of emergency arbitration awards.

Arbitration is commonly understood to be a process in which each party acts independently. One of the main draws of arbitration as a means of resolving commercial disputes as opposed to traditional litigation is the autonomy of the parties involved. A component of the arbitration process can be defined and shaped by each party individually. Instruments should follow the law and common practise. The courts should give the parties the most leeway to proceed with their preferred procedure once they have determined that the instrument does not contravene the guidelines of the law. Sections 10–13, 16–17, 21–23, 27–29A, and 30 of the Arbitration Act grant complete discretion to the parties involved in the dispute and authorise emergency arbitrators to issue interim orders (also known as "awards"). Furthermore, since one law may not be the same in another country and vice versa, the question of jurisdiction will be mostly settled on the basis of the principle of party autonomy. Another notable issue is the debate between the Venue Vs. Seat of arbitration in respect of location.

The Arbitration Act, Section 34 (2) (B) (II), allows for the setting aside of an award based on a change in public policy, which can be interpreted in a number of ways. An equitable, efficient, and tailored to the needs of the arbitration at hand arbitral procedure is what the Arbitration Act is all about. The Court's Exercise of Power under Section 34 of the Arbitration and Conciliation Act, 1996, and the "Doctrine of Severability" also matters much. Another legal issue discussed is that of "Res Judicata". Originating in English common law, the concept of "Res Judicata" has been defined and refined through various judicial pronouncements ever since its inception. There were some complications that surfaced after the Geneva Protocol on Arbitral Clauses which was put into effect. For example, the award's recipient now has to prove to the executing court that the award has become final in the country where it was issued. When compared to the Convention's stated goal of easy and quick enforcement of an arbitral award, the aforementioned procedure falls short. For the recognition and enforcement of foreign arbitral awards, the United Nations Convention on the Recognition and Enforcement of Foreign Arbitral Awards emerged as the result of lengthy negotiations (the New York Convention, 1958). For the purpose of establishing a solid mechanism whereby the commercial disputes of contracting countries can be referred to arbitration, the Indian legislature adopted the New York Convention, 1958 and enacted the Foreign Awards (Recognition and Enforcement) Act, 1961 in 1961. The purpose was to ensure that the foreign awards were quickly and efficiently resolved, so they could be enforced without any technical glitches. The First and Second Schedules of the Arbitration (Protocol and Convention) Act, 1937 respectively include the Geneva Protocol and the Geneva Convention. Like the New York Convention of 1958, the Schedules were incorporated into the Foreign Awards (Recognition and Enforcement) Act of 1961. On July 13, 1960, India became the 58th country to ratify the Convention on the Recognition and Enforcement of Foreign Arbitral Awards. Both the Arbitration (Protocol and Convention) Act of 1937 and the Foreign Awards (Recognition and Enforcement) Act of 1961 were nullified by the Arbitration and Conciliation Act of 1996[6] ("the Arbitration Act, 1996"). For this reason, the UNCITRAL Model Law and Rules were taken into account when crafting the Arbitration Act of 1996. If you need to enforce a foreign award in India, you should know that this is covered in Section II of the Arbitration Act, 1996. In order to protect an arbitral award, the term "recognition" is typically used as a defensive strategy. An arbitral award is "recognised" when it is upheld in a subsequent arbitration between the same parties to the same convention. A party contesting an arbitration award may seek recognition of the award as a defence against any other claim the parties to the arbitration may have against one another, even if the issues raised by the arbitration have already been settled. On the other hand, if fresh concerns have emerged that were not addressed in the prior arbitration round(s), those concerns may be investigated, and the process of having the award recognised may grind to a halt.

But "enforcement" takes a more aggressive stance. When a party seeks enforcement of an award, they are doing so with the intention of having the award recognised and then having the award enforced through the courts. The terms "recognition" and "enforcement" are often used interchangeably because of the way they work together. The Supreme court of India has given award need not be enforced for it to be recognised, but enforcement does make recognition a prerequisite. It's possible that the award's recipients will ask for public acknowledgment as a deterrent against reviving the issues the award addresses. In cases where an award must be enforced, the court must not only recognise the award's legal effect but also use legal sanctions to ensure the award is carried out.

A definition of "foreign award" is also pertinent. The definition of a "foreign award" can be found in Section 44 of the Arbitration Act, 1996[8]. A "foreign award" is defined as "an arbitral award on differences between persons arising out of legal relationships, whether contractual or not, considered as commercial under the law in force in India, made on or after the 11th day of October, 1960." in accordance with the First Schedule Convention and a written arbitration agreement, and in one of those areas where the Central Government has determined that reciprocal provisions have been put into place and has decided to announce it through an official gazette. According to the New York Convention of 1958, "arbitral award" refers to decisions made by both individual arbitrators and permanent arbitral bodies to which the parties have agreed to submit. In Serajuddin & Co. v. Michael Golodetz, the High Court of Calcutta made the observation that the term "foreign arbitration" would also include arbitrations where one of the parties belongs to a country that has not ratified the Geneva Convention. In its subsequent analysis, the Court determined that the terms "foreign arbitration" and "foreign award" were associated with the following in the decisions where they were used.

Although the definitions under the Arbitration (Protocol and Convention) provisions are not exhaustive, the Court noted that the countries that have ratified the Geneva Conventions have included certain classes of such arbitrations and awards within the definitions. In this case, one of the parties was an Indian national and the other was an American, so the Court determined that the arbitration was considered to be foreign arbitration because it did not fall within the purview of the Indian Arbitration (Protocol and Convention) Act, 1937 and because American law applied.

The Foreign Awards (Recognition and Enforcement) Act of 1961 and the Arbitration (Protocol and Convention) Act of 1937 were two of the first laws to address the recognition and enforcement of foreign awards. The Arbitration and Conciliation Act of 1996 outlines the process for “recognising” and “enforcing” an arbitral award.

While the Code of Civil Procedure, 1908 (CPC, 1908) governs the process for enforcing court orders, the Arbitration Act, 1996 (the “Act”) is the primary legal framework for upholding arbitral awards in India. To give just one example, there are certain requirements. Both Section 44 and Section 49[13] of the Arbitration Act, 1996 deal with the “recognition” and “enforcement” of arbitral awards.

Both the Geneva Convention of 1927 for the Enforcement of Foreign Arbitral Awards and the United Nations Convention of 1958 (New York Convention of 1958) have been ratified by India (Geneva Convention, 1927). Once an award is received by a country that is a signatory to one of the Conventions, the provisions of that Convention will govern the award’s recognition and enforcement.

The steps involved in enforcing a foreign award can be broken down into three main categories. The first step in enforcing an arbitration award is for the party seeking enforcement to file an application with the court that has jurisdiction over the matter, as required by Section 47 of the Arbitration Act, 1996. An invalid arbitration clause in the agreement, improper notice of the appointment of an arbitrator, or an error in law or fact on the part of the Arbitral Tribunal are all grounds on which a party or judgment-debtor can later seek to have a ruling upholding the award set aside in court. The grounds of challenge available under Section 34 of the Arbitration Act, 1996 cannot be used to challenge a foreign award because it has been held in numerous judgements that Part I of the Arbitration Act, 1996 is not applicable to arbitrations seated in a foreign country.

The award must meet the mandatory requirements of the Arbitration Act of 1996 before it can be enforced. In the same way that a court decree under CPC, 1908 is carried out once the award has met the necessary requirements of the Arbitration Act, 1996. Section 47 of the Act, 1996, establishes the minimum requirements for the enforcement of an award. In order to be enforceable in the country of its intended use, the award must be in original form or in a form recognised by the laws of that country. Second, the award must be accompanied by the original or a certified copy of the agreement from which the dispute arose, as well as any other evidence that may be required to establish that the award is a "foreign award." A more enforcement-friendly climate was sought by the Supreme Court in PEC Ltd. v. Austbulk Shipping Sdn. Bhd. ruled that the word "shall" under Section 47 read as "may" must be limited to the initial stage of filing the application. This means that the applicant may delay submitting the necessary paperwork until after the application has been made. The Court noted that some courts have taken a strict view with respect to the filing of documents, while others have held that non-filling of documents does not necessarily call for ejection of the application.

The need for a proper stamp when executing an award has been the subject of debate. However, the Supreme Court's decision in Shriram EPC Ltd. v. National Environmental Tribunal addressed the issue of award stamping. Specifically, Rioglass Solar SA stated unequivocally that stamping is not required. The Supreme Court ruled that there is no need to register the award before it can be enforced as a court decree.

Enforcement of Foreign Arbitral Awards

An independent proceeding seeking an order to file execution of a foreign award is not necessary, as the Supreme Court ruled in Fuerst Day Lawson Ltd. v. Jindal Exports Ltd. The Supreme Court's decision was relied on by the Bombay High Court in Noy Velissina Engineering Spa v. Jindal Drugs Ltd. which determined that a foreign award could be executed as a decree of the court. For purposes of the Arbitration Act, 1996, Section 2(1)(e)[20] defines "court" as follows: Except in the case of international commercial arbitration, (1)(e)....(i) means the Principal Civil Court of original jurisdiction in a district, and includes the High Court in exercise of its ordinary civil jurisdiction, having jurisdiction to decide the questions forming the subject-matter of the arbitration if the same had been the subject-matter of a suit, but does not include any civil court or any Court of Small Causes; (ii) a High Court having jurisdiction to hear appeals from decrees of courts subordinate to that High Court, and in other cases, a High Court having jurisdiction to decide questions forming the subject-matter of the arbitration if the same had been the subject-matter of a suit. According to a decision by the Supreme

Court in State of Maharashtra v. Atlanta Ltd. the court where the judgement debtor's assets are located is the proper venue for an application to enforce an overseas arbitral award. Moreover, the application for execution of the award can be filed simultaneously in all such courts having jurisdiction, even if the judgment-assets debtors are located within the territory of more than one court. In addition, the Supreme Court in Sundaram Finance Ltd. v. Abdul Samad, while providing some clarity as to the appropriate court to approach for enforcement of a foreign award held that a foreign award-holder can initiate execution of the award before any court in India having territorial jurisdiction where the assets are located. It's crucial to remember that since the Commercial Courts Act, 2015 established specialised commercial courts, any dispute involving a commercial enterprise must be resolved in a commercial court.

If the amount of the foreign award exceeds a certain threshold, it will be enforced by the commercial court of the appropriate court with territorial and pecuniary jurisdiction.

Since the passage of the Commercial Courts Act, 2015 and the Arbitration and Conciliation (Amendment) Act, 2015, the Commercial Division of the particular High Court where the assets of the judgment-debtor are situated, has jurisdiction over the awards arising out of arbitrations seated in India, despite the fact that such arbitrations are international commercial arbitrations.

It is also important to note the arbitral awards passed in both reciprocating and non-reciprocal countries; for enforcement in both the countries. Judgment rendered by a court located outside of the country in question is what is meant by the term "foreign judgement" in Section 2(6) of the CPC, 1908. A judgement rendered by a court located outside of India is considered to be a "foreign judgement" because it is not issued by a court within India's borders. Confusion arises for a party seeking enforcement of a foreign award in one of two scenarios: when the award is passed by a country that does not reciprocate, and when the award is passed by a country that does.

A petition for execution may be filed by a party seeking enforcement of an award passed by a reciprocating country with the court having appropriate jurisdiction under Section 44-A of the Code of Civil Procedure. For enforceability, the execution must be submitted to the court that has jurisdiction over the judgement debtor's assets. Furthermore, if there is money/claim which is to be realised out of the award passed, the execution shall be filed accordingly in the appropriate high court, after the establishment of commercial divisions in various high courts of the country. Otherwise, the location of the judgement debtor's assets will determine the place of execution.

However, under Orders 5, 6, and 7 of the Civil Procedure Code of 1908, a new suit must be filed by the party seeking enforcement of an award passed by a non-reciprocal country. Following the filing of the written statement in accordance with Order 8 CPC, 1908, the issues will be framed in accordance with Order 9 CPC, 1908, and the evidence stage (the recording of evidence) will follow. The court will issue a ruling after hearing arguments from both sides, and a decree will be drawn up within 15 days. Keep in mind that you only have three years from the date the award was made to file an enforcement action in the proper court. Furthermore, the foreign award attached to a new suit will be considered evidence in accordance with Section 86 of the Evidence Act, 1872.

It is crucial to keep in mind that for a foreign judgement to be binding in either case, the execution or suit must meet the requirements set forth in Section 13 CPC, 1908. This section lays out the prerequisites that must be met before a foreign judgement can be recognised as final.

There is a connect between public policy and enforcement. The term "public policy" has been a point of contention among Indian expatriate judges recently. This is one of the defences that can be used to challenge the enforcement of an arbitral award. The age of "pro-enforcement stance" was a dark cloud in the regime of Indian jurisprudence until the landmark decision in Bharat Aluminum Co. v. Kaiser Aluminium Technical Services Inc. (Balco). In the Balco case, a panel of five judges distinguished between the jurisdictional scope of domestic and foreign-seated arbitration and ruled that Part I of the Arbitration Act, 1996 would not apply to the latter. This judgement also upheld the validity of Section 34(2) of the Act, 1996, which states that a foreign award cannot be challenged unless it violates public policy. Again using some self-control, the Supreme Court in Renusagar Power Co. Ltd. v. General Electric Co., it was determined that "public policy" cannot be used as a reason to refuse to enforce an award solely because it was obtained through illegal means.

Later, while departing from its "pro-enforcement stance," the Supreme Court, in ONGC v. Saw Pipes Ltd., broadened the test of "public policy" and held that awards which violate Indian laws would be held to be "patently illegal" and the same would be held to be against the "public policy" of India. Such an interpretation would allow the disputing party to raise the same arguments it had during the arbitration, further delaying the process of enforcing the award.

In addition, the Supreme Court, in Phulchand Exports Ltd. v. O.O.O. Patriot [33], further broadened the scope of "public policy" under Section

48 of the Arbitration Act, 1996 and interpreted the scope in accordance with Section 34. The Supreme Court reversed course after Saw Pipes with the judgement in Phulchand, allowing the parties to the appeal to challenge the merits of the award as final.

It should be borne in mind that if the adjudication is made by an arbitral tribunal that enjoys considerable latitude and play at the joints in making awards, it will be subject to challenge and may be thrown out or modified depending on whether or not the arbitrators failed to draw an inference which ought to have been drawn on the facts proved before them.

The court in Associate Builders v. DDA agreed with the premise in ONGC and ruled that the term “public policy” must be given a broad interpretation. Due to the Supreme Court’s retrograde interpretation of Sections 48 and 34 of the Act, 1996, the parties were granted access to the merits of the arbitral award in these decisions.

A foreign arbitral award was recently not enforced by the Delhi High Court under the Arbitration Act, 1996 in the case of Campos Brother Farms v. Matru Bhumi Supply Chain (P) Ltd. The Court ruled that an award cannot be enforced on the basis of “public policy” if the arbitrator, while rendering the award, failed to take into account a material issue relating to the arbitral proceedings’ maintainability. The court found that this strategy would run counter to the very foundations of fairness.

In National Agricultural Coop. v. USDA, the U.S. Mktg. The “public policy of India” test has been noted in the case of Federation of India v. Alimenta SA . This case may be seen as a tribute to a narrow view of the extent to which foreign interference can derail the process of enforcing an overseas arbitration ruling. The aforementioned decision, however, marked a significant departure from the Supreme Court’s earlier decision in Vijay Karia v. Prysmian Cavi E Sistemi SRL, in which the court took a pro-arbitration stance. There is a question of public policy and the foreign award enforcement.

The Supreme Court reversed the premise established in the judgement of Phulchand and brought the scope of “public policy” into conformity with the New York Convention, 1958, in Shri Lal Mahal Ltd. v. Progetto Grano Spa. It was argued in Shri Lal Mahal that the award violated Indian law and thus could be overturned under Section 48 of the Act, 1996. The Court determined that the “patently illegal” ground for challenging an award is not covered by Section 48 of the Act, 1996, and that it is instead covered only by Section 34. The Court determined that it has a narrow discretionary role in deciding whether or not to enforce an overseas award, and that Section 48 of the Arbitration Act, 1996 does not permit a review of the award’s merits.

In 2015, an amendment was made that added a Second Explanation to clause (b) of subsection (1) of Section 48, which states that the enforcing court shall be given very little leeway in assessing the prospects of "public policy." The terminology employed in that Explanation makes this abundantly clear.

Second, "the test as to whether there is a contravention with the fundamental policy of Indian law shall not entail a review on the merits of the dispute,"

The Delhi High Court established a balancing test to decide whether or not to enforce a foreign arbitral award in Cruz City Mauritius Holdings v. Unitech Ltd. It also determined that the grounds for rejecting an international arbitration award are high and that the discretion to do so is narrow.

In the case of Union of India v. Vedanta Ltd., a three-Judge Bench of the Supreme Court rejected the Supreme Court's retrograde stance in the Alimenta case, and ruled that courts should only minimally interfere with the enforcement of foreign arbitral awards regardless of the involvement of the government.

In Vijay Karia case, the Supreme Court made reference to the "pro-enforcement bias" of the New York Convention, 1958, upon which Section 48 of the Act, 1996 is wholly based. Public policy cannot be used as a justification for a court to overturn an award on its merits, and the New York Convention of 1958 establishes strict limits on such interference.

In addition, in Centro trade Minerals and Metals Inc. v. Hindustan Copper Ltd. the Supreme Court interpreted Section 48(1)(b) of the Act, 1996 to uphold an award made pursuant to the rules of the International Chamber of Commerce. Keeping in mind the primary object of Section 48(1)(b), namely the enforcement of a foreign award, the Supreme Court ruled that the word "otherwise" cannot be read and interpreted "ejusdem generis" and ruled that a narrower meaning and interpretation should be afforded.

It can be seriously noted that the Indian law is constantly developing for settling legal disputes. As a result of the country's economic reforms and the subsequent expansion of trade and FDI, Indian courts have adapted to the new realities. Investment from abroad into India depends critically on the efficiency and effectiveness of commercial dispute resolution. Foreign investors gain confidence in a country's investment climate when that country has a robust dispute resolution mechanism. An outdated and retrograde system will only slow down the entire dispute resolution process.

Different interpretations of "recognition" and "enforcement" in Indian jurisprudence have converged in an attempt by the judiciary to make it work along the lines of the New York Convention, 1958, which has been in effect since the advent of the Arbitration and Conciliation Act, 1899 and continues today with the Arbitration Act, 1996. Although the Supreme Court and other High Courts have issued rulings, we believe that victory is still far from assured. While some countries have made strides towards "recognition" and "enforcement" of foreign arbitral awards, India is still not among them.

Enforcement of a foreign arbitral award was debated over how much the Indian judiciary should be involved. In some cases, the Indian judiciary has weighed in on the merits of the award itself, which has resulted in a rehearing of the case and thrown a spanner into efforts to smoothly implement the "recognition" and "enforcement" of the award. A return to the retrograde mentality that prevailed during the time when the Arbitration Act of 1940 governed the dispute resolution mechanism is brought about by such legislation. The Arbitration Act of 1996 adds another layer of complexity to the enforcement process by requiring multiple High Courts to issue opinions and rulings on the same question of law and facts.

The sole intent of Section 48 of the Arbitration Act, 1996 is to facilitate an easy enforcement procedure. Article V of the New York Convention of 1958 is equivalent to Section 48. It is essential to remember that the words "may be" have been used for refusing the enforcement of an award in Section 48 and Article V of the New York Convention, 1958, thereby making the intention and objective of the section very clear. Despite the fact that the grounds for refusing to enforce an award shall be construed narrowly, as evidenced by the judgements passed by various High Courts of India, the courts have occasionally breached the carefully guarded wall of interference.

CONCLUSION

This article provides a brief overview of commercial dispute resolution in India and how a foreign arbitral award can be enforced in the country. It may not be completely out of place to say that the entire process of recognition and enforcement is sped up a bit thanks to the efforts of the Indian judiciary. To be consistent with the spirit of Article V of the New York Convention of 1958, however, India must work towards establishing a pro-enforcement regime. Decisions in recent cases like Vijay Karia and Centro trade show promise for a more effective enforcement system. Although the actions of National Agricultural Co-operative Marketing Federation of India were an attempt to undo the improvements the Indian judiciary has made to make India a pro-enforcement destination. Forcing the "recognition" and "enforcement" mechanism was to trawl the search for a formidable shore for the enforcement of the arbitral awards.

REFERENCES

Anusornsena, A, (2012). *Arbitrability and Public Policy in Regard to the Recognition and Enforcement of Arbitral Award in International Arbitration: the United States, Europe, Africa, Middle East.* Digital Commons. digitalcommons.law.ggu.edu.

Baboolal, R. (2022). *A Review of Judicial Enforcement of Arbitral Awards in South Africa, Conflict Resolution Quarterly*. Wiley Online Library.

Bambach, L.A. (2009). The Enforceability of Arbitration Decisions Made by Muslim Religious Tribunals: Examining the Beth Din Precedent. *Journal of Law and Religion,* cambridge.org

Bersani, M. D. (1993). *The Enforcement of Arbitration Awards in China.* Journal International Arbitration, HeinOnline. doi:10.54648/JOIA1993013

Choi, S. (1995). Judicial enforcement of arbitration awards under the International Centre for Settlement of Investment Disputes and New York Conventions. Online *New York University Journal of International Law and Politics.*

Gharavi, H & Liebscher, C, (2002). *The International Effectiveness of the Annulment of an Arbitral Award: Challenge in International Commercial Arbitration*. books.google.com.

Kleinheisterkamp, J. (2009). *The impact of internationally mandatory laws on the enforceability of arbitration agreements*. World Arbitration & Mediation Review. papers.ssrn.com

Kojovic, T. (2001). Court Enforcement of Arbitral Decisions on Provisional Relief How Final is Provisional? *Journal of International Arbitration.*

Mistelis, L. A. (2013). Award as an investment: The value of an arbitral award or the cost of non-enforcement. *International Centre for Settlement of Investment Disputes Review*. academic.oup.com

Peerenboom, R. (2001). Seek truth from facts: An empirical study of enforcement of arbitral awards in the PRC. *The American Journal of Comparative Law*. academic.oup.com

Rivkin, D. W. (1993). *Enforceability of Arbitral Awards Based on Lex Mercatoria*, Arbitration International. academic.oup.com

Schachter, O, (1960). The Enforcement of International Judicial and Arbitral Decisions. *American Journal of International Law*

Van den Berg, AJ, (2014). *Should the setting aside of the arbitral award be abolished?* International Centre for Settlement of Investment Disputes Review.

Villiers, L. (2011). Breaking in the 'unruly horse': The status of mandatory rules of law as a public policy basis for the non-enforcement of Arbitral awards. *Australian International Law Journal*, search.informit.org

Zafarovich, T.S. (2022). Different Approaches in Enforcement of Arbitral Award Annulled at the Place of Arbitration. Miasto Przyszłości;.

KEY TERMS AND DEFINITIONS

Enforcement of Award: It refers to the process of enforcing an arbitral award, which is a binding decision made by an arbitrator or arbitral tribunal in an arbitration proceeding. The award can be enforced in a court of law.

Foreign Award: It is an arbitral award on differences between persons arising out of legal relationships, whether contractual or not, considered as commercial under the law in force in India[1]. It is a result of foreign arbitration and is enforceable in India if it is made in a territory which has been notified as a convention country by India. India is a signatory to the Convention on the Recognition and Enforcement of Foreign Arbitral Awards, 1958 ("New York Convention") as well as the Geneva Convention on the Execution of Foreign Arbitral Awards, 1927 ("Geneva Convention").

Foreign Award: It refers to an arbitral award made in a country other than the country where enforcement is sought.

Inherent Jurisdiction: It refers to the power of a court to hear and determine cases within its jurisdiction, independent of any statutory provisions.

Lex Mercatoria: It is a body of commercial law that is used by merchants and traders to govern their transactions. It is based on a few substantive and procedural principles, under which the reasonable expectations of the parties to a particular contract become the single source of law.

National Court System: It refers to the hierarchy of courts within a country that interpret and apply the law. In some countries, higher echelons of the judiciary are involved in the administration of justice. For example, in India, the judiciary is structured in three levels with subsidiary parts: the Supreme Court, High Courts, and District Courts. The Supreme Court is the top court and ultimate appellate court in India, led by the Chief Justice of India. High Courts are the top judicial bodies in individual states, controlled and managed by state Chief Justices. Below the High Courts are District Courts, also known as subordinate courts, that are controlled and managed by District and Sessions Judges

Secular Law: This refers to laws put forward by secular institutions, such as the monarchy, the city, or the manor. It aims to deal with conflicts between people and ideas, pursuing the overarching goal of social peace. Secularism is most commonly defined as the separation of religion from civil affairs and the state.

Chapter 6
International Arbitral Procedures

ABSTRACT

The legal framework for international arbitration agreements is established. Issues arising from any dispute will be examined within a legal framework, even though the arbitral awards are enshrined within the legally enforceable contracts of the parties. When comparing arbitration as an ADR method to other modes, the advantages and disadvantages of the resulting arbitration agreements are readily apparent. However, there are necessary conditions for the end result to be justifiable. Procedural laws play a significant role in ensuring this as well. For instance, the New York Convention and the established national arbitration statutes which apply in the case of individual countries specify and define the matters relating to the agreements, such as what constitutes an international commercial agreement by looking at each of the specific terms like "arbitration agreement," "international," "commercial," "disputes," "differences," etc. This chapter aims to discuss these terms contextually.

BACKGROUND

Arbitration for dispute settlement has become a universal practice now under the modern alternate dispute redressal system and there are global methods and practices which are usually according to the cultural practices and legal and judicial systems prevalent in any country. The arbitration methods are,

DOI: 10.4018/978-1-6684-4040-7.ch006

therefore, different for each condition. The legally enforceable contracts have their specific requirements. The arbitration methods accordingly vary in each of the situations. This chapter will discuss the issues concerning the arbitration methods internationally.

In this chapter, an attempt is made to discuss the following:

1. To give a brief survey of previous literature
2. To discuss the institutions and procedures for international arbitration
3. To comprehend the laws for overseas arbitration contracts

For the purpose of this study, a descriptive research methodology is used analysing the secondary data gathered from the secondary published print and electronic material.

PREVIOUS RESEARCH LITERATURE

There are several aspects to the arbitration agreement as in the case of contract. Defining the arbitration, enclosure of the arbitration clause, people to accept the arbitration procedure, free will and commitment to end conflicts and matters associated with all these. On each of such aspects, there should be legal provisions enacted in the countries which adopt alternate mechanism for dispute redressal. A review of the arbitration laws relating to some of these issues can help gather the correct perspectives of the arbitration laws at the global level. On Dispute settlement relating to International Commercial Arbitration, the United Nations Conference on Trade and development (UNCTAD) has produced a document 5.2 as the Arbitration agreement. It is the law governing the judicial proceeding that will determine whether an appeal can be made to the court's decision to admit the defendant's request (UNCTAD,2005). The issues relating to the law governing the validity of the arbitration agreement were examined (Nazzini, R; 2016). The nature of agreement was peer reviewed (Nevisandeh, M; 2016). A discussion on the applicable law to international arbitration agreements was provided pleading for a uniform law (Flecke-Glammarco; 2015). A jurisdictional overview of the effects of assignments of contractual rights on arbitration agreements was studied (Girsberger,D; 1992). A question was raised as to whether the distinctive status of international arbitration agreements is a private international law (Phus,M; 2020). An explanation is provided on the legal framework used to determine the capacity of parties to enter into an arbitration agreement (Kimani,E; 2021). The problem of the law governing the validity of the arbitration agreement was also examined (Nazzini, R; 2016). The method of determining the law governing an arbitration agreement was examined (Campbell, M; 2021) It was questioned whether the possibility of using the proper law is a reality or only a utopia (Thilakaratna, KAAN; 2021). Empirical studies support Carrington and Haagen's diagnosis (Chua-Rubenfeld, S; 2019). Where judicial proceedings have become electronic, arbitration proceedings too have taken the electronic shape and arbitration agreements in electronic form are in place as well. However, there are problems of proving the electronic agreement in different contexts of the national laws (Al Dalaein, MN; 2021). Arbitration agreement is especially important in the process of arbitration as an alternate dispute resolution mechanism (Vlahna, K; 2008). While comparing the Common Law and the Law of Singapore, it is argued that the party autonomy should be taken more seriously in arbitration agreements (Yand, TJ; 2020). The arbitration agreement has to be addressed by considering the ways in which the agreement has been addressed under various arbitral rules, national laws and judicial decisions (Ugarte, R; 2010) . When the law governing the arbitration agreement is not specifically mentioned or expressly given, a new agreement scenario arises for dispute settlement (SCC On line ;2021).

INSTITUTIONS AND PROCEDURES FOR INTERNATIONAL ARBITRATION

The legal foundation for international arbitration agreements is discussed here, by contrasting international arbitration with other methods of conflict resolution and analysing their relative merits and shortcomings. The definitional issue of what constitutes an "arbitration agreement," an "international" arbitration agreement, a "commercial" relationship, and a "difference" or "dispute," as well as the jurisdictional requirements of the New York Convention and leading national arbitration statutes (such as the UNCITRAL Model Law) as they apply to international arbitration agreements are provided.

The businesses and other organisations opt to have their international commercial disputes settled by arbitrators instead of courts. Courts, administrative tribunals, and other forms of dispute resolution are provided by nations and other political organisations, with some having a focus on commercial disputes specifically. The parties agree to submit to the decisions of international arbitral tribunals rather than utilise the aforementioned dispute resolution mechanisms, and what exactly is it about the "arbitration" process that makes this possible. A discussion on these issues can be explored in the narrative given here. In a given situation, the parties fought over the house on Kuelol street in front of the dioketes (administrative tribunals) of the castron (district) of Jeme. After much wrangling in front of the dioketes, a proposal was finally advanced that all the parties could get behind and elect the arbitrators from the castron, and the dioketes sent them into the house to divide the things up. The most serious cases might be heard by multiple courts with overlapping jurisdictions. Certain rules undoubtedly existed that, in theory, determined the limits of competence of the various courts; however, uncertainty persisted. There are numerous charters in the surviving feudal records that deal with conflicts between different regions. Litigants, at a loss to determine before which authority to bring their suits, often agreed to set up arbitrators of their own, or they opted to settle out of court. In many cases, reaching an agreement with a stubborn opponent was the only way to ensure that a favourable ruling was actually carried out. In some cases, after spending a lot of money on lawyers and time and effort preparing for hearings term after term, one might change the mind seven years later to submit to the arbitration one may currently oppose.

The 2013 Global Corruption Barometer by Transparency International looks at the impact that corruption has on people's daily lives in a variety of countries. According to the report, corruption is seen as running through the foundations of the democratic and legal process in many countries, affecting public trust in political parties, the judiciary, and the police, among other basic institutions. These findings are based on the results of a Transparency International survey of more than 114,000 respondents in 107 countries. Twenty-four percent of those who deal with the legal system, admit to having paid a bribe. More than 20% more bribes were reported to have been paid to the judiciary in Ghana, Indonesia, Mozambique, Solomon Islands, and Taiwan than in the previous report's time period. Justice is seen as the most corrupt branch of government by citizens in 20 nations (Afghanistan, Albania, Algeria, Armenia, Azerbaijan, Bulgaria, Cambodia, Croatia, Democratic Republic of the Congo, Georgia, Kosovo, Kyrgyzstan, Lithuania, Madagascar, Moldova, Peru, Serbia, Slovakia, Tanzania, and Ukraine). In these countries [for which data is available], an estimated 30 percent of those who have dealt with the legal system have admitted to paying a bribe.

There is a need for the arbitrator to have some relevant experience of the business or another field. Many judges serving on national courts are generalists who hear civil, criminal, domestic, and other disputes despite having little to no experience in the commercial sector (either in business or as a practising lawyer advising businesses). In contrast, parties often choose arbitrators who have extensive and/or specialised knowledge in the subject matter and/or law of the dispute (e.g., arbitrators with experience in construction, joint ventures, insurance, or maritime disputes). These factors make the tribunal's decision more predictable and commercially reasonable.

Moreover, the parties may stipulate in their contract that the arbitrators must possess a certain level of expertise or meet certain qualifications. The parties to an oil and gas contract may insist that the arbitrators have experience with oil and gas disputes, the parties to an insurance or reinsurance policy may insist that the arbitrator is a licensed insurance practitioner or a former employee of the insurance industry, and so on. Alternately, the parties can agree to have the dispute arbitrated in accordance with the rules of a specific institution that has been established to handle (and having institutional lists of arbitrators with specialised expertise and experience).

In international arbitration, it is fairly confident that the court will act impartially. One of the benefits of international arbitration is that it allows disputing parties to choose a third-party arbitrator who is not affiliated with the government of either party's home country and who is not a citizen of either party's home country. Alternatively, the parties may agree to have the presiding arbitrator be of a neutral nationality while selecting a co-arbitrator of their choosing (including a co-arbitrator with the party's own nationality). An American or Canadian arbitrator could serve as the presiding member of a tribunal that included French and Japanese parties.

International arbitration agreements are enforceable. As discussed previously, the 2014 ratification of the Convention requires Contracting States to recognise and enforce international arbitration agreements by referring their parties to arbitration. Take into account the proposed Hague Convention on Choice of Court Agreements, which was written under the auspices of the Hague Conference on Private International Law. However, Article 2 and Article 9 of the proposed Convention contain some important caveats.

Awards made in international arbitration must be enforceable. Challenges existed in international arbitration in mediaeval Europe. Similar challenges exist today in securing effective recognition of judgements made in one country by courts in another. Situations involving parallel proceedings and jurisdictional disputes in various national courts are highly likely to make it difficult to enforce judgements made by national courts.

It should be noted that no analogous multilateral treaty for the recognition and enforcement of foreign court judgements exists at the present time. This means that there is a "enforceability premium" for international arbitral awards compared to judgements issued by domestic courts. When deciding whether or not to enter into an international arbitration agreement, this is a critical factor.

Confidentiality is an inherent part of the international arbitration. Many international arbitrations are held in secret. Generally, third parties (including the press) are not permitted access to the documents and proceedings of an international commercial arbitration, and neither party is permitted to disclose any information related to the arbitration to any third party. Take into account the opinions of arbitration's business users on the subject of privacy, as reported in the Buhring-Uhle study. Keeping the details of a business dispute private could be advantageous for a number of reasons. A forum selection clause can be an alternative to an international arbitration agreement. A forum selection clause will either be exclusive (requiring all disputes to be resolved exclusively in the specified contractual forum) or non-exclusive (allowing disputes to be resolved in any court with jurisdiction over the parties) (permitting either party to pursue litigation in the specified contractual forum, but not precluding litigation in other forums). Resolution of differences between states through arbitration is another important aspect. The signatory powers of international arbitration have "recognised international arbitration as the most effective, and at the same time the most equitable, means of settling disputes which diplomacy has failed to settle". The example of the USA and UK going for international arbitration is available for perusal. Similarly, the acceptance of Abyei agreement for arbitration between Sudan and South Sudan is another example. Investment disagreements can be arbitrated. A foreign investor in the United States goes for the settlement of disputes arising from investment to be handled in a venue other than U.S. courts. UK-Bosnia-Herzegovina BIT is another example where international arbitration is used to settle investment disputes. Over the course of the last century, international arbitration has become an increasingly common method of resolving legal disputes. Caseloads at leading arbitral institutions have steadily increased over the past 20 years, with the number of reported cases increasing by a factor of two to ten. Over the past 60 years, the number of requests for new arbitrations at the International Court of Arbitration of the International Chamber of Commerce has increased from 32 in 1956 to 210 in 1976 to 337 in 1992 to 452 in 1997 to 529 in 1999 to 593 in 2006 to 767 in 2013. International arbitration agreements must comply with the jurisdictional requirements set forth by the applicable International Arbitration Convention and any applicable national arbitration law. Most modern national arbitration statutes (again, such as the UNCITRAL Model Law) are "pro-arbitration," as they provide effective and robust mechanisms for enforcing international arbitration agreements and arbitral awards. It is not always easy to determine which international arbitration agreements fall under the purview of the New York Convention, despite the gravity of the issue. In contrast, nothing in Article II of the Convention (or otherwise) expressly addresses which arbitration agreements are subject to Article II's "recognition" requirement. The New York Convention's jurisdictional requirements place significant constraints on its applicability. Most modern state statutes governing international arbitration follow the New York Convention by including express or implied jurisdictional limitations. These jurisdictional requirements are of great practical importance, just as they are under the Convention, because they determine when the generally "pro-arbitration" substantive provisions of modern arbitration legislation apply to arbitration agreements and arbitral awards.

Arbitration Clause is another important procedure of arbitration. An agreement to "arbitrate," as opposed to an agreement to do something else, is required for most international commercial arbitration conventions and national arbitration statutes to apply. The same is true for investment and state-to-state arbitrations. This gives rise to the thorny definitional question of what exactly constitutes a "arbitration agreement." The parties to a contract might agree to expert determination, conciliation, mediation, or some other form of alternative dispute resolution; they might also agree to a forum selection clause that would have any litigation take place in a particular national court; or they might agree to arbitration. None of these methods are "arbitration" as defined by the New York Convention (or other international arbitration conventions) or domestic arbitration statutes.

International Arbitration: Appointing, Challenging, and Replacing Arbitrators

The selection of arbitrators, including by the parties' agreement and by non-judicial appointing authorities, as this is one of the most crucial aspects of international arbitral proceedings. The chapter also discusses the function of national courts in the appointment of arbitrators. In the third section, we look at the criteria that must be met in terms of the arbitrators' identities.

These criteria include the arbitrators' impartiality and independence, as well as any contractually imposed or other criteria. The arbitrators' appointment and subsequent challenge and removal are discussed in the fourth chapter. The emphasis is first on the appointment by non-judicial appointing authorities, and then on the appointment by national courts. Finally, the difficulties of "truncated" tribunals are discussed, in which some or all of the members of the tribunal decline to take part in making an award.

One of the distinguishing features of international arbitration is that disputes are generally not submitted to any particular "court" or tribunal that has already been established. This holds true not only in investment and inter-state arbitration, but also in international commercial arbitration. In contrast to national courts and many international tribunals (such as the International Court of Justice), which have a pre-existing complement of judges who are assigned randomly to cases and generally applicable, comprehensive procedural rules, there is no such thing as a "standing tribunal." On the other hand, an arbitral tribunal must be independently constituted for most arbitral proceedings, either by the parties themselves or otherwise in accordance with the terms of the arbitration agreement and applicable law. Selection of Arbitrators is Left to the Parties. The principle of party autonomy is prevalent throughout the international arbitral process, including the selection of the tribunal. As will be shown below, parties are given considerable leeway by international arbitration conventions, national law, and institutional rules to choose the arbitrators who will preside over "their" arbitration, either directly or through the mechanisms of their choosing. To ensure an impartial arbitral tribunal and to protect other similarly important national and international public policies, this independence is subject to narrow restrictions.

There is often a procedure for choosing the arbitrator(s) in international commercial arbitration agreements, either explicitly or through the incorporation of institutional arbitration rules. 1. If the parties to an arbitration cannot agree on the identity of the arbitrators themselves, the most common contractual mechanism for selecting an arbitrator is the appointment of a neutral "appointing authority" to make those selections.2 All major institutional rules provide for such a role by the sponsoring institution when the parties agree to arbitrate under the institution's rules.3 Furthermore, international arbitration conventions and most national arbitration statutes require that the arbitrator be appointed by the sponsoring institution.

Arbitrators in a Global Business Dispute Case

It has to be kept in mind that under most arbitration laws, the disputing parties get to decide on the total number of arbitrators. Most cases of international commercial arbitration involve sole or multi-member tribunals.

How do one-arbitrator tribunals and three-arbitrator tribunals compare in terms of their benefits and drawbacks? If there are laws from more than one jurisdiction at play, what can a three-person tribunal decide? What would a three-person tribunal allow in a case with intricate technical background? What are the potential advantages and safeguards of a three- or five-member tribunal and how would they be implemented? Could it be explained what and why are the potential procedural and logistical drawbacks of a three (or five) member tribunal? Can a preference for a specific number of arbitrators be stated unequivocally?

Number of Arbitrators in Cases Involving the Disputes Between Different Countries

The number of arbitrators agreed upon in the Alabama Arbitration and the Abyei Arbitration is an important consideration. Article IV of the Treaty of Washington provides greater details regarding this. A summary of the articles discussed is available in the appendix. However, there arises questions like does each agreement specify a minimum number of arbitrators or if there is a difference between commercial and inter-state arbitrations in terms of the preferred number of arbitrators, and if so, the reasons need to be established.

Methods for determining the number of arbitrators when the parties have not already done so.

It is not uncommon for parties to have disagreements over the agreed-upon number of arbitrators to hear disputes. Rules or presumptions regarding the number of arbitrators are provided by both national law and institutional rules in the absence of an agreement. Section 5 of the FAA states that "the arbitration shall be by a single arbitrator" in cases where the parties have not agreed on the number of arbitrators. In contrast, Article 10 of the UNCITRAL Model Law adopts a different approach, adopting a presumption in favour of three arbitrators. Similarly, the number of arbitrators is decided on a case-by-case basis in the Netherlands (Article 1026(2) of the Netherlands Code of Civil Procedure). Here, the article states that the number of arbitrators shall be designated by the court. It is also specified in the arbitration rukled of the various institutions which anticipate dispute resolution through arbitration. Article 7 of the UNCITRAL Rules from 2010 and Article 12 of the ICC Rules from 2012 handle the issue of how many arbitrators will be involved. Article 6(2) of the 2012 Swiss Rules ("As a rule, the Court shall refer the case to a sole arbitrator, unless the complexity of the subject matter and/or the amount in dispute justify that the case be referred to a three-member arbitral tribunal."). There cannot be a value judgement of the strategy. The parties have the right to choose the arbitrators, and they can do so either by doing so themselves or by agreeing on an appointing authority or other selection mechanism. Arbitrator selection is a highly nuanced process that takes place against a web of legal requirements and strategic considerations for the parties.

The parties must take into account the arbitration clause's procedural mechanisms when choosing an arbitrator (including any institutional rules). They must also take into account any relevant national law, the arbitration clause, and any institutional rules in determining the arbitrators' qualifications and independence. The parties should also think about the qualities, skills, and experience they'd like an arbitrator to have, as well as how the appointing authority is likely to use its discretion in the absence of a mutual agreement. The below-referenced excerpts investigate the myriad problems that can crop up when the parties to an international arbitration exercise their right to choose the arbitrator(s).

There is another case of international arbitration where the ruler of Qatar, a nation in the Middle East and an oil company named as International Marine Oil Company Ltd. Rrived at an arbitral agreement. It was agreed that beginning one year from the date of this Agreement's signature, "the Company shall pay to the Ruler the sum of Qatari Riyal 1,000,000 annually." If and when commercial quantities of oil are discovered, this annual rental will end, but the Ruler will always be entitled to a minimum annual royalty payment of Riyal 1,000,000 under the terms of Article 8 hereof. At the end of each year following the signing of this agreement, the aforementioned calculations will be made. If the Ruler wants a loan of 1,000,000 Riyal from the Company when oil is discovered in commercial quantities in the concession area, and the Company will give it to him. The Company shall be entitled to recover such loan by making a deduction of up to fifty percent (50%) of the royalties accruing thereafter to the Ruler, provided that the amount paid to the Ruler in any one year shall not be reduced below the sum of Riyal One Million (QR. 1,000,000) as provided above.

The Principal Agreement, drafted in both Arabic and English, defined "discovery of oil in commercial quantities" as "the time when a well or wells are drilled, tested, and found capable of producing no less than 15,000 barrels of oil of satisfactory quality per day, for thirty consecutive days, according to good oil field practise." This Agreement has been written in both Arabic and English; both versions are equally valid; however, it is understood that the Ruler will refer to the Arabic version when interpreting the terms of this Agreement. (Cambridge University Press, 2021).

From this case, it had to be decided whether Islamic law or natural justice and equity were to be used in interpreting the Principal Agreement. There is a famous case 1917 case Bearman v. Dux Oil Co., in which Mr. Justice Hardy of the Oklahoma Supreme Court made some pertinent comments. Mr. Justice Hardy remarked on a case involving an oil concession, stating:

"On the construction of contracts, it is the duty of the Court to place itself as far as possible in the position of the parties at the time their minds met upon the terms of the agreement, and from a consideration of the writing itself ascertain their intention; and if this cannot be done by the instrument itself, the circumstances under which it was made and the subject matter to which it relates may be considered; and with these aids, it is the duty of the Court so to construe and interpret the instrument as nearly as may be required" . The court emphasised on the contractual position of consensus ad idem.

CONCLUSION

The preceding discussions attempted to present the legal framework for international arbitration proceedings, including the selection, challenge, and replacement of arbitrators in international arbitration, the rights and duties of international arbitrations, the selection of arbitral seats, the procedures, disclosures, and provisional relief in international arbitration, consolidation, joinder, intervention, and finally the choice of substantive law in international arbitration. There are several issues at stake in deciding the international arbitration and as such different strategies are adopted from situation to situation in deciding about all matters concerning international commercial arbitration.

REFERENCES

Al Dalaien, M. N. (2021). Problems of Proving the Electronic Arbitration Agreement. Taylor & Francis. https://www.tandfonline.com

Cambridge University Press. (2021). *Ruler of Qatar v. International Marine Oil Company, Ltd., International Arbitrations.* Cambridge University Press.

Campbell, M. (2021). *How to determine the law governing an arbitration agreement.* Research Information. bris.ac.uk https://research-information

Chendil, K. (2021). *The Governing Law of Arbitration Agreement: Settling the Unsettled.* SCC Online. https://www.scconline.com

Chua-Rubenfeld, S, (2019). Religious Arbitration of Federal Rights. *The Yale Law Journal.*

Flecke-Giammarco, G, (2015). CISG and Arbitration Agreements. *Korea Science.*

Gisbergen, D. (1992). *Assignment of Rights and Agreement to Arbitrate.* Oxford University Press. https://academic.oup.com

Kimani, E. (2021). *A Critique of The Law Governing Capacity of Parties to Arbitrate.* Social Science Research Network. https://papers.ssrn.com

Nazzini, R. (2016). *The Law Applicable to the Arbitration.* JSTOR. https://www.jstor.org › stable

Nazzini, R. (2016). *The Law Applicable to the Arbitration.* Cambridge University Press & Assessment. https://www.cambridge.org

Nevisandeh, M. (2016). *The Nature of Arbitration Agreement.* Science Direct. https://www.sciencedirect.com

Phua, M. (2020). *Distinctive status of international arbitration agreements.* Academic. https://academic.oup.com

Thilakarathna, K.A.A.N. (2021). *A Utopia or Reality: Possibility of Using the Proper Law.* Scientific Research Publishing.

Ugarte, R. (2010). *Journal of International Arbitration.* Winston & Strawn LLP, https://www.winston.com

Vlahna, K, (2008). *Arbitration and the Importance of the Arbitration Agreement.* Dergi Park. dergipark.org.tr https://dergipark.org.tr

Yang, T. J. (2020). Ascertaining the Proper Law of an Arbitration Agreement. *Kluwer Law Online.* https://kluwerlawonline.com › JOIA2020030

KEY TERMS AND DEFINITIONS

Administrative Tribunal: An administrative tribunal is a type of court that specializes in administrative law, particularly disputes concerning the exercise of public power. Their role is to review decisions made by governments and government agencies.

Arbitration Clause: An arbitration clause is a provision in a contract that requires the parties to resolve their disputes through an arbitration process.

Arbitration Procedure: Arbitration procedure refers to the process by which disputes are resolved through arbitration. The parties must agree to submit the dispute to arbitration in writing, either before or after the conflict arises. The arbitration process involves filing a claim and an answer, selecting an arbitrator or a panel, exchanging documents and evidence, and holding a hearing.

Arbitration Proceedings: Arbitration is a way of resolving disputes between parties without going to court, by choosing a neutral person or a panel to hear and decide the issues. The parties agree on the arbitration process, which usually involves filing a claim and an answer, selecting an arbitrator or a panel, exchanging documents and evidence, and having a final hearing. Arbitration is binding, meaning that the parties have to follow the arbitrator's decision.

Enforceability procedure: Enforceability refers to the ability of a contract or agreement to be enforced in a court of law. The enforceability procedure would depend on the jurisdiction and the type of contract or agreement in question.

Swiss Rules: The Swiss Rules of International Arbitration have been drafted to be efficient, flexible and cost-effective for the resolution of international or domestic disputes. The parties are free to designate their arbitrator(s), to select the applicable law, the language of the proceedings, the seat of the arbitration, and their own legal counsel, in Switzerland or abroad. If the seat of the arbitration is in Switzerland, the parties will enjoy many advantages offered by Swiss arbitration law.

Treaty of Washington: There have been several treaties known as the Treaty of Washington. One such treaty was signed and ratified by the United Kingdom and the United States in 1871. It settled various disputes between the countries, including the Alabama Claims for damages to American shipping caused by British-built warships, as well as illegal fishing in Canadian waters and British civilian losses in the American Civil War. Another treaty known as the Washington Treaty or North Atlantic Treaty forms the basis of the North Atlantic Treaty Organization (NATO).

Chapter 7
Arbitral Decisions from Around the World:
A Brief Analysis

ABSTRACT

According to the rules of the arbitration court, any agreement, submission, or reference made or evidenced in writing with a duly signed or unsigned document shall be deemed to have been agreed in by the parties. The parties agree that the arbitration court's rules must also be taken into account. More in-depth discussions are required to shed light on such topics as the legal framework for international arbitral awards, the form and contents of international arbitral awards, the correction, interpretation, and supplementation of international arbitral awards, the annulment of international arbitral awards, the recognition and enforcement of international arbitral awards, and the application of preclusion, Lis Pendis, and Stare Decisis in international arbitration awards. The purpose of this chapter is to present these within the legal framework of specific arbitral courts, most notably the London Court of International Arbitration.

DOI: 10.4018/978-1-6684-4040-7.ch007

BACKGROUND

Arbitral decisions have different issues of concern. The arbitral decisions have to be eventually enforced and they should lead to the settlement of conflicts which can promote commercial transactions smoothly. The arbitral decisions have to be transparent, just, ease-giving for the parties, and acceptable without causing concern and having to approach the formal courts. To that extent the arbitral decisions are difficult, challenging and would need talent and skills. Empirical studies have been conducted to assess arbitral decision at a global level.

An effort is made here to achieve the following objectives

1. To understand the international arbitral awards
2. To understand the supplementation of international arbitral awards
3. To discuss such issues as Lis Pendis and Stare Decisis

The methodology used here is secondary data analysis from the secondary materials available in the various published sources of the print media as well as the web sources.

PREVIOUS RESEARCH LITERATURE

Arbitrary decisions across the globe provide their interconnect to the various national laws including the administrative laws. The nature of the decisions taken during the arbitration procedures are also viewed carefully. Questions are raised as to whether the arbitral decisions are balanced or just arbitrary. The rationality in the arbitration decisions are also reviewed. A good number of studies have raised similar issues and analysed the arbitrary decisions globally to arrive at a pattern of the arbitrary decisions. It is questioned as to how the administrative law should face the uncertainties arising out of probabilities which cannot be ascribed to the results (Vermeue,A; 2015). There is an ongoing debate about the similarity and differences of the arbitrary decisions and deliberate decisions (OUP,) A question was raised whether the decisions are arbitrary in the international business ranking study (Shichun Xu et. al,; 2008). It is argued that numerical associations reliably alter spatial response choices in arbitrary decisions(Schroeder, PA; 2015). The European Court of Human Rights decisions in comparative law were examined (Brill, 2021) . Studies have found neural correlates of decision processes through an analysis of variance along the decision type (Maoz,U, 2019). It is pointed out that all formal and substantive notions are certainly related. Experts argue against any indecision-making, legal certainty, and avoidance of arbitrariness(un.org, 2023). Arbitrariness is to be avoided in all arbitral awards. The situation is explained using the international covenant that no one shall be subjected to arbitrary arrest or detention or exile. Similar principles are applicable even in the case of arbitral decisions (Brody,R; 1991) Arbitrariness can be given a different metaphysical explanation or arbitrary grounding (Warner,J; 2022). The Administrative Procedure Act instructs federal courts to invalidate agency decisions that are "arbitrary" or "capricious (Miles, TJ, 1983). In this context the argument that reasonableness requires revitalised justification (Dindjer,H; 2021) Previous studies have shown that iconic graphical signs can evolve and the cultural evolution of real-world symbols might occur leading to arbitrariness(Caldell, CA; 2012).

LONDON COURT OF INTERNATIONAL ARBITRATION RULES

International arbitral awards can be legally enforced within specific parameters. For the necessary arbitration, the rules and regulations must be laid down in detail. Arbitration procedures are regulated by the London Court of Arbitration. The LCIA rules, which are those of the London Court of International Arbitration, can be discussed asunder:

The parties are deemed to have agreed in writing that any arbitration between them shall be conducted in accordance with the LCIA Rules or such amended rules as the LCIA may adopt from time to time. This includes situations where an agreement, submission, or reference is made or evidenced in writing (whether signed or not) and provides for arbitration under the rules of the LCIA, the London Court of International Arbitration, the London Court of Arbitration, or the London Court. This preamble, the articles, and the index, along with the annexure to the LCIA Rules and the Schedule of Costs, as each may be amended from time to time by the LCIA, constitute the LCIA Rules.

The LCIA rules have been such that any party seeking to initiate arbitration under the LCIA Rules ("Claimant") shall deliver to the Registrar of the LCIA Court ("Registrar") i. a written request for arbitration ("Request"), containing or accompanied by the full name, nationality, and all contact details (including email address, postal address, and telephone number) of the Claimant for the purpose of receiving delivery of all documentation in the arbitration pursuant to Article 4; and the same particulars of the Claimant's authorised representatives (if any) and of all other parties to the arbitration; (ii) a copy of any contractual or other documentation in which the terms of the Arbitration Agreement (other than the LCIA Rules) invoked by the Claimant to support its claim are contained and to which the Claimant's claim relates; (iii) a statement briefly summarising the nature and circumstances of the dispute, the estimated amount or value of the dispute, the transaction(s) at issue, and the claim advanced by the Claimant against any other party to the arbitration (each such other party being herein separately described as a "Respondent"); (iv) a statement of any procedural matters for the arbitration upon which the parties have already agreed in writing or in respect of which the Claimant makes any proposal under the Arbitration Agreement (such as the arbitral seat, the language(s) of the arbitration, the number of arbitrators, their qualifications and identities); (v) the Claimant's nominee's full name, email address, postal address, and telephone number if party nomination of arbitrators is required by the Arbitration Agreement (or any other written agreement, however drafted); (vi) evidence that the LCIA has received or is being sent the registration fee specified in the Schedule of Costs, failing which the Registrar shall treat the Request as not having been delivered and the arbitration as not having been commenced under the Arbitration Agreement; and (vii) confirmation that copies of the Request (including all accompanying documents) have been or are being delivered to all other parties to the arbitration in accordance with Article 4 by one or more means to be identified specifically in such confirmation, to be supported then or as soon as possible thereafter by documentary proof satisfactory to the LCIA Court of actual delivery (including the date of delivery); or, if actual delivery is demonstrated to be impossible, confirmation that the Request (including all accompanying documents) has been filed with the LCIA. If all these requirements are met to the LCIA Court's satisfaction in respect of each arbitration, a Claimant may serve a composite request in respect of all such arbitrations (whether against one or more respondents and under one or more Arbitration Agreements). In particular, in any consolidated request, the Claimant must separately identify the disputed transaction(s), the amount or value of the claim, and the other party against whom the claim is being asserted. Unless otherwise determined by the LCIA Court or the Arbitral Tribunal, each arbitration so initiated shall be conducted in accordance with the LCIA Rules.

Further, Article 4.1, mandates that the Registrar must receive the request (and any supporting materials) in electronic format.

For all purposes, an arbitration is considered to have begun on the date the request (and all supporting documents) are received by the Registrar via electronic transmission (the "Commencement Date"), provided the LCIA has received the registration fee. In cases where the registration fee is paid at a later time, the LCIA will use the date it actually receives the fee as the Start Date.

The LCIA Court may permit a Claimant to supplement, modify, or amend its Request to correct any error in computation, any clerical or typographical error, any ambiguity, or any mistake of a similar nature at any time after the Commencement Date but prior to the appointment of the Arbitral Tribunal, after affording the parties a reasonable opportunity to state their views and upon such terms as the LCIA Court may determine. The term "Claimant" shall be so interpreted under the Arbitration Agreement if there are one or more Claimants (whether or not jointly represented).

Then, the Respondent shall deliver to the Registrar a written response to the Request (the "Response") within 28 days of the Commencement Date, or such lesser or greater period as determined by the LCIA Court upon application by any party or upon its own initiative (pursuant to Article 22.5). The Response shall contain or be accompanied by i. a format where the full name, nationality, and contact details of the respondent and its authorised representatives (if any), including email and postal addresses and telephone numbers, for the purpose of receiving delivery of all documentation in the arbitration in accordance with Article 4; (ii) a decision on whether or not the Claimant's Request, which includes the Claimant's invocation of the Arbitration Agreement in support of its request, is granted in whole or in part; (iii) in the absence of full confirmation, a statement briefly summarising the nature and circumstances of the dispute, the estimated monetary amount or value, the transaction(s) at issue, and the defence advanced by the Respondent, and also indicating any counterclaim advanced by the Respondent against any Claimant and any cross-claim against another Respondent; (iv) a response to any statement of procedural matters for the arbitration contained in the Request under Article 1.1(iv), such as the respondent's own statement relating to the arbitral seat, the language(s) of the arbitration, the number of arbitrators, their qualifications and identities, and any other procedural matter upon which the parties have already agreed in writing or in respect of which the respondent makes any proposal under the Arbitration Agreement; (v) the Respondent's nominee's full name, email address, postal address, and telephone number if party nomination of arbitrators is required by the Arbitration Agreement (or any other written agreement, however drafted); and (vi) confirmation that copies of the response (including all accompanying documents) have been or are being delivered to all other parties to the arbitration in accordance with Article 4 by one or more means of delivery to be identified specifically in such confirmation, to be supported then or as soon as possible thereafter by documentary proof satisfactory to the LCIA Court of actual delivery (including the date of delivery); or, if actual delivery is demonstrated to the LCIA Court, a statement that the LCIA Court has jurisdiction to hear the arbitration. If the respondent satisfies the requirements of Article 2.1 in respect of each arbitration to which the respondent responds, the LCIA Court will accept a composite response in case the request is a composite request. In each arbitration, the Respondent must specify the estimated amount or value in a dispute, the transaction or transactions at issue, and the specific defence, counterclaim, or crossclaim that the Respondent is asserting against the other party. All materials should be submitted electronically.

Any party that fails to nominate or propose an arbitrator candidate by the time the response is due or such other time period as the parties may agree upon shall be deemed to have waived forever the right to do so. A Respondent's denial of any claim or the advancement of any defence, counterclaim, or crossclaim in arbitration shall not be precluded (on its own) by the Respondent's failure to deliver all or any part of a Response within the time limit or at all.

After affording the parties an opportunity to express their views and on such terms as the LCIA Court may determine, and subject to Article 2.4, the LCIA Court may permit a party to supplement, modify, or amend its Response to correct any error in computation, any clerical or typographical error, any ambiguity, or any mistake of a similar nature.

If there are more than one Respondents (whether or not they are jointly represented), the term "Respondent" in the Arbitration Agreement will be interpreted accordingly. The President of the LCIA Court (or any Vice President, Honorary Vice President, or former Vice President of the LCIA Court) or a division of three or more members of the LCIA Court appointed by its President or any Vice President (the "LCIA Court") shall perform the functions of the LCIA Court under the Arbitration Agreement in its name. The LCIA Court will oversee the Registrar's or a deputy Registrar's performance of their duties under the Arbitration Agreement. The Registrar of the LCIA Court shall be the recipient of all communications from the parties to the arbitration, their authorised representatives, the arbitrators, the tribunal secretary, and the experts. Each party or authorised representative of a party must ensure that all other parties receive a copy of all communications with the Registrar. Further, the Claimant shall submit the request and the respondent shall submit the response electronically, including by email or any electronic filing system operated by the LCIA. If you need to submit your Request or Response in a format other than what is specified above, you must first get written permission from the Registrar, acting on behalf of the LCIA Court. Any written communication relating to the arbitration shall be delivered via email or any other electronic means of communication that provides a record of its transmission, unless otherwise approved or directed in writing by the Arbitral Tribunal or, prior to the constitution of the Arbitral Tribunal, the Registrar acting on behalf of the LCIA Court. A written communication sent by electronic means shall be treated as received by a party on the day it is transmitted (such time to be determined by reference to the recipient's time zone) for the purpose of determining the commencement of any time limit, unless otherwise ordered by the Arbitral Tribunal or the Registrar acting on behalf of the LCIA Court. Any written communication permitted or required to be delivered pursuant to this Article 4 shall be deemed to have been received by a party on the day it is delivered (such time to be determined by reference to the recipient's time zone).

Unless otherwise ordered by the Arbitral Tribunal or the Registrar acting on behalf of the LCIA Court, for the purpose of determining compliance with a time limit, a written communication shall be treated as having been made by a party if transmitted or delivered prior to or on the date of the expiration of the time limit (such time to be determined by reference to the sender's time zone).

If a deadline is to be observed, it will start counting down the day after the addressee receives the written communication. If the last day of such period falls on a holiday or a day when businesses are closed in the location of the addressee (or the location of the party against whom time is being calculated), the period shall be extended until the first business day following such last day. Any weekends or legal holidays that fall within the time frame in question must also be factored in. As soon as reasonably practicable after any change to the full name and contact details (including email address, postal address, and telephone number) of a Party or its authorised representatives, that Party shall notify the Registrar, the Arbitral Tribunal, and all other Parties.

Any dispute between the parties regarding the sufficiency of the Request or the Response shall not prevent the LCIA Court from forming the Arbitral Tribunal. If either the Request or the Response is missing, late, or incomplete, the LCIA Court may still move forward with the arbitration. The term "Arbitral

Tribunal" refers to either a single arbitrator (including an Emergency Arbitrator, if necessary) or, if there are multiple arbitrators, all of them collectively. The arbitrators shall at all times be and remain objective and totally separate from the parties, and no arbitrator shall act as an advocate for or authorised representative of any party in the arbitration. The arbitrator is not permitted to offer advice to either party regarding the merits of the dispute or the likely outcome of the arbitration. Each candidate for appointment as an arbitrator before the LCIA Court must provide the Registrar (upon the latter's request) with a brief written summary of his or her qualifications and professional positions (past and present); agree in writing to fee rates that are consistent with the Schedule of Costs; and sign a written declaration answering the following questions: I whether there are any circumstances currently known to the candidate which are likely to give rise to a conflict of interest; and (ii) whether the candidate has any The candidate is required to provide the Registrar with the signed agreement and declaration as soon as possible. Each arbitrator shall be under an ongoing obligation, until the arbitration is finally concluded, to promptly disclose in writing to the LCIA Court, any other members of the Arbitral Tribunal, and all parties I any circumstances becoming known to that arbitrator after the date of his or her written declaration (under Article 5.4) that are likely to give rise in the mind of any party to any justifiable doubts as to his or her impartiality or independence. Promptly after the Registrar receives the Response or, if no Response is received, after 28 days from the Commencement Date, the LCIA Court will appoint the Arbitral Tribunal (or such other lesser or greater period to be determined by the LCIA Court pursuant to Article 22.5).

The LCIA Court alone has the authority to appoint arbitrators under the Arbitration Agreement, and no other party or third party may do so (albeit taking into account any written agreement or joint nomination by the parties or nomination by the other candidates or arbitrators). Unless the parties agree in writing otherwise or the LCIA Court finds that a three-member tribunal is appropriate under the circumstances, 5.8 a single arbitrator will be appointed (or, exceptionally, more than three). The LCIA Court will select arbitrators in accordance with any procedures or criteria for doing so that the parties have previously agreed to in writing. The LCIA Court must also consider the amount in dispute, the number of parties involved, the location of the parties, the languages spoken by the parties, and any other factors it deems relevant to the case at hand. The President of the LCIA Court and the Vice Presidents of the LCIA Court, as well as the Chair of the LCIA Board of Directors (the latter being an ex officio member of the LCIA Court), may only be appointed as arbitrators if nominated in writing by a party or parties or by the other candidates or arbitrators. The President of the LCIA Court shall only be eligible to be appointed as an arbitrator if the parties agree in writing to nominate as the sole arbitrator. If the Registrar asks, each party must reveal its nationality to the Registrar and the other parties. A sole arbitrator or the presiding arbitrator shall not be of the same nationality as any party where the parties are of different nationalities, unless all parties who are not of the same nationality as the arbitrator candidate agree otherwise in writing. In the context of Article 6.1, "nationality" refers to a natural person's citizenship, which can be obtained through birth, naturalisation, or whatever other means are necessary under the laws of the country in question. For a corporation or other legal entity, "nationality" refers to the country where it was formed and where its primary place of business is located. A company that is formally established in one country but has its administrative hub in another is considered a dual citizen of those two states. If one of the parties is a corporation or other legal entity, then that entity's nationality will be considered to include that of its controlling shareholders or interests. A person who is a citizen of two or more States shall be treated as a citizen of each State; citizens of the European Union shall be treated as nationals of its different Member States and shall not be treated as having the same nationality; a citizen of an overseas territory of a State shall be treated as a national of that territory and not of that State; and a legal person incorporated in an overseas territory of a State shall be treated as such and not (by such fact a national of that State).

To the extent that the parties have agreed, in any manner other than through the LCIA Court, on the appointment of any arbitrator, such agreement shall be treated for all purposes under the Arbitration Agreement as an agreement to nominate an arbitrator. The LCIA Court may appoint such nominee as arbitrator only if the nominee satisfies the requirements of Articles 5.3 through 5.5; the LCIA Court may refuse to appoint any nominee if it finds that the nominee does not satisfy these requirements. In the event that neither the Claimant nor the Respondent, or any third person (other than the LCIA Court) makes a timely nomination of an arbitrator (in the Request, the Response, or otherwise), the LCIA Court may appoint an arbitrator. Any late nomination may be considered by the LCIA Court; however, the Court is under no obligation to do so. No party may appoint an arbitrator or the arbitrator who will preside over the case without the other parties' consent (in writing). If there are more than two parties to a dispute and they have not all agreed in writing that the disputant parties represent collectively two separate "sides" for the formation of the Arbitral Tribunal (as Claimants on one side and Respondents on the other, each side nominating a single arbitrator), then the LCIA Court shall appoint the Arbitral Tribunal without regard to any agreement between the disputant parties as to the composition of the Arbitral Tribunal. In such a case, the Arbitration Agreement shall be treated for all purposes as if the parties had expressly agreed in writing to have the LCIA Court nominate and appoint the Arbitral Tribunal. In cases of extreme urgency, either party may petition the LCIA Court to have an Arbitral Tribunal convened under Article 5 of the Rules of Arbitration immediately. Such an application shall be made to the Registrar in writing by electronic means, along with a copy of the Request (if made by a Claimant) or a copy of the Response (if made by a Respondent), and shall be delivered or notified forthwith to all other parties to the arbitration. The application must detail the exceptional circumstances that call for the swift establishment of the Arbitral Tribunal. The application shall be decided by the LCIA Court as soon as practicable under the circumstances. If the application is approved, the LCIA Court may extend or shorten any time period specified in the Arbitration Agreement or any other agreement of the parties in order to convene the Arbitral Tribunal (pursuant to Article 22.5). Any party may apply to the LCIA Court for the immediate appointment of a temporary sole arbitrator to conduct emergency proceedings pending the formation or expedited formation of the Arbitral Tribunal (under Articles 5 or 9A) in the event of an emergency at any time prior to the formation or expedited formation of the Arbitral Tribunal.

Any such application to the Registrar shall be made in writing via electronic means, and shall be accompanied by a copy of the Request (if made by a Claimant) or a copy of the Response (if made by a Respondent), which shall be delivered or notified promptly to all other parties to the arbitration. The application must detail I why the appointment of an Emergency Arbitrator is necessary in light of the urgency of the situation, and (ii) the nature of the emergency and the reasons for it. The LCIA Court will not consider the application unless the applicant certifies in writing that the Special Fee required by Article 9B has been paid or is being paid to the LCIA. The terms of the Cost Schedule shall apply to the Special Fee. The amount of this deposit is set forth in the Schedule and will be used to pay for the LCIA's administrative charges and expenses, as well as the Emergency Arbitrator's fees and expenses. After the Emergency Arbitrator has been appointed, the LCIA Court may increase the Special Fee payable by the applicant in accordance with the Schedule. Any Special Fee paid to the LCIA shall not be subject to Article 24 except as provided in Section 5(vi) of the Schedule of

Costs. The application must be decided as quickly as possible by the LCIA Court. If the request is approved, the LCIA Court will appoint an emergency arbitrator within three days of the Registrar receiving the request (or as soon as possible thereafter).

The Emergency Arbitrator may conduct the emergency proceedings in any manner deemed appropriate in the circumstances, taking into account the nature of such emergency proceedings, the need to afford to each party, if possible, an opportunity to be consulted on the claim for emergency relief (whether or not it avails itself of such opportunity), the claim and reasons for emergency relief, and the parties' further submissions (if any). The Emergency Arbitrator may make a decision on the claim for emergency relief based solely on the documents submitted to him or her by the parties, and is not required to hold any hearing with the parties, either in person or virtually via conference call, videoconference, or other communications technology.

As soon as possible, but in no event later than 14 days after the Emergency Arbitrator's appointment, the Emergency Arbitrator shall render a decision on the claim for emergency relief. Only in extraordinary circumstances (as per Article 22.5) or with the written consent of all parties to the emergency proceedings may this deadline be extended by the LCIA Court. The Emergency Arbitrator has the same authority to make orders and awards as the Arbitral Tribunal does under the Arbitration Agreement, and can also make orders referring all or part of the claim for emergency relief back to the proceedings before the Arbitral Tribunal (when formed).

The Urgent Arbitrator's decision must be made in writing and must include an explanation for the decision. Any award made by the Emergency Arbitrator must be in accordance with Article 26.2 and will be binding under Article 26.8. (subject to Articles 9.11 and 9.12). The Registrar shall promptly electronically transmit to the parties any order or award issued by the Emergency Arbitrator.

The LCIA Court will decide the amount of the Arbitration Costs, which will include the Special Fee paid in accordance with Article 28.1. Any party's Legal Costs, including those for emergency proceedings, shall be included in the Legal Costs under Article 28.3. The Emergency Arbitrator has the authority to decide the total amount of Legal Costs associated with the emergency proceedings, as well as the breakdown of costs between the parties. If the Emergency Arbitrator so chooses, the Arbitral Tribunal may decide all or a portion of the costs associated with the emergency proceedings.

The Arbitral Tribunal may confirm, vary, discharge, or revoke, in whole or in part, any order or award of the Emergency Arbitrator (except for any order adjourning to the Arbitral Tribunal, when formed, any part of the claim for emergency relief) upon application by any party or on its own initiative.

If a party requests it, or if the Emergency Arbitrator decides to do so on its own, the Emergency Arbitrator can do the following before the Arbitral Tribunal is formed: A statement as follows will be made available. i. I uphold, modify, discharge, or revoke all or a portion of an Emergency Arbitrator's order, and/or issue a new order; (ii) clarify or amend any award made by the Emergency Arbitrator due to a computation error, clerical error, typographical error, ambiguity, or mistake of a similar nature; and/or Any claim for emergency relief brought forward in the emergency proceedings but not decided in any award of the Emergency Arbitrator is subject to (iii) an additional award.

A party is not precluded from seeking interim or conservatory measures from a state court or other competent authority prior to the formation of the Arbitral Tribunal, and nothing in Article 9B shall be construed as a waiver or substitution for the exercise of such right. During the emergency proceedings, the Emergency Arbitrator, the Registrar, and all other parties shall be promptly notified in writing of any application to and any order by such court or authority.

All questions concerning the conduct of the emergency proceedings not specifically addressed in the articles shall be resolved by the LCIA Court in its discretion.

There are provisions of replacement of arbitrator appointment time line also.

Either party may request that a new arbitrator be appointed quickly by the LCIA. Requests to appoint a replacement arbitrator quickly must be submitted in writing to the Registrar via electronic means and either delivered to or immediately communicated to all other parties to the arbitration. The application will be heard and decided as quickly as possible by the LCIA Court. For the purpose of speeding up the appointment of the replacement arbitrator, the LCIA Court may set or shorten any period of time in the Arbitration Agreement or any other agreement of the parties if the application is granted.

The LCIA Court may, on its own initiative, at the written request of all other members of the Arbitral Tribunal, or upon a written challenge by any party, terminate the appointment of any arbitrator if: I the arbitrator resigns from his or her position as arbitrator by providing written notice to the LCIA Court of his or her intent to resign as arbitrator, with copies to the parties and the other members of the Arbitral Tribunal (if any); or (ii) the arbitrator

If an arbitrator (i)wilfully violates the Arbitration Agreement, (ii)does not act fairly or impartially as between the parties, or (iii)does not conduct or participate in the arbitration with reasonable efficiency, diligence, and industry, the LCIA Court may find that the arbitrator is unfit to act under Article 10.1.

Within 14 days after the formation of the Arbitral Tribunal, or (if later) within 14 days of becoming aware of any grounds described in Article 10.1 or 10.2, the party challenging the arbitrator must provide the LCIA Court, the Arbitral Tribunal, and all other parties with a written statement of the reasons for the challenge. This statement must include the name of the arbitrator being challenged and a brief explanation of the nature of the challenge. It is only after the LCIA Court has confirmed the appointment of an arbitrator that the nominating or participating party can raise objections to the impartiality of the arbitrator. The LCIA Court shall withdraw the appointment of the challenged arbitrator if all other parties agree in writing to the challenge within 14 days of receipt of the written statement (without reasons).

If the challenged arbitrator does not resign in writing within 14 days of receipt of the written statement, or if the parties do not agree to have the LCIA Court decide the challenge, then the challenged arbitrator will be removed from office. The LCIA Court may conduct the challenge proceedings in any manner it deems appropriate in the circumstances, but it must give the other parties and the challenged arbitrator a fair chance to respond to the challenging party's written statement. Additional information and materials may be requested at any time by the LCIA Court from the challenging party, the challenged arbitrator, other parties, any authorised representative of a party, other members of the Arbitral Tribunal, and the tribunal secretary (if any).

The Registrar will send a copy of the LCIA Court's written decision and the reasons for it to the parties, the challenged arbitrator, and the other members of the Arbitral Tribunal (if any). Once the LCIA Court rules on the challenge, the arbitrator's appointment will be revoked. The written resignation of a challenged arbitrator prior to a decision by the LCIA Court shall not be construed as an admission on the part of the arbitrator challenging the written statement.

Fees and expenses (if any) for the former arbitrator's services shall be determined by the LCIA Court in a manner it deems appropriate under the circumstances (see section 10.7). The LCIA Court may also decide whether, how much, and to whom any party should pay the challenge's costs; and the LCIA Court may refer all or any part of such costs to the later decision of the Arbitral Tribunal and/or the LCIA Court under Article 28.

If the LCIA Court has reasonable doubts about the independence or impartiality of any candidate for the arbitrator, if a nominee declines appointment as an arbitrator, or if an arbitrator is to be replaced for any reason, the LCIA Court may decide whether or not to revert to the original nominating process for such arbitral appointment.

If a party is given the chance to nominate a new arbitrator, under the Arbitration Agreement or otherwise, and that party doesn't do so within 14 days (or such lesser or greater time as the LCIA Court may determine), the LCIA Court may decide that the party waived its chance to do so and appoint the new arbitrator anyway.

As to whether and to what extent the prior proceedings in the arbitration shall stand, the Arbitral Tribunal (when reconstituted) shall decide. In the event that one of the arbitrators refuses or continues to miss meetings without good cause, the remaining arbitrators may jointly notify the LCIA Court, the parties, and the absent arbitrator in writing of the arbitrator's refusal or failure to participate. As long as the LCIA Court gives its written consent, the remaining arbitrators can decide to proceed with the arbitration (including the making of any award) even if one of the arbitrators is absent. The remaining arbitrators shall consider the stage of the arbitration, any explanation made by or on behalf of the absent arbitrator for his or her refusal or failure to participate, the likely effect upon the legal recognition or enforceability of any award at the seat of the arbitration, and such other matters as they deem appropriate in deciding whether to continue the arbitration. If the remaining arbitrators rule without the absent arbitrator's input, they must explain their reasoning in the award they issue. If the remaining arbitrators decide at any time after giving written notice of such refusal or failure not to continue the arbitration with the participation of the absent arbitrator, the remaining arbitrators shall notify the parties and the LCIA Court in writing of such decision; and, in that event, the remaining arbitrators or any party may refer the matter to the LCIA Court for the revocation of the absent arbitrator's appointment and the appointment of a new arbitrator.

Once the Arbitral Tribunal is formed, it will communicate directly with the parties (with a copy to the Registrar) and disregard the Registrar unless the Arbitral Tribunal specifically decides otherwise.

Each party shall be provided with a copy of any written communication sent by the Registrar on behalf of the Arbitral Tribunal or the LCIA Court to any one party. If a party submits a statement or document to the Arbitral Tribunal under Article 15, they must also provide a copy to the other parties and the Registrar, and they must notify the Arbitral Tribunal in writing that they have done so.

No party shall, knowingly and intentionally, make or attempt to make any contact with any member of the LCIA Court exercising any function in relation to the arbitration, or, from the formation of the Arbitral Tribunal onwards, any member of the Arbitral Tribunal or the tribunal secretary (if any), unless such contact has been disclosed in writing prior to or shortly after the time of such confabulation. However, despite Article 3.3, a party is allowed to contact the Registrar on its own initiative for administrative purposes.

Except as the parties may otherwise agree in writing, any arbitrator, candidate, or nominee who is required to participate in the selection of a presiding arbitrator may consult any party to obtain the views of that party as to the suitability of any candidate or nominee as presiding arbitrator prior to the formation of the Arbitral Tribunal, provided that such arbitrator, candidate, or nominee promptly informs any other arbitrator, candidate, or nominee involved in the arbitration. The Arbitral Tribunal shall, at all times during the arbitration, perform the following general duties as set forth in the Arbitration Agreement:

(i.) Has a duty to treat all parties fairly and impartially, without favouring any one over another; and (ii) a duty to provide each side with a fair and reasonable opportunity to present its case and address that of their opponent(s). (iii) the responsibility to establish procedures that are appropriate for the circumstances of the arbitration, so that the dispute is resolved in a timely, cost-effective, and fair manner.

Subject to the mandatory provisions of any applicable law or any rules of law the Arbitral Tribunal may decide to be applicable, 14.2 the Arbitral Tribunal shall have the broadest discretion to discharge these general duties, and the Parties shall at all times do everything necessary in good faith for the fair, efficient, and expeditious conduct of the arbitration, including the Arbitral Tribunal's discharge of its general duty.

Within 21 days of the Registrar's written notification of the formation of the Arbitral Tribunal, the parties and the Arbitral Tribunal shall make contact (either through a hearing in person or virtually by conference call, videoconference, or using other communications technology or exchange of correspondence). The Arbitral Tribunal may take into account any joint proposals the parties make regarding the conduct of their arbitration. Without limiting the Arbitral Tribunal's general discretion, after affording the parties a fair opportunity to present their case, the Arbitral Tribunal may, subject to the following, make a final decision on the dispute. According to the LCIA Rules, the arbitrator may issue any order it deems necessary for the fair, efficient, and prompt administration of the arbitration.

The Arbitral Tribunal may, in its discretion and pursuant to its authority under Article 14.5, issue any order necessary to facilitate the procedure to be adopted in the arbitration, including, but not limited to:

(i.) reducing or eliminating the need for any written statement to be delivered under Article 15; (ii) limiting any witness' written and oral testimony in accordance with Article 20.4; (iii) utilising technological means to quicken and improve the arbitration process (including any hearing); (iv) determining which issues, and in what order, will be resolved at each stage of the arbitration process, as set forth in the articles (v) waiving the right to a hearing; Using its authority to make an Early Determination under Section 22.1(viii);(vii) determining a reasonable time frame for the conduct of any arbitration-related proceedings, including the holding of any hearing;(viii) shortening a time period in accordance with Section 22.1(ii); and (x) if the Arbitral Tribunal so determines, making any other order that it deems appropriate under the circumstances of the arbitration. If there is more than one arbitrator on the Arbitral Tribunal, the person in charge of the proceedings may act unilaterally if all parties and the other arbitrators agree.

The Arbitral Tribunal may retain the services of a tribunal secretary in connection with an arbitration, subject to Articles 14.9 through 14.15 and any applicable law. An Arbitral Tribunal may not delegate its power to decide matters to a secretary under any circumstances. The Arbitral Tribunal, which shall retain responsibility for ensuring that all tasks are performed to the standard required by the LCIA Rules, shall retain authority and control over all work performed by the Tribunal Secretary on its behalf and under its supervision.

Each candidate for the position of secretary of an Arbitral Tribunal must sign a written declaration answering the following questions before being considered for the position: I does the candidate know of any circumstances which are likely to give rise in the mind of any party to any justifiable doubts as to the candidate's impartiality or independence, and if so, does the candidate fully disclose the nature and extent of such circumstances? Such a written declaration must be provided by the candidate without undue delay to the Arbitral Tribunal and the Registrar.

Only after receiving consent from both parties may an Arbitral Tribunal hire a tribunal secretary to assist it. A court secretary receives initial approval when:

i. all parties have reached an agreement on the scope of the tribunal secretary's authority; (ii) if the tribunal secretary is to be paid an hourly rate and reimbursed for expenses, the parties have agreed on the hourly rate and the right to reimbursement; (iii) the written declaration referred to in Article 14.9 has been made available to the parties; and (iv) The person serving as the tribunal secretary has been mutually agreed upon by all parties.

If the Arbitral Tribunal wants the tribunal secretary to do work beyond what was agreed upon in Article 14.10(i), or if it wants to increase the hourly rate to be charged by the tribunal secretary, it must first get the parties' consent.

If a party does not raise an objection within the time limit established by the Arbitral Tribunal, that party will be deemed to have accepted the terms of Articles 14.10 and 14.11.

After the LCIA Court has made its determination under Article 28.1 as to the amount of the Arbitration Costs, any fees charged by or expenses reimbursed to a tribunal secretary shall be included in those costs.

A tribunal secretary shall be under an ongoing obligation, until the arbitration is finally concluded, to promptly disclose in writing to the LCIA Court, the Arbitral Tribunal, and all parties in the arbitration any circumstances becoming known to that tribunal secretary after the date of his or her written declaration (under Article 14.9) which are likely to give rise in the mind of any party to any justifiable doubts as to his or her impartiality or independence.

The Arbitration Court, in its sole discretion, may fire the court secretary. Any secretary of a tribunal shall be subject to Article 10 above with any necessary modifications.

Unless the parties have agreed or jointly proposed in writing otherwise, or unless the Arbitral Tribunal should decide otherwise, the written stage of the arbitration and its procedural timetable shall be as set forth in this Article 15.

The Claimant shall deliver to the Arbitral Tribunal and all other parties either: I a written election to have its Request treated as its Statement of Case complying with this Article 15.2; or (ii) a written Statement of Case setting out in sufficient detail the relevant facts and legal submissions on which it relies, together with the relief claimed again, within 28 days of receipt of the Registrar's written notification of the formation of the Arbitral Tribunal.

Within 28 days after receipt of the Claimant's Statement of Case or the Claimant's election to treat the Request as its Statement of Case, the Respondent shall deliver to the Arbitral Tribunal and all other parties either: I its written election to have its Response treated as its Statement of Defense and (if applicable) Counterclaim complying with this Article 15.3; or (ii) its written Statement of Defence and (if applicable) Statement of Counterclaim setting out the Respondent's position with respect to the Claim

The Claimant shall deliver to the Arbitral Tribunal and the other parties within 28 days of receipt of the Respondent's Statement of Defence and (if applicable) Statement of Counterclaim or the Respondent's election to treat the Response as its Statement of Defence and (if applicable) Statement of Counterclaim, a written Statement of Reply which, where there is any counterclaim, shall also include a Statement of Defence to Counterclaim in the same manner as required for a Statement.

If the Response Statement includes a Statement of Defence to Counterclaim, the Respondent must submit a written Statement of Reply to the Defence to Counterclaim, along with any supporting documents, to the Arbitral Tribunal and the other parties within 28 days of receipt of the Statement of Reply.

Except as otherwise directed by the Arbitral Tribunal, after the last of these Statements has been submitted, neither party may submit any further written statement. The Arbitral Tribunal may issue supplemental or alternative instructions for any aspect of the written phase of the arbitration, including but not limited to: i. additional written comments (ii) declarations made in writing with respect to any party's counterclaims; iii) the submission of sworn testimony from any fact or expert witness in writing; iv) the service of any other form of written evidence; and (v) the procedures, deadlines, and parties involved in the arbitration's written phase.

The Arbitral Tribunal may proceed with the arbitration (with or without a hearing) and make one or more awards even if the Respondent does not submit a Statement of Defence or the Claimant does not submit a Statement of Defence to Counterclaim, or if at any time any party fails to avail itself of the opportunity to present its written case in the manner required under this Article 15 or as otherwise ordered by the Arbitral Tribunal.

As soon as reasonably possible after the written stage of the arbitration, the Arbitral Tribunal shall proceed in such manner as has been agreed to in writing by the parties or pursuant to its authority under the Arbitration Agreement.

The Arbitral Tribunal shall, in any event, seek to make its final award as soon as reasonably possible, and shall endeavour to do so no later than three months following the last submission from the parties (whether made orally or in writing), in accordance with a timetable notified to the parties and the Registrar as soon as practicable (if necessary, as revised and re-notified from time to time). As soon as practicable after receiving what it believes to be the final submission from the parties (whether written or oral), the

Arbitral Tribunal (other than a sole arbitrator) shall set aside adequate time for deliberations (in person or otherwise) and notify the parties of the time it has set aside.

The seat (or legal place) of the arbitration may be determined by written agreement between the parties prior to the formation of the Arbitral Tribunal, or with the prior written consent of the Arbitral Tribunal after the formation of the Arbitral Tribunal.

Absent any such agreement, the arbitration shall take place in London (England), unless and until the Arbitral Tribunal orders that another arbitral seat is more appropriate given the circumstances and after providing the parties with a reasonable opportunity to submit written comments to the Arbitral Tribunal. The LCIA Court will not use the existence of a default seat as a factor when making appointments of arbitrators and emergency arbitrators under Articles 5, 9A, 9B, 9C, and 11.

If a personal hearing is required, it can be held wherever the parties and the Arbitral Tribunal agree is best. If the Arbitral Tribunal needs to hold a meeting in person, it can do so wherever it sees fit. For all purposes, the arbitration shall be deemed to have been conducted at the arbitral seat, and any order or award shall be deemed to have been made at that seat, even if any hearing or deliberation takes place other than in person (in whole or in part).

Subject to Article 16.5 below, the law applicable to the Arbitration Agreement and the arbitration shall be the law applicable at the seat of the arbitration, unless and to the extent that the parties have agreed in writing on the application of other laws or rules of law and such agreement is not prohibited by the law applicable at the seat of the arbitration.

Despite Article 16.4's provisions, the LCIA Rules are interpreted in accordance with English law.

Until the Arbitral Tribunal is formed, the proceedings of the arbitration shall be conducted in the language or language of predominance of the Arbitration Agreement.

If the Arbitration Agreement has been drafted in more than one language, the LCIA Court will decide which language will be used for the initial stages of the arbitration unless the Arbitration Agreement specifies that the arbitration proceedings will be conducted in more than one language.

If the LCIA Court and the Registrar communicate in the language(s) chosen at the outset of the arbitration or the language(s) of the arbitral seat, the non-participating or defaulting party will have no grounds for complaint.

If the parties cannot agree on the language(s) to be used in the arbitration after the Arbitral Tribunal is formed, the Arbitral Tribunal will make that decision, taking into account the initial language(s) of the arbitration and any other matter it may consider appropriate in the circumstances, after giving the parties a reasonable opportunity to make written comments.

If any document is expressed in a language other than the language(s) of the arbitration and no translation of such document is submitted by the party relying on the document, the Arbitral Tribunal may order or (if the Arbitral Tribunal has not been formed) the Registrar may request that party to submit a translation of all or any part of that document in any language(s) of the arbitration or of the arbitral seat.

It is possible for one or more authorised representatives to appear in person before the Arbitral Tribunal on behalf of any party in the arbitration.

Prior to the formation of the Arbitral Tribunal, the Registrar may request the following information from any party to the arbitration proceeding: I written confirmation of the authority granted by that party to any authorised representative designated in its Request or Response; and (ii) written confirmation of the names, email and postal addresses of all such party's authorised representatives in the arbitration. At any time after its formation, the Arbitral Tribunal can request similar evidence or confirmation from any party in whatever form it sees fit.

Any party intending to make a change or addition to its authorised representatives after the Arbitral Tribunal has been formed must give prompt written notice to the other parties, the Arbitral Tribunal, the tribunal secretary (if any), and the Registrar; and any such change or addition must be approved by the Arbitral Tribunal before it can be implemented in the arbitration.

The Arbitral Tribunal may refuse to approve a proposed change or addition to a party's authorised representatives if it believes that the composition of the Arbitral Tribunal or the finality of any award would be jeopardised as a result (on the grounds of possible conflict of interest or other like impediment). The Arbitral Tribunal shall consider the general principle that a party may be represented by an authorised representative chosen by that party, the stage which the arbitration has reached, the efficiency resulting from maintaining the composition of the Arbitral Tribunal (as constituted throughout the arbitration), and any likely wasted costs or loss of time resulting from such change in determining whether to grant or withhold such approval.

As a condition of appearing before the Arbitral Tribunal, each party must ensure that its authorised representatives have agreed to follow the general guidelines set forth in the Annex to the LCIA Rules. A party's consent to the appearance of an authorised representative is deemed to be an agreement by the party that the representative will abide by the terms of this provision.

If a party files a complaint against another party's authorised representative who has appeared before the Arbitral Tribunal by name (or if the Arbitral Tribunal files such a complaint on its own initiative), the Arbitral Tribunal will have the authority to determine, after consulting with the parties and giving the alleged infringing representative a reasonable opportunity to respond, whether or not the alleged infringing representative has violated the general guidelines. If the Arbitral Tribunal determines that the authorised representative has violated this provision, the Arbitral Tribunal may impose any or all of the following sanctions upon the authorised representative: I a written reprimand; (ii) a written caution as to future conduct in the arbitration; and (iii) any other measure necessary to fulfil within the arbitration the general duties required of the Arbitral Tribunal under Articles 14.1(i) and 14.2. (ii).

Any party may request a hearing before the Arbitral Tribunal before it rules on its jurisdiction and authority (in accordance with Article 23) or makes an award on the merits. Unless the parties agree in writing to a documents-only arbitration, the Arbitral Tribunal can decide at any point whether or not a hearing is necessary. For this reason, a hearing might be broken up into several shorter sessions (as decided by the Arbitral Tribunal).

Any hearing shall be conducted in accordance with procedures established by the Arbitral Tribunal and agreed upon in advance by the parties. The Arbitral Tribunal shall have exclusive authority under the Arbitration Agreement to determine the date, time, place, format, substance, procedure, deadlines, and other aspects of the conduct of any hearing (if applicable). A hearing can be held in person, over the phone, via videoconference, or through some other means of communications with people in one or more locations (or in a combined form). The content of the arbitration may depend on whether or not the parties answer certain questions or address certain issues raised by the arbitrator. The scope of the Arbitral Tribunal's consideration of any question or issue may be limited as well.

The Arbitral Tribunal shall provide written notice to the parties of any hearing with reasonable advance notice.

Except where the parties agree in writing otherwise, all hearings shall be held in confidence.

Any fact or expert witness upon whose testimony a Party relies shall be subject to the provisions of this Article 20.

Prior to any hearing, the Arbitral Tribunal may require any party to provide written notice of the identity of each witness that party intends to call (including rebuttal witnesses), as well as the subject matter, content, and relevance of that witness's testimony.

Unless the Arbitral Tribunal orders otherwise, a party may submit a signed statement or similar document in lieu of oral testimony from a witness.

The Arbitral Tribunal has the authority to determine the time, manner, and form in which these written materials shall be exchanged between the parties and presented to the Arbitral Tribunal, as well as the authority to admit, reject, or limit the oral and written testimony of witnesses.

Any party or the Arbitral Tribunal can ask for a witness whose written testimony is relied on by the other side to appear in person for oral questioning during the hearing. If the other party is ordered by the Arbitral Tribunal to ensure the attendance of a witness, and that witness refuses or fails to appear at the hearing without good cause, the Arbitral Tribunal may give the written testimony as much weight, or none at all, as it sees fit.

Any party or its authorised representatives may interview any potential witness for the purpose of submitting written testimony to the Arbitral Tribunal or producing such person as an oral witness at any hearing, subject to the mandatory provisions of any applicable law, rules of law, and any order of the Arbitral Tribunal to the contrary.

Unless the Arbitral Tribunal rules otherwise, any person who intends to testify before it will be treated as a witness regardless of whether that person is a party to the arbitration or was, is, or becomes an officer, employee, owner, shareholder, or otherwise identified with any party.

At any hearing, the Arbitral Tribunal shall have the right (but not the obligation) to administer any appropriate oath or affirmation to any witness prior to that witness's oral testimony, subject to the mandatory provisions of any applicable law.

Each party is entitled, under the supervision of the Arbitral Tribunal, to question any witness who testifies orally during a hearing before the Arbitral Tribunal. There is no set order in which the Arbitral Tribunal must question the witness.

After consulting with the parties, the Arbitral Tribunal may appoint one or more experts to provide a written report to the Arbitral Tribunal and the parties regarding issues in the arbitration.

Any such expert must sign a written declaration attesting to his or her independence and impartiality, which must be delivered to the Arbitral Tribunal and copied to all parties.

The Arbitral Tribunal may, at any time and on such terms as the Arbitral Tribunal considers appropriate in the circumstances, order any party to provide to such expert any information or to provide access to any relevant documents, goods, samples, property, site, or thing under that party's control for inspection.

After delivery of the written report, the Arbitral Tribunal may, at the request of any party or if it deems it necessary, require the expert to appear for a hearing at which the parties shall have a reasonable opportunity to question the expert on the report and to present witnesses to testify on relevant issues arising from the report. This paragraph, Section 214, is intended to apply only if the Arbitral Tribunal determines that such a hearing is necessary. Any expert to the Arbitral Tribunal shall be subject to Articles 20.8 and 20.9 of the LCIA Rules, as amended as appropriate.

Any expert appointed by the Arbitral Tribunal pursuant to this Article 21 may have his or her fees and expenses paid from the Advance Payment for Costs payable by the parties under Article 24 and shall be included in the Arbitration Costs under Article 28.1.

On the application of a party or (except as provided in paragraph (x)below) on its own initiative, but only after affording the parties a fair opportunity to present their positions and on such terms (as to costs and otherwise) as the Arbitral Tribunal may decide, the Arbitral Tribunal shall have the authority to:

i. to permit a party to supplement, modify, or amend any claim, defence, counterclaim, crossclaim, defence to counterclaim, defence to crossclaim, and reply, including a Request, Response, and any other written statement submitted by such party;
ii. to shorten or lengthen (even after the time has run out) any period of time prescribed under the Arbitration Agreement, any other agreement of the parties, or any order made by the Arbitral Tribunal;
iii. to enquire into such matters as it deems necessary or advisable, including whether and to what extent the Arbitral Tribunal should take the lead in identifying issues and determining facts and the law(s) or rules of law applicable to the Arbitration Agreement, the arbitration, and the merits of the parties' dispute;
iv. require any party to allow the Arbitral Tribunal, any other party, any expert to such party, and any expert to the Tribunal access to inspect any documents, goods, samples, property, site, or thing under that party's control;
v. require any party to provide the Arbitral Tribunal and the other parties with any documents or copies of documents in that party's possession, custody, or power that the Arbitral Tribunal determines to be relevant;

vi. to determine the time, manner, and form in which any material tendered by a party on any issue of fact or expert opinion should be exchanged between the parties and presented to the Arbitral Tribunal; and to determine whether or not to apply any strict rules of evidence (or any other rules) as to the admissibility, relevance, or weight of such material;

vii. to determine the stage of the arbitration at which any issue or issues shall be determined, the order in which they shall be determined, and the procedure to be adopted at each stage in accordance with Article 14 above;

viii. to issue an order or award (an "Early Determination") finding that a claim, defence, counterclaim, crossclaim, defence to counterclaim, or defence to crossclaim is manifestly outside the jurisdiction of the Arbitral Tribunal or is inadmissible or manifestly without merit;

ix. to require a party to an arbitration agreement or a land contract to comply with that agreement's terms or pay damages for a breach of that agreement's terms;

x. after the Commencement Date or (if earlier) in the Arbitration Agreement, to allow one or more third persons to be joined in the arbitration as a party, and to make a single final award, or separate awards, in respect of all parties so implicated; and (y) to make a single final award, or separate awards, in respect of all parties so implicated;

After giving the parties a fair chance to air their grievances, the arbitrator may rule that the proceedings should be terminated if it appears that either party has abandoned the arbitration or both parties have withdrawn all claims, counterclaims, and crossclaims.

By agreeing to arbitration under the Arbitration Agreement, the parties are deemed to have agreed that they will not apply to any state court or other legal authority for any order available from the Arbitral Tribunal (if formed under Article 22.1) without the written consent of all parties to the arbitration.

The Arbitral Tribunal shall render its award in accordance with the applicable law(s) or rules of law selected by the parties. If the Arbitral Tribunal finds that the parties have not made such a choice, then it will apply whatever law(s) or rules of law it deems applicable.

Unless the parties agree otherwise in writing, the Arbitral Tribunal will not consider principles of "ex aequo et bono," "amiable composition," or "honourable engagement" when deciding the merits of the dispute.

The LCIA Court may also fix, shorten, or extend any period of time under the Arbitration Agreement or other agreement of the parties, subject to any order of the Arbitral Tribunal under Article 22.1(ii) (even where the period of time has expired).

Notwithstanding Article 22.1(xi), and after affording the parties a reasonable opportunity to present their positions, the LCIA Court may order that the arbitration be terminated if it appears to the LCIA Court that the parties have abandoned the arbitration or that all claims, counterclaims, and crossclaims have been withdrawn.

Article 22A Arbitral Consolidation and Concurrent Proceedings

Upon the application of any party and after giving all affected parties a reasonable opportunity to state their views, and upon such terms (as to costs and otherwise) as the Arbitral Tribunal may decide, the Arbitral Tribunal shall have the power to order, subject to the approval of the LCIA Court:

i. where all parties to the other arbitrations agree in writing, the arbitration may be consolidated with one or more other arbitrations into a single arbitration subject to the LCIA Rules;
ii. the consolidation of the arbitration with one or more other arbitrations subject to the LCIA Rules and commenced under the same arbitration agreement or any compatible arbitration agreement(s), and between the same disputing parties or arising out of the same transaction or series of related transactions, provided that no arbitral tribunal has yet been formed by the LCIA Court for such other arbitration(s) or, if already formed, that such arbitral tribunal(s) is/are compatible with the LCIA Rules.
iii. where the same arbitral tribunal is constituted in respect of each arbitration, the same arbitral tribunal shall conduct the arbitrations concurrently where the same disputing parties are involved or where the arbitrations arise out of the same transaction or series of related transactions and are subject to the LCIA Rules.
iv. where all parties to the arbitrations to be consolidated agree in writing, consolidate one or more arbitrations into a single arbitration subject to the LCIA Rules; and
v. after giving the parties an opportunity to be heard, determine that two or more arbitrations subject to the LCIA Rules have been commenced under the same arbitration agreement or any compatible arbitration

> agreement(s) and are either between the same disputing parties or arise out of the same transaction or series of related transactions, and that these arbitrations shall be consolidated to form a single arbitration subject to the LCIA Rules; provided, however, that no arbitral tribunal shall have the authority to consolidate more than one arbitration.

Regarding any challenge to the Arbitration Agreement's initial or continued existence, validity, effectiveness, or scope, the Arbitral Tribunal shall have the authority to rule upon its own jurisdiction and authority (23.1).

For these purposes, an arbitration clause that is or was supposed to be a part of another agreement shall be deemed to be a separate arbitration agreement. This arbitration provision shall remain in full force and effect notwithstanding any determination by the Arbitral Tribunal that any other agreement is null and void or otherwise unenforceable.

Respondent's objection to the Arbitral Tribunal's jurisdiction must be made as soon as possible but in no event later than the time for Respondent's Statement of Defence, and any party responding to a counterclaim or crossclaim must make a similar objection as soon as possible but in no event later than the time for that party's Statement of Defence. Any claim that the Arbitral Tribunal is acting outside its jurisdiction must be made as soon as possible after the Arbitral Tribunal has signalled its intention to act on the matter. However, if the Arbitral Tribunal finds that the delay was warranted under the circumstances, it may still admit an untimely objection to its jurisdiction or authority.

The Arbitral Tribunal, in its discretion, may rule on the challenge to its jurisdiction or authority in an award as to jurisdiction or authority or in a subsequent award on the merits.

After the Arbitral Tribunal is formed, the parties' agreement to arbitrate under the Arbitration Agreement shall be deemed to be an agreement not to apply to any state court or federal court for a judicial review of any award or ruling made by the Arbitral Tribunal.

the Arbitral Tribunal's jurisdiction or authority, except I with the prior written agreement of all parties to the arbitration, (ii) with the prior authorization of the Arbitral Tribunal, or (iii) following the latter's award on the objection to its jurisdiction or authority.

To guarantee payment of the Arbitration Costs under Article 28.1, the LCIA Court may order the parties to make an advance payment to the LCIA (the "Advance Payment for Costs") in such amounts and at such times as the LCIA Court deems appropriate. All payments made to the LCIA shall be applied by the LCIA in accordance with the LCIA Rules towards the payment of the Arbitration Costs, including the LCIA's own fees and expenses.

The LCIA shall own the Advance Payment for Costs, which it may disburse or apply as it sees fit in accordance with the LCIA Rules and invest in a manner consistent with the LCIA's interests. In no event shall the LCIA serve as trustee, and the LCIA's sole obligation to the Parties with respect to the Advance Payment for Costs shall be to act in accordance with these LCIA Rules.

If the Advance Payment for Costs is more than the total amount of the Arbitration Costs as determined by the Arbitral Tribunal pursuant to Article 28.1, then the LCIA shall transfer the excess amount to the parties in such proportions as the parties may agree in writing or, failing such agreement, in the same proportions and to the same parties as the Advance Payment for Costs was paid to the LCIA, subject to any order of the Arbitral Tribunal.

The LCIA will use the parties' contact information provided during the proceedings to make reasonable attempts to contact them and arrange for the transfer of the excess amount. The LCIA will give the party written notice of its intention to retain the excess amount if it does not hear back from that party within 30 days. A party's right to claim and/or receive the excess amount is considered waived permanently if the party does not respond within an additional 60 days.

Unless there are exceptional circumstances, the Arbitral Tribunal should not move forward with the arbitration before confirming with the Registrar that the LCIA has sufficient funds to cover all outstanding and anticipated Arbitration Costs.

The LCIA Court may order the other party or parties to make an additional Advance Payment for Costs in an equivalent amount if a party fails or refuses to make a payment on account of the Arbitration Costs as directed by the LCIA Court (subject to any order or award on Arbitration Costs).

If this happens, the party who made the additional Advance Payment for Costs can ask the arbitrator to rule that the defaulting party owes them the money plus interest, and they can force the defaulting party to pay it.

Any failure by a party asserting a claim, counterclaim, or crossclaim to make any required payment promptly and in full may be deemed by the LCIA Court or the Arbitral Tribunal to be a waiver of the claim, counterclaim, or crossclaim, thereby relieving the Arbitral Tribunal of any jurisdiction it may have under the Arbitration Agreement with respect to such claim, counterclaim, or crossclaim (as the case may be), subject to any terms decided by the LC.

Even if a party withdraws a claim, counterclaim, or crossclaim, it may still defend against the claim, counterclaim, or crossclaim as a respondent.

The LCIA will deal with any party on the understanding that it is complying with all applicable requirements relating to bribery, corruption, terrorist financing, fraud, tax evasion, money laundering, and/or economic or trade sanctions ("Prohibited Activity").

If the LCIA determines (in its sole discretion and without the need to state any reasons) that acting on such an instruction may involve Prohibited Activity, or breach any law, regulation, or other legal duty which applies to it, or that such action may otherwise expose the LCIA to enforcement action or censure from any regulator or law enforcement agency, then the LCIA may refuse to act on such instruction and/or accept or make any payment.

For the purpose of complying with laws relating to Prohibited Activity, the parties agree in 24.11 to provide the LCIA with any information and/or documents reasonably requested by the LCIA. Any information or documents related to Prohibited Activity may be disclosed by the LCIA to courts, law enforcement agencies, or regulatory authorities as the LCIA deems necessary to comply with applicable obligations.

Upon the application of any party, and after affording all other parties a reasonable opportunity to respond to such application, the Arbitral Tribunal shall have the authority, upon such terms as the Arbitral Tribunal deems appropriate under the circumstances:

i. to require any defendant to a claim, counterclaim, or crossclaim to deposit funds with a financial institution or provide some other form of security for all or a portion of the amount in dispute;
ii. to direct that any funds, documents, goods, samples, property, site, or thing under the control of any party and relevant to the subject matter of the arbitration be preserved, stored, sold, or otherwise disposed of; and

Any relief that the Arbitral Tribunal would have power to grant in an award, such as the payment of money or the disposition of property as between any parties, may be ordered on a provisional basis, subject to a final decision in an award.

Any costs or losses incurred by the Respondent Party in complying with the Arbitral Tribunal's order may be covered by a cross-indemnity provided by the Applicant Party, secured in such manner as the Arbitral Tribunal deems appropriate. The Arbitral Tribunal may issue one or more awards in the arbitration deciding the amount payable under such cross-indemnity and any consequential relief.

The Arbitral Tribunal shall have the power, upon the application of a party, after giving all other parties a reasonable opportunity to respond to such application, to order any claiming, counterclaiming, or crossclaiming party to provide or procure security for Legal Costs and Arbitration Costs by way of deposit or bank guarantee or in any other manner and upon such terms as the Arbitral Tribunal considers appropriate under the circumstances. The applicant may be required to provide a cross-indemnity to cover any expenses or losses incurred by the claimant, counterclaimant, or cross-claimant as a result of complying with the Arbitral Tribunal's order. The Arbitral Tribunal may issue multiple awards in the arbitration proceeding to determine the amount of any cross-indemnity payment and any consequential relief. If a party who is making a claim, counterclaim, or crossclaim does not comply with an order to provide security, the Arbitral Tribunal has the right to stay or dismiss that party's claims, counterclaims, or crossclaims.

Interim or conservatory measures that the Arbitral Tribunal would have power to order under Article 25.1 may be sought from a competent state court or other legal authority I prior to the formation of the Arbitral Tribunal; and (ii) after the formation of the Arbitral Tribunal, in exceptional cases and with the authorization of the Arbitral Tribunal, until the final award. All applications for interim measures and all orders for such measures after the Commencement Date shall be communicated promptly in writing by the applicant party to the Registrar and, after the formation of the Arbitral Tribunal, also to the Arbitral Tribunal and, in both cases, also to all other parties.

The parties are deemed to have agreed that they will not seek an order for security for Legal Costs or Arbitration Costs from any state court or other legal authority as a condition of agreeing to arbitration under the Arbitration Agreement.

Claims, counterclaims, and cross-claims may all be resolved by the Arbitration Tribunal in separate awards, which may be issued at any time (including Legal and Arbitration Costs under Article 28). The validity of such awards shall be the same as the validity of any other award rendered by the Arbitral Tribunal.

Unless all parties agree in writing to the contrary, the Arbitral Tribunal shall make any award in writing and shall state the reasons upon which such award is based. The award must be signed by the Arbitral Tribunal or by those members of the Tribunal who agree with the award, and it must include the date the award is made and the location of the arbitration. Except as otherwise agreed by the parties or as directed by the Arbitral Tribunal or the LCIA Court, any Award may be executed electronically and/or in counterparts and assembled into a single instrument.

Unless otherwise agreed upon by the parties, an award may be denominated in any legal tender.

Unless the parties agree otherwise, the Arbitral Tribunal may order that simple or compound interest shall be paid by any party on any sum awarded at such rates as the Arbitral Tribunal determines to be appropriate (without being bound by rates of interest practised by any state court or other legal authority) with respect to any period which the Arbitral Tribunal determines to be appropriate ending not later than the date upon which the award is complied with.

If there are more than one arbitrator and the Arbitral Tribunal can't come to a unanimous decision, then the issue will be decided by a simple majority. In the absence of a majority vote, the presiding arbitrator shall make the final decision.

The signatures of the majority arbitrator(s) or (in the absence of a majority) the presiding arbitrator(s) shall be sufficient if and only if the reason for any absent signature is stated in the award by the majority arbitrator(s) or the presiding arbitrator(s).

If all Arbitration Costs have been paid to the LCIA in accordance with Articles 24 and 28, the sole or presiding arbitrator is responsible for delivering the award to the LCIA Court, which will then forward the award to the parties after it has been authenticated by the Registrar as an LCIA award. Transmission may be made electronically or (at a party's request or if electronic transmission to a party is not possible) in writing. The electronic form shall take precedence over the paper form in the event of a discrepancy.

All awards (and the reasoning behind them) made under this section shall be final and binding on the parties. Unless prohibited by applicable law, the parties agree to immediately and without further delay carry out any award; and the parties irrevocably waive any right to appeal, review, or recourse to any state court or other legal authority.

If the parties reach a final resolution to their dispute, the Arbitral Tribunal may decide to issue an award recording the settlement if they both request it in writing (a "Consent Award"), but only if the award clearly states on its face that it was issued at the parties' request and with their consent. No explanation or decision regarding the arbitrator's or attorney's fees need be included in a Consent Award. Upon written confirmation by the parties to the LCIA Court that a final settlement has been reached, and subject to payment by the parties of any outstanding Arbitration Costs in accordance with Articles 24 and 28, the LCIA Court shall discharge the Arbitral Tribunal and conclude the arbitration proceedings.

A party may request that the Arbitral Tribunal rectify any error in computation, any clerical or typographical error, any ambiguity, or any mistake of a similar nature in an award by giving written notice to the Registrar (with copies to all other parties) within 28 days of receipt of such award. The Arbitral Tribunal shall make the correction by recording it in an addendum to the award within 28 days of receiving the request, provided that it finds the request to be justified after consulting with the parties. Even if the Arbitral Tribunal does not think the request is warranted after consulting with the parties, it may still issue an addendum to the award dealing with the request and any Arbitration Costs and Legal Costs related to the request.

After consulting with the parties, the Arbitral Tribunal has the discretion to issue an addendum to the award within 28 days of the date of the award to correct any error (including any error in computation, any clerical or typographical error, any ambiguity or any mistake of a similar nature).

To request an additional award from the Arbitral Tribunal as to any claim, counterclaim, or cross-claim presented in the arbitration but not decided in any award, a party must give written notice to the Registrar (with copies to all other parties) within 28 days of receiving the final award. The Arbitral Tribunal shall make the additional award within 56 days of receipt of the request if, after consulting with the parties, it determines that the request is justified. Even if the Arbitral Tribunal does not believe the request is warranted after consulting with the parties, it may still issue an addendum to the award dealing with the request and any Arbitration Costs and Legal Costs related thereto.

In addition, the Arbitral Tribunal may, within 28 days of the date of the award and after consulting with the parties, make an additional award on its own initiative as to any claim, counterclaim, or crossclaim presented in the arbitration but not decided in any award.

Any supplement or additional award made hereunder shall be subject to the provisions of Articles 26.2 through 26.7. Any supplement to an award will be considered a part of the award itself.

The LCIA Court will determine the arbitration fees ("Arbitration Costs"), excluding any legal or other fees incurred by the parties themselves, based on the Schedule of Costs. Each party will be responsible for their own share of the Arbitration Costs owed to the LCIA and the Arbitral Tribunal.

When the LCIA Court has determined the amount of the Arbitration Costs, the Arbitral Tribunal must specify that amount in order or award. In the absence of a final settlement between the parties as to liability for such costs, the Arbitral Tribunal shall decide the proportions in which the parties shall bear such Arbitration Costs. The party that paid the LCIA the Arbitration Costs pursuant to Article 24 shall be entitled to recover from the other party the amount of the Arbitration Costs that the Arbitral Tribunal determined should be paid by that other party.

All or a portion of a party's legal or other expenses ("Legal Costs") may be awarded or ordered to be paid by the other party by the Arbitral Tribunal. The amount of such Legal Costs shall be determined by the Arbitral Tribunal based on such reasonable criteria as it deems appropriate. The arbitrators aren't bound by the rates or methods used by state courts or other authorities to determine costs.

For purposes of determining the amount of the Arbitration Costs and the Legal Costs, the Arbitral Tribunal shall apply the general principle that costs should reflect the parties' relative success and failure in the award or arbitration or under different issues, unless the Arbitral Tribunal determines that such an application would be inappropriate under the Arbitration Agreement or otherwise. The Arbitral Tribunal may also consider the parties' and their authorised representatives' behaviour during the arbitration, including whether they cooperated to expedite the proceedings in terms of time and cost, or whether they did not cooperate, resulting in unnecessary delay and expense. The Arbitral Tribunal shall provide an explanation for its decision on costs in the order or award in which that decision is included (unless it is a Consent Award).

After the Commencement Date, the parties must confirm in writing any prior oral or written agreement regarding who will pay what portion of the Legal Costs and/or Arbitration Costs, regardless of the outcome of any dispute, arbitration, or award.

The parties shall remain jointly and severally liable to pay to the LCIA and the Arbitral Tribunal the Arbitration Costs determined by the LCIA Court even if the arbitration is abandoned, suspended, withdrawn, or concluded, by agreement or otherwise, prior to the final award being made.

Unless otherwise directed by the LCIA Court, the LCIA Court's determinations on all issues relating to the arbitration shall be final and binding on the parties and the Arbitral Tribunal. Such determinations shall be treated as administrative in nature, and the LCIA Court shall not be required to provide reasons for any such determination, with the exception of reasoned decisions on challenges to arbitral awards under Article 10.

No party shall have the right to appeal or seek review of any determination and decision of the LCIA Court in any state court or before any other legal authority to the extent permitted by any applicable law. In cases where an appeal or review is required by applicable law or otherwise, the LCIA Court has the authority to rule on whether or not the arbitration should proceed.

Unless disclosure is required by law, is necessary to protect or pursue a legal right, or is necessary to enforce or challenge an award in legal proceedings, the parties to an arbitration agree to keep all awards, materials created for the arbitration's purposes, and documents produced by another party in the proceedings confidential. All authorised representatives, witnesses of fact, experts, and service providers involved in the arbitration must provide the same confidentiality undertaking as the parties.

The Arbitral Tribunal, any tribunal secretary, and any expert to the Arbitral Tribunal shall also be subject to Article 30.1 of the LCIA Rules, with the necessary modifications. Unless otherwise required by applicable law or to the extent that disclosure of an arbitrator's refusal to participate in the arbitration is required of the other members of the Arbitral Tribunal under Articles 10, 12, 26.6, and 27.5, the deliberations of the Arbitral Tribunal shall remain confidential to its members and, if appropriate, any tribunal secretary.

Without the prior written consent of all parties and the Arbitral Tribunal, the LCIA will not publish any award or any part of an award.

The LCIA's data protection notice is available on the LCIA website, and any personal data processing by the LCIA is subject to applicable data protection legislation.

The Arbitral Tribunal shall, in early stages of the arbitration, in accordance with its duties under Article 14.1, consult with the parties and, where appropriate, the LCIA to determine whether it is appropriate to adopt:

I any specific information security measures to safeguard both paper and digital documents exchanged during the arbitration; and

(ii) any mechanism for dealing with the processing of personal data generated or exchanged during the arbitration, taking into account any data protection or equivalent laws that may be in effect.

Subject to the mandatory provisions of any applicable law or rules of law, the LCIA and the Arbitral Tribunal have the authority to issue directions addressing information security and data protection, and such directions shall be binding on the parties and, in the case of the LCIA, also on the members of the Arbitral Tribunal.

There shall be no liability to any party for any act or omission in connection with an arbitration hearing on the part of the LCIA (including its officers, members, and employees), the LCIA Court (including its President, Vice Presidents, Honorary Vice Presidents, former Vice Presidents, and members), the LCIA Board (including any board member), the Registrar (including any deputy Registrar), any arbitrator, any Emergency Arbitrator, any tribunal secretary, or any expert to the Arbitral Tribunal.

After the award has been made and all opportunities for any addendum to the award or additional award under Article 27 have lapsed or been exhausted, no member of the LCIA (including its officers, members, and employees), the LCIA Court (including its President, Vice Presidents, Honorary Vice Presidents, former Vice Presidents, and members), the LCIA Board (including any board member), the Registrar (including any deputy Registrar), any arbitrator, any Emergency Arbitrator, or any member of

The parties irrevocably submit to the exclusive jurisdiction of the courts of England and Wales to hear and decide any action, suit, or proceedings between the parties and the LCIA (including its officers, members, employees), the LCIA Court (including its President, Vice Presidents, Honorary Vice Presidents, former Vice Presidents and members), the LCIA Board (including any board member), or the LCIA.

If a party proceeds with the arbitration despite knowing that a provision of the Arbitration Agreement has not been complied with, but fails to raise an objection as to such non-compliance promptly to the Registrar (before the formation of the Arbitral Tribunal) or the Arbitral Tribunal (after the formation of the Arbitral Tribunal), then the party will be deemed to have irrevocably waived its right to object.

The LCIA, the LCIA Court, the Registrar, the Arbitral Tribunal, any tribunal secretary, and each of the parties shall at all times act in good faith, respecting the spirit of the Arbitration Agreement, and shall make every reasonable effort to ensure that any award is legally recognised and enforceable at the arbitral seat, unless otherwise expressly provided in the Arbitration Agreement.

If and to the extent that any provision of the Arbitration Agreement is determined by the Arbitral Tribunal, the Emergency Arbitrator, or any court or other legal authority of competent jurisdiction to be invalid, ineffective, or unenforceable, such determination shall not, of itself, adversely affect any order or award by the Arbitral Tribunal or the Emergency Arbitrator or any other provision of the Arbitration Agreement which shall remain in full force and effect, except as may be prohibited by law.

Guidelines for the Parties' Authorized Representatives in General

The authorised representatives of the parties appearing by name within the arbitration shall comply with the general guidelines set forth in this paragraph 1 in order to promote the good and equal conduct of the parties. These rules are not intended to change the terms of the Arbitration Agreement or to relieve an authorised representative of his or her primary duty of loyalty to the party represented in the arbitration or of the obligation to present that party's case effectively before the Arbitral Tribunal. Moreover, if and to the extent that any mandatory laws, rules of law, professional rules, or codes of conduct are shown to apply to an authorised representative appearing in the arbitration, these rules shall not deviate from those requirements.

If an authorised representative knows that he or she is making a frivolous challenge to the appointment of an arbitrator or to the Arbitral Tribunal's jurisdiction or authority, then that representative should not make those challenges. This is because it could delay the arbitration process and could cast doubt on the finality of any award.

Any authorised representative who knowingly makes a false statement to the Arbitral Tribunal or the LCIA Court is in violation of paragraph 3.

It is forbidden for an authorised representative to knowingly present false evidence to the Arbitral Tribunal or the LCIA Court, or to rely on such evidence in any way. An authorised representative must not knowingly conceal or aid in the concealment of any document (or part thereof) that is ordered to be produced by the Arbitral Tribunal.

With respect to any member of the LCIA Court exercising any function in relation to the arbitration or, from the formation of the Arbitral Tribunal onwards, any member of the Arbitral Tribunal or the tribunal secretary (if any), the Authorised Representative shall not, without the prior written disclosure to the Parties, intentionally initiate or attempt to initiate any unilateral contact relating to the arbitration or the parties' dispute with any member of the Arbitral Tribunal or, from the formation of the Arbitral Tribunal onwards, any member of the LCIA Court. The Registrar may be contacted directly by an authorised representative, but only on administrative matters.

Articles 18.5 and 18.6 give the Arbitral Tribunal the authority to determine whether or not an authorised representative has violated these general guidelines and, if so, to exercise its discretion to impose any or all of the sanctions set forth in Article 18.6.

International Arbitration Award Structure and Content

The 1958 Convention on the Recognition and Enforcement of Foreign Arbitral Awards gives arbitral awards special recognition and enforcement powers under international law (the New York Convention).

Arbitral awards rendered in the territory of one contracting state shall be recognised as binding and enforced in another contracting state pursuant to the New York Convention, subject only to the limited grounds for refusal of recognition and enforcement set forth in Article V of the Convention.

The form and substance of an arbitral award are thus of paramount importance, given its unique status. Specifically, this chapter addresses the following concerns:

how an award was rendered, including the different kinds of awards that can be made and the formalities that must be met in accordance with the New York Convention and certain national laws; differences between what is required by some national laws and arbitration rules and what is considered standard practise for arbitral awards; and the finality of an arbitration award, the availability of challenges to arbitration awards, the limited availability of appeals to arbitration awards, and the ability to enforce arbitration awards.

What's the difference between an arbitral award and an arbitration award? The term "arbitral award" appears in the New York Convention, UNCITRAL's Model Law, and the UNCITRAL's Rules on Arbitration. However, many sets of arbitration rules simply use the term "award," such as those under the International Chamber of Commerce (ICC), the London Court of International Arbitration (LCIA), the International Centre for Dispute Resolution (ICDR), the Stockholm Chamber of Commerce (SCC), and the Singapore International Arbitration Centre. Although the long title of the Act refers to "arbitration awards," and the term "arbitral award" appears in Sections 2(b) and 81, the English Arbitration Act also primarily uses the term "award" (c).

That's why "arbitral award" is the proper term, though "arbitration award" and "award" can also be used.

To "the recognition and enforcement of arbitral awards made in the territory of a State other than the State where the recognition and enforcement of such awards are sought and arising out of differences between persons, whether physical or legal," the New York Convention applies. Furthermore, "arbitral awards not considered as domestic awards in the State where recognition and enforcement of such awards is sought" are subject to the Convention under Article 1(1). As an added bonus, Article 1(2) specifies that "arbitral awards" include "awards made not only by arbitrators appointed for each case but also by permanent arbitral bodies to which the parties have submitted."

Accordingly, the following distinctions can be made between the various forms of awards:

In the context of international arbitration, a "domestic award" refers to a decision rendered by an arbitrator within a single state.

A "foreign award" is an arbitration award that was issued, or is deemed to have been issued, in a country other than the one in which the parties are located. Even if London is the "seat" of arbitration, the arbitral tribunal may still sign the award in another country for practical reasons. According to Section 53 of the English Arbitration Act of 1996, however, the award will be recognised as having been made at the seat.

Award that is not yet finalised is called a "interim award" or "provisional award" (see, for example, Section 39 of the English Arbitration Act). Generally speaking, an interim award is not enforceable because it has not become binding as required by Article V(1)(e) of the New York Convention. However, some US courts have ruled that an interim order issued by an arbitral tribunal or even by an emergency arbitrator can be enforced as an award if it definitively and conclusively resolves a single issue.

A "partial award" resolves only some of the claims at issue.

An "agreed award" is a formal record of a settlement reached through arbitration that was entered into with the consent of all parties and the arbitral tribunal.

Arbitral awards, as opposed to other decisions or orders made within an arbitration, are enforceable both internationally (under the New York Convention) and nationally (under national arbitration laws). It is important to note that the nomenclature used by the arbitral tribunal is not conclusive, even though awards are usually labelled as such.

The rules of arbitration or the laws of the country in which the arbitration is taking place will typically dictate any formality requirements that must be met. Here's an illustration:

The UNCITRAL Model Law (Article 31) and many other national arbitral laws require that the award be made in writing, signed by the arbitrator or arbitrators, and include the date of the award and the place of arbitration; and additionally, it is customary to require the arbitral tribunal to provide an explanation of the reasoning behind its award.

The parties are free to agree on the form of the award, which is reflected in some national arbitration laws such as the English Arbitration Act 1996 (Section 52(1)).

Even though having an award signed is not required by the New York Convention, it is a fundamental requirement in practise.

Time must be allotted for the final agreed award to be couriered among the three arbitrators in the case of a three-person tribunal with arbitrators in different countries in order to obtain their respective signatures. The arbitrators must also make sure there are enough originals: one for each of the arbitrators and one for the arbitral institution (if applicable).

Even if there is a dissenting opinion, it is customary for all arbitrators to sign the award. However, in some cases, a single arbitrator may refuse to sign the award because of his or her disagreement with the majority. Most cases can be resolved by having the remaining arbitrators (or at least the chair or presiding arbitrator) sign the award and providing an explanation for the absent arbitrator's absence.

Even if the award is signed in a different location, that location should be designated as the seat of arbitration. For purposes of the New York Convention, the award will be considered to be of the nationality of the seat of the governing body.

As was previously mentioned, many laws and rules governing arbitration require arbitrators to provide an explanation for their decisions.

The SCC Rules do, however, necessitate that reasons be provided for awards, despite the fact that the Swedish Arbitration Act of 1999 does not.

Although it is often stated that the obligation to provide reasons is not mandatory, if there is such an obligation and the parties agree to dispense with it, it is crucial that the award itself clearly reflects the parties' agreement to forego providing reasons.

While "Minimum requirements" are stipulated, some national laws impose additional requirements that must be met for arbitral awards made in that specific seat of arbitration, in addition to the aforementioned requirements. Just to give one illustration:

An award in Sweden must specify in detail what a challenging party must do in order to comply with the Swedish Arbitration Act of 1999. if there is no determination of the merits and the award ends the proceedings; and concerns Sections 36 and 41 of the Act, which govern challenges to the arbitrators' compensation amounts; and

Scotland's Arbitration (Scotland) Act of 2010 requires, by default, that awards include a notation about whether or not a provisional or partial award was previously made under Rule 51 of Schedule (and the extent to which any previous provisional award is superseded or confirmed).

Before proceeding with arbitration, arbitrators should always verify whether or not any additional local, state, or federal regulations apply.

In international arbitrations, the rendering of an award is not typically subject to a deadline stipulated by national arbitration laws. Some arbitration rules, however, set deadlines for completing arbitration. If we look at the ICC Rules of 2021 as an example, Article 31(1) states that the arbitral tribunal must issue its final award within six months of the date of the terms of reference. However, the ICC Court can extend the deadline if it so chooses or if the arbitral tribunal requests an extension and explains why. A similar provision can be found in the 2017 SCC Rules, which stipulates that the arbitral tribunal must make a decision within six months of receiving the case for arbitration (Article 43).

Article 30(1) of the 2014 ICDR Rules states that the arbitral tribunal shall make every effort to deliberate and prepare the award as quickly as possible after the hearing and, unless otherwise agreed by the parties, specified by law, or determined by the ICDR administrator, no later than 60 days after the closing of the hearing.

In order to ensure that the award is made in a timely manner, it is beneficial to establish a deadline at the outset of the proceeding that applies pressure to both the arbitral tribunal and the parties. However, the six-month time limit under the ICC and SCC Rules is commonly extended, at least in larger cases, and this can be combined with a general obligation on all participants to act efficiently, with potential costs consequences on a party that fails to do so.

An arbitral tribunal's productivity and self-control can be improved by setting a deadline for the issuance of an award following the conclusion of a case. The parties are less likely to be kept waiting for too long to receive the award, and the arbitrators are more likely to give careful consideration to the evidence and the parties' arguments if they do so quickly after the hearing. Institutional sanctions against arbitrators who take too long to issue awards are not uncommon.

But there is a clear risk that an award issued after such a deadline would be liable to be set aside, so institutions are generally careful to ensure that time limits are extended where necessary, either at the request of the arbitral tribunal or on the institution's own initiative.

In the extremely unlikely event that a firm deadline is stipulated in the arbitration agreement (without any provision for extension), the arbitral tribunal must ensure that it meets the applicable deadline. However, a statutory possibility of extending a time limit may be provided by national arbitration laws. For instance, the English Arbitration Act states in Section

50(1) that "[w]here the time for making an award is limited by or pursuant to the arbitration agreement, then, unless otherwise agreed by the parties, the court may... by order extend that time" if the parties have not agreed to an extension of time.

Communication of an arbitral award to the parties is typically required as soon as possible under national arbitration laws. In accordance with the Swedish Arbitration Act, for instance, "award shall be delivered to the parties immediately" .

The English Arbitration Act states in Section 55(2) that "the award shall be notified to the parties by service on them of copies of the award, which shall be done without delay after the award is made." This provision applies if the parties have not agreed otherwise. Most types of rules within institutions have something very similar.

The chair of the arbitral tribunal typically gives the award to the parties involved. The institution itself may issue the award in some cases of institutional arbitration, such as those conducted in accordance with the ICC, LCIA, or ICDR Rules.

However, if the parties are located on different continents, the unfortunate result of one party receiving the award several days before the other could arise if the award were delivered by courier. To prevent this from happening, arbitral tribunals typically send the award to the parties via email first, with hard copies sent via courier.

Acceptance of the award is generally acknowledged by the parties after it has been issued by the arbitral tribunal. This is critical for multiple reasons, including checking that the award has been properly delivered and determining whether or not there is enough time to make corrections or seek to have the award nullified.

In accordance with English law, the arbitral tribunal may delay award delivery pending full payment of its fees and expenses, although a party may seek intervention from the English court in this regard. In contrast, the arbitrators are expressly forbidden from doing so by Section 40 of the Swedish Arbitration Act. It is customary in institutional arbitration for the arbitral institution to ensure that all fees and costs have been paid in a timely manner prior to the delivery of the arbitral award.

Any clerical, computational, or typographical error in an arbitration award may be challenged by either party to the proceeding before the arbitral tribunal within a certain period of time, usually 30 days from the date of the award as specified by the applicable law or rule. In the same time frame, a party may also seek an interpretation of a narrow portion of the award. Additionally, a party may request a separate award in respect of any claim for which the arbitral tribunal has not yet rendered a decision.

It is important to distinguish between the minimum content that may be deemed necessary for the award to be considered to be valid and enforceable pursuant to the applicable arbitration law at the seat of arbitration and international best practises when analysing the content of an arbitral award.

Minimum requirements are typically set quite low due to the fact that there are good policy reasons for arbitral awards to be enforceable. However, international arbitration would not be acceptable as a system of international dispute resolution if arbitrators and arbitral institutions were content to merely meet the bare minimum.

Rules for Drafting Arbitral Awards

Still, it is increasingly common for arbitral institutions and other organisations to publish guidelines for arbitrators on the proper drafting of arbitral awards. Here are some of the rules:

The following can be considered as minimum requirements for an arbitral award:

1. Specifics on the contending groups and their lawyers;
2. Methodological background;
3. Particulars of the Contract at Issue, including the Arbitration Clause;
4. Information about the events leading up to this point;
5. The evidence and reasoning provided by each side;
6. A compiled list of problems where applicable;
7. Any applicable reasoning by the arbitral tribunal on the issue of jurisdiction;
8. In-depth explanations of the arbitrators' thinking on the case's merits, addressing each contested issue individually; and
9. A crucial component of the prize.
10. The bare minimum
11. Procedures obligatory

As was previously mentioned, most national laws and arbitration rules have various formal requirements that must generally be met.

Since the applicable formal requirements are usually mandatory, an award that does not comply with them may be subject to annulment at the seat of the arbitration. Although Article V of the New York Convention does not provide a basis for non-recognition, this may be used as an argument against recognition in other jurisdictions. However, in practise, these formal requirements rarely cause problems, and when they do, they can usually be corrected as mentioned above (see "Correction of the award").

Whether or not a failure to give reasons for all or part of the decision constitutes a valid ground for seeking to set aside the award depends on whether or not giving reasons is required under the applicable arbitration law or the applicable arbitration rules, or both. Partially because of the general policy requirement to ensure that arbitral awards are generally enforceable, and partly because it is recognised that arbitrators are not required to be legally trained and it would be wrong to impose the same standards as may be required of a judge, courts generally set a rather low standard for the requirement to give reasons.

Bremer HandelsgesellschaftmbH v. West Zucker GmbH (No. 2), an English case, was decided by Lord Justice Donaldson, who ruled as follows:

All that's required is for the arbitrators to lay out what happened and why they think it happened that way, and then state their decision and explain why it's justified in light of the evidence. To what extent does [an]. . . The arbitrators are not required to evaluate the law and the authorities, which is how the award differs from a judgement. Having them detail their reasoning for reaching that conclusion will suffice.

Similar to Navigation Sonamar Inc v. Algoma Steamships Limited, where an attempt to vacate an arbitral award for lack of reasons was rejected, the court there considered not only what was explicitly stated but also what was implicit in the award and ultimately upheld the decision. The arbitrators' expressions as businessmen, rather than lawyers, were upheld by the court as legitimate.

The Swedish Supreme Court ruled in the Soyak II case that in order to have an award nullified, there must be an absolute absence of any rationale for the decision. It was a case where one of the parties filed a motion to vacate the award for lack of reasons under the SCC Rules. The highest court in the land made the following declarations:

There may be a variety of motivations for including a requirement that the award include reasoning in the arbitration agreement. A lack of specific provisions regarding what should be included in the reasons allows the parties to have varying expectations for the arbitral tribunal's justification of its decision. However, whether the arbitral tribunal's reasoning is so lacking that it constitutes a ground for setting aside the award must be distinguished from the question of what the parties reasonably or unreasonably expected and what can be said to be good practise among arbitrators.

Since it compels the arbitral tribunal to examine the issues and evidence, providing adequate reasoning in an arbitral award ensures legal certainty. The importance of finality must be weighed against the value of having complete explanations for the outcome in cases where grounds for a reversal were previously set aside. To evaluate the merits of the arbitral tribunal's findings would go beyond the scope of deciding a challenge to an award. Therefore, only a total lack of reasons, or reasons that in the circumstances must be considered to be so insufficient that they can be equated with a lack of reasons, can be sufficient to constitute a procedural irregularity. This is because a qualitative judgement of the reasoning would give rise to significant difficulties in drawing the line between procedure and substance. However, in cases where there is a major procedural flaw, it is reasonable to assume that the lack of explanations contributed to the award's final result.

Some other institutions' regulations have been modelled after the ICC's strictures. The standard of review at the China International Economic and Trade Arbitration Commission (CIETAC) is low. According to Article 51 of the 2015 CIETAC Rules, the CIETAC "may bring to the attention of the arbitral tribunal issues addressed in the award on the condition that the arbitral tribunal's independence in rendering the award is not affected." Therefore, CIETAC may bring up issues for the arbitral tribunal to consider, but formal approval of the arbitral award is not necessary.

There is a less rigorous review process available through the Danish Institute of Arbitration. The Secretariat, as stated in Article 28 of the 2013 Rules, "may propose modifications as to the form of the award and without affecting the Arbitral Tribunal's jurisdiction, draw its attention to other issues, including issues of importance to the validity of the award and its recognition and enforcement." However, the responsibility for the contents of the award rests solely with the arbitral tribunal.

Rules for reviewing awards issued by the German Arbitration Institute in 2018 also permits this.

An award is considered "final" with respect to the issues it resolves, regardless of whether all of the issues submitted to the arbitral tribunal were resolved or not. However, the term "final award" refers only to awards that resolve all issues in an arbitration proceeding. An arbitration panel is considered to be functus officio once a final award has been issued. Having rendered its final award, the arbitral tribunal has fulfilled its responsibilities.

An arbitration agreement typically includes language stating that the arbitrator's decision is "final and binding" on all parties. Additionally, "[e] ach Contracting State shall recognise arbitral awards as binding and enforce them according to the rules of procedure of the territory where the award is relied upon," as stated in Article III of the New York Convention. The arbitration award is final and binding on the parties as is customary under national law and arbitration rules.

The "finality" will depend on the grounds for setting aside awards at the seat of arbitration and the enforcement regime in any place where the arbitral award is sought to be enforced. If both the state in which the award was made and the state in which enforcement is sought have ratified the New York Convention, the award is considered final and cannot be challenged unless there has been a serious procedural irregularity or the award is contrary to public policy. When it comes to the recognition and enforcement of foreign arbitral awards, the New York Convention contracting states' arbitration laws are largely in line with the rules established by the Convention.

In the case of some settlement through arbitrations, parties may review a Final Award and note that while there may not be any serious legal errors or serious procedural issues with the Award - amounting to grounds for annulment or non-recognition - there are other shortcomings or imperfections that do not seem right or consistent with the parties' submissions. This could be because the tribunal made a basic typographical error (such as referring to the wrong party by name or omitting negation from a sentence), a mathematical error, or an explanation of the tribunal's finding on a particular issue that raises additional questions or that the parties cannot agree on its interpretation. Even if the tribunal has addressed all of the claims and issues that were briefed to it, it is possible that it has overlooked some of the parties' arguments. In all of these cases, the final award may be improved by the arbitral rules and national law governing the procedure of the arbitration to avoid controversy when enforcing the award.

Any nation that is a UN member, a member of a UN specialised agency, or a party to the International Court of Justice's Statute may ratify the Convention and become a member of the ICJ. The ICSID Convention mandates that a Tribunal's award is final and binding on all parties to the proceeding, and all parties are required to abide by the award's terms. To have the award's monetary obligations recognised and enforced in the courts of any ICSID Member State as though it were a final judgement of the courts of that state, the non-complying party must submit to the competent court (or other authority which the State has designated for this purpose) a copy of the award certified by the Secretary-General. Each Member State must recognise and enforce the award, but each State's laws relating to sovereign immunity from execution remain in effect (Article 55 of the ICSID Convention). ICSID itself has no formal role in the recognition and enforcement of an award under the ICSID Convention, and certified copies are sent to the parties on the date of dispatch. However, if one party notifies ICSID that the other party is not complying with an award, ICSID will usually get in touch with the non-complying party to enquire about the steps that party has taken or plans to take to comply with the award.

LAWS OF PRECLUSION, LIS PENDENS, AND STARE DECISIS IN INTERNATIONAL ARBITRATION

International Arbitration has paid attention to such legal concepts like preclusion, Lis Pendens, Stare Decisis and res judicata. These in investment arbitration proceedings remain a subject of academic discussions, especially with regard to the application of the "triple identity test." Amidst widespread criticism of the investor-state arbitration system, the need for a more unified strategy has become an urgent matter. Improving the rule of law in investment arbitration requires finding workable solutions to avoid multiple/concurrent proceedings and inconsistent decisions. Topics covered include: investor-state arbitration; res judicata; lis pendens; general principles of law; collateral estoppel; issue estoppel/preclusion; and the triple identity test. In this article, we'll discuss the state of res judicata and lis pendens in international investment arbitration and then discuss some of the most recent developments in this area.

However, in a mixed arbitration case involving an international investment dispute, the tribunal did not reject res judicata as a principle of international law that it was bound to uphold. In fact, it reaffirmed res judicata as "a principle of international law, and even a general principle of law within the meaning of Article 38 (1) (c) of the Statute of the International Court of Justice," with the arbitrators making it clear that: "the present Tribunal in no way denies the value of the principle of res judicata, nor its potential application in the present proceedings to the extent that any issue already decided between the parties may prove to be relevant to the determination of Although the first proceedings did not make it to a decision on the merits, they did reach a negative decision on the issue of jurisdiction by finding that the waiver requirement of Article 1121 NAFTA had not been met when the proceedings were initially instituted in 1998. Since the first proceedings never even got to the substance of the dispute, the second proceedings had to be instituted. It is the tribunal's position that "the point is simply that a decision which does not deal with the merits of the claim, even if it deals with issues of substance, does not constitute res judicata as to those merits."

CONCLUSION

International arbitrations have been advocated for, along with the various rules and regulations that are followed depending on the country. While the arbitration process is being initiated, there are several procedural details of the award that need to be considered. The rules of various institutions like LCIA, New York Convention, ICDR etc through their articles, sections and sub sections make it amply clear as to the different aspects that demand attention in the formulation of International Commercial Arbitration Policies and their execution in different situations.

REFERENCES

Brill. (2021); *Arbitrary Judicial Interference in Human Rights Guaranteed.* Brill. https://brill.com

Brody, R. (1991). *The United Nations Creates a Working Group on Arbitrary.* Cambridge University Press & Assessment. https://www.cambridge.org

Caldwell, C. A. (2012). *Cultural Evolution and Perpetuation of Arbitrary.* PLOS. https://journals.plos.org

Dindjer, H. (2021). *What Makes an Administrative Decision Unreasonable.* Wiley. https://onlinelibrary.wiley.com

Jye, I. B. (2022). *How are arbitrary and deliberate decisions similar and different?* Oxford University Press., https://academic.oup.com

Maoz, U. (2019). *Neural precursors of decisions that matter—an ERP study.* eLife Sciences. https://elifesciences.org

Miles, T. J. (1983). *Neither Arbitrary nor Capricious.* International Budget Partnership. https://internationalbudget.org

Org, U. N. (2023). *Rule of Law and Democracy: Addressing the Gap*. UN. https://www.un.org

Schroeder, P. A. (2015). *Arbitrary numbers counter fair decisions*. National Institutes of Health. https://www.ncbi.nlm.nih.gov

Vermeule, A. (2015). *Rationally Arbitrary Decisions in Administrative Law*. JSTOR. https://www.jstor.org

Warner. (2022). Arbitrary grounding. Springer. https://link.springer.com

Xu, S. (2008). *Are decisions "Arbitrary" in our International Business*. Research Gate. https://www.researchgate.net

KEY TERMS AND DEFINITIONS

Agency Theory: Agency theory is a principle that is used to explain and resolve issues in the relationship between business principals and their agents. Most commonly, that relationship is the one between shareholders, as principals, and company executives, as agents.

Commencement Date: The date of commencement of arbitration is the date on which a request for a dispute to be referred to arbitration is received by the respondent. This date is also known as the "Arbitration Commencement Date."

Issue Preclusion: The principle of collateral estoppel, also known as "issue preclusion," is a legal doctrine that prevents parties from relitigating issues that have already been decided in a prior legal proceeding. This means that once an issue has been fully and fairly litigated and decided, the parties are bound by that decision in subsequent actions on different causes of action between them (or their privies) as to the same issues actually litigated and essential to the judgment in the first action.

Lis Pendens: Lis Pendens Arbitralis refers to parallel and competing proceedings between international courts and tribunals, just as between international and domestic tribunals. The filing of a Lis pendens is a vital tool for protecting a party's rights in enforcing a purchase and sale agreement for real estate, but if the claim at issue falls within a mandatory arbitration clause, the party may not have the right to file a Lis pendens.

Schedule of Costs: A schedule of costs is a document that outlines the fees and expenses associated with an arbitration proceeding. These costs can include administrative charges, fees for the arbitral tribunal, and expenses incurred by the parties during the course of the arbitration.

Stare Decisis: Stare decisis is the principle that prior arbitration decisions should serve as a guide or precedent and control the determination of the arbitrator's decision in the case at hand.

Statement of Defence: In an arbitration conducted under certain rules, such as CAM Rules, the Statement of Defence is the first opportunity for the Respondent to present its position on the Claimant's assertions. The Respondent can also make any objections to the Tribunal's jurisdiction, attempt to join in the proceedings any other parties, and assert any counterclaims that it may have against the Claimant. The Statement of Defence should be submitted within the period of time agreed upon by the parties or determined by the arbitral tribunal.

Chapter 8
Confidentiality of Arbitrations: A Review

ABSTRACT

Arbitration is confidential in nature. The parties to a dispute must agree to keep the matter under wraps at all times. It should be noted that the UNCITRAL model law does not include a provision guaranteeing confidentiality in international commercial arbitration, which is a major reason why this is not guaranteed legally in many countries. However, countries like Scotland, New Zealand, Peru, and Australia have strict regulations governing the privacy of their citizens' personal information. The exact situation is unique in each country. Even though there is no express provision for confidentiality in UK statutes, case law has evolved to protect such information. As a result, it's important to examine and discuss the circumstances in various nations. This chapter will make an effort to shed light on the confidentiality clause per se, as well as the confidentiality of international arbitration.

BACKGROUND

Confidentiality in arbitration is a very important feature for the success of arbitration. The line of the demarcation between transparency and secrecy in arbitration is very thin and has to be built with skill. It is one issue that can make or mar the effort of ADR. Until the arbitral award is decided and made enforceable, the parties will maintain confidence based on the extent of confidentiality and secrecy retained at all levels. The method of approach to

DOI: 10.4018/978-1-6684-4040-7.ch008

the arbitration should not cause any misgiving or suspicion which will lead to the unnecessary discussion beyond the parties to the arbitration. Therefore, confidentiality in arbitration has to be an in-built mechanism.

This chapter aims to achieve the following objectives;

1. To study the various dimensions of confidentiality in arbitration
2. To study the clause regarding non-disclosure
3. To study the rules relating to the confidentiality of the arbitrators
4. And to arrive at inferences useful for the understanding of confidentiality in arbitration

For the purpose of this research, a descriptive method is used. Data have been collected from secondary sources like scientific journals, books, and other print and digital media relating to law and arbitration.

PREVIOUS RESEARCH LITERATURE

Confidentiality is an important aspect of any arbitration agreement. Confidentiality has different significant issues that need to be perused. Scientific investigations have been carried out by previous scholars. Questions like who, why, and when of confidentiality in arbitration have been raised. It is argued that confidentiality is one of the reasons for choosing arbitration over judicial court procedures for dispute settlement (SCC Online, 2021). The scope of confidentiality binding upon the participants in arbitration proceedings has been examined (Fabian, K; 2021).A study of confidentiality in arbitration has pointed out that in most of the cases, confidentiality is essential and justified the provision(Cremades, BM; 2013). It is argued that the public interest in judicial proceedings that are supposed to drive the decisions of the court requires confidentiality(Zamoff, M; 2022). At the same time, some argue that arbitration process is not an inherently confidential process as the arbitrator is bound by the applicable rules which are publicly known(Singer,DC; 2020). Confidentiality in arbitration is considered as a principled approach and allowing the disclosure of the documents to third parties would defeat the purpose of private arbitrations(Bennett,DR & Hodgson,MA; 2017). The basic assumption of confidentiality in arbitration is that it is done in good faith. If it is violated, it can end up in fishing (Reuben,RC; 2006). Confidentiality in arbitration and public interest is an exception and not a rule always(Tweeddale,A; 2022). However, another scholar justifies confidentiality and states that confidentiality is a fundamental principle in arbitration(Bhagner, H; 2001). The European view on choice of law in licencing is that arbitration should contain the confidentiality clause (Dessemontet,F;1996). International arbitral awards also provide for enforcement retaining the confidentiality(Dolinger,J;1983). The confidentiality of international arbitration proceedings is an area of common interest from mercantile law to academic discussions(Sales,Jeffrey W; 2022). The issues raised by confidentiality in international arbitration were examined (Poorooye,A; 1958).The confidential requirement of the proceedings of the arbitrators in international arbitrations is provided in the arbitration instrument for foreign arbitrations(Yu,HL; 2021). It is emphasized that confidentiality and arbitral proceedings are closely interrelated (Campbell,CM; 2018). Protection of confidentiality in arbitration has to be ensured (Brown,JCP; 2021).

SIGNIFICANCE OF CONFIDENTIALITY IN ARBITRATION

In order to avoid further complications from public airings of grievances, it is often necessary to keep disputes behind closed doors. Secrecy and personal privacy are two of the many advantages attributed to international commercial arbitration.

ICA's inherent confidentiality appears to be a selling point for those looking to resolve their disputes through the organization. The parties' obligation to keep the arbitration proceedings secret seemed unquestioned for a long time because of the private setting in which they took place. However, since certain judgments were issued in some countries beginning in the mid-1980s, it was held that confidentiality was not an essential attribute of arbitration.

When comparing the laws of different countries, it becomes clear that there is no uniform approach to the issue but rather significant differences, with some countries having no regulations at all, others having very general regulations, and a few having even stricter ones. Even in circles where diversity is acknowledged, there are often vast disagreements over what exactly constitutes diversity.

For this reason, it should come as no surprise that many commentators deny the existence of an implied confidentiality duty in ICA. Confidentiality in ICA, it turns out, can be deceptive to the point that it has been called a "myth".

Many nations do not safeguard ICA confidentiality, possibly because the UNCITRAL Model Law on ICA, which is adopted in whole or in part by many nations, does not address this issue. Confidentiality is strictly regulated by law in countries like New Zealand, Peru, Scotland, and Australia.

The countries chosen to host the ICA typically have wildly different situations. In the United Kingdom, for instance, there is no statutory regulation on confidentiality for ICA, but there has been a significant development in case law to protect confidentiality. The Federal Arbitration Act and the Uniform Arbitration Act, which is used as a model by most States, do not include any provisions mandating the protection of parties' private information during the arbitration process. However, unless both parties agree to it, ICA is not required to maintain confidentiality under French law, despite a 2011 amendment that mandated it for domestic arbitration.

RULES FOR CONFIDENTIALITY IN ARBITRATION

The arbitrators and employees at each centre for arbitration must follow certain rules regarding the protection of client confidentiality. Even though there may be Codes of Ethics for arbitrators or more in-depth rules, they do not necessarily create a duty of confidentiality for the parties. Article 6 of Appendix I, and Article 1 of Appendix II, of the ICC Rules, only impose duties on arbitrators and the staff of the International Court of Arbitration, but not on the parties, although Article 22.3 permits the Arbitral Tribunal to make orders concerning confidentiality at the request of any party. Similarly, article 37.1 of the AAA's ICDR rules only imposes duties of confidentiality on arbitrators and the Administrator, and article 37.2 establishes that the tribunal may make orders concerning confidentiality; additionally, there is a Code of Ethics with provisions on confidentiality for arbitrators that applies to both domestic AAA arbitrations and international ICDR arbitrations.

Article 30 of the LCIA Rules, on the other hand, establishes clear guidelines for the obligation of confidentiality. Despite not being explicitly addressed, the award appears to be implicitly confidential under article 34.5 of the UNCITRAL Arbitration Rules, which requires the consent of both parties before it can be made public.

The existence or nonexistence of a duty of confidentiality is not the only topic up for debate; the nature and scope of any such duty also depend on the specific circumstances. Those who may have a duty of confidentiality include the parties and their representatives and advisors, as well as the arbitrators, secretaries, witnesses, experts, court reporters, translators, and interpreters who are all part of the arbitration process.

The existence of the arbitration itself, the parties' pleadings and memorials, the documents produced or other evidence such as witness statements or experts' reports, the award and other arbitration decisions, and information contained in such filings could all fall within the scope of the material.

Information disclosed in arbitration filings may include confidential business information that could cause harm to one or both parties in an ICA, such as financial data, production costs, pricing policies, know-how, or trade secrets. A company's financial woes or the existence of a faulty product could also be made public, which would hurt their reputation and give an advantage to their rivals.

In case of an award issued in an ICA is challenged, either for annulment or for recognition and enforcement, the award and all information contained therein become public record as a result of the judicial process. Interim injunctions in an ICA may similarly necessitate the intervention of the courts. In these cases, there is no need to maintain complete secrecy.

There are situations in which one or both parties to an arbitration agreement are required by law to disclose information, such as when a tax, criminal, or judicial authority requests it or when a regulatory agency (for banking, securities, or insurance matters) requests it. Although the parties may have an interest in keeping the arbitration out of the public eye, we are faced with exceptions to confidentiality in these cases due to the public interest being imposed over the private interest of the parties.

Some legislation, arbitration rules, or case law in some countries have also admitted as exceptions to the duty of confidentiality in other circumstances that do not fit with the inescapable situations described above. To protect the legitimate interests of one party vis-à-vis third parties, or to protect or enforce a right against a third party acting as a plaintiff or defendant, which has been qualified as a matter of procedural public order, it may be necessary to disclose that arbitration is taking place. In addition, it has been taken into account that disclosing some information concerning the arbitration when there is a good reason to do so does not constitute a breach of the duty of confidentiality. Similarly, a parent company, shareholders, auditors, insurers, and a potential acquirer with a due diligence interest are all entitled to know about the arbitration and its results.

An ICC publication cites the example of a subcontractor, who would be entitled to know the terms and circumstances of an arbitral dispute between a main contractor and the owner of the works (Craig, Park & Paulsson; 2000)

We would add that the owner of the works has every right to be informed of any subcontractor disputes that may arise and be heard by an arbitrator. While each of these contracts stands on its own, the exception seems reasonable given that they are linked contracts that share a common object or cause.

Therefore, unless prohibited by applicable legislation or arbitration rules, or by agreement among the parties, the parties may disclose details of their own arbitration, including to interested third parties, if there are legitimate reasons to justify that they are acting in good faith.

The duty of confidentiality of the arbitrators in the performance of their tasks, but not of the parties or other people involved in the arbitration proceedings, is the only thing that tends to be recognized almost unanimously in national legislations or in the arbitration rules regarding ICA in matters of confidentiality. That's why ICA arbitrators typically recommend including a clause in the Terms of Reference committing the parties to keep the arbitration proceedings private.

There is no presumption of confidentiality in ICA, and there does not appear to be any general principle on the matter, because the bound individuals and protected contents can vary widely even in situations where the applicable rules recognize the duty of confidentiality.

In view of the fact that the law applicable to the arbitration agreement, the law of the contract, or the law of the seat of arbitration may govern the confidentiality of ICA disputes depending on the facts of each case and the parties' agreement, those who wish to keep their ICA disputes private or avoid potentially unfavorable or harmful publicity should investigate the applicable law regarding confidentiality. Still, it's smart to have explicit provisions in the arbitration agreement that address privacy concerns.

One of the hallmarks of private arbitration is that the parties are free to design their own rules and procedures for resolving disputes. However, just as the free market can "fail" (by requiring limits on the freedom of market players), so too may defects in the machinery of international arbitration cry out for a bit of enlightened intervention. It is argued that it was against the law to talk about what happened during a private commercial arbitration. The scope of arbitral confidentiality is "far from a settled issue.

There is increasing disagreement over whether or not such an implied duty of confidentiality exists, as evidenced by two recent pronouncements from courts in different countries. Due to this discrepancy in authority, there is a lot of mystery surrounding the level of confidentiality that can be expected in ostensibly private arbitrations. If the any arbitration clause in the contract guarantees privacy, then keeping the proceedings private shouldn't be too much of an issue. However, confidentiality is rarely addressed in pre-dispute arbitration agreements. In their eagerness to reach an agreement, the parties rarely consider the future. Even if they do consider the confidentiality issue, they might not know how it would affect the resolution of their dispute in arbitration. In most cases, the parties will use a "generic" arbitration clause of the type recommended by arbitration institutions. When a dispute arises, the parties often cannot agree on even the most basic issues, such as whether or not the proceedings should be kept private. The issues raised by varying levels of privacy protection are serious. When settling legal disputes, businesspeople frequently seek anonymity or at least a reliable estimate of how much secrecy they can expect to enjoy. Uncertainty in this regard can only lead to mistrust of the arbitration procedure. There are a lot of challenges in the way of finding a solution to this issue. A solution in the form of a default rule is likely to be accepted by most participants in the arbitration process was sought. Therefore, it attempted to summarise several countries' conflicting confidentiality standards, and then present the role of institutional rules, the effect on contracting parties, and the challenges in resolving the conflicts. A possible conclusion is to present a system of a uniform default rule and some suggestions for implementing it. For example, confidentiality is not imposed in some countries. A recent decision of the Swedish Supreme Court, Bulgarian Foreign Trade Bank Ltd. v. AI Trade Finance Inc. in which it was held that there is no implied duty of confidentiality in private arbitrations. It has received widespread attention because of the dramatic circumstances surrounding the case. The Bulgarian bank argued that it was not bound by the arbitration clause because it was not a party to the contract that led to the arbitration, which was initiated by the finance company located in Stockholm.

Mealey's International Arbitration Report, which apparently received the arbitrators' ruling from counsel for the finance company, reported that the bank was bound by the clause. The finance company, upon learning of the publication, claimed that the award was null and void because the bank had breached its duty of confidentiality under the UN-ECE arbitration rules and Swedish law. Swedish law does not make arbitration proceedings secret unless the parties contract for secrecy (and even then, not if 4 Case No. T 1881-99), and the Swedish Supreme Court ruled that the UN-ECE rules do not prohibit disclosure of the outcome of an arbitration proceeding (Swedish Sup. Ct. 27 Oct. 2000).

Due to Swedish law's requirement that a party seeking to enforce an award produce a copy of it4, confidentiality in arbitration proceedings can only be guaranteed through either an express contractual provision or the adoption of arbitration rules that expressly provide for it. Sweden isn't the first country to reject the concept of an implied duty of privacy. A decision by the High Court of Australia in Esso Australia Res. "crashed like a giant wave - a veritable Australian tsunami" on the shores of jurisdictions around the world. Ltd. v. Plowman, confidentiality is not "an essential attribute" of commercial arbitration. This is in contrast to privacy. Since the Minister for Energy and Minerals was not a party to the arbitration, the Court ruled that he was entitled to the discovery of arbitration documents and information. In the United States, where no federal court above the district court level has ruled on this issue, the few district court decisions reject any implied duty of confidentiality. An ICC arbitration between a Panhandle subsidiary and the Algerian state oil company was at the center of the leading case, United States v. Panhandle E. Corp. The federal government sought to compel Panhandle, a U.S. company, to produce documents from the arbitration.

The parties expect the arbitration to be private, and any disclosure would be disappointing. The court ruled that the ICC Rules do not impose any obligation of confidentiality on the parties to the arbitration process, and that there is no inherent duty of confidentiality absent a contract to the contrary. As a result, it granted the government's motion to compel the production of the records.10 II. This is especially important because London is frequently the situs of international arbitrations, and English law holds that arbitral parties are subject to an implied duty of confidentiality. An English court held in the seminal case of Ali Shipping Corp. v. Shipyard Trogir that this obligation is implicit in every arbitration agreement as "an essential corollary of the privacy of arbitration proceedings." This obligation extends to the outcome of the arbitration as well as the "pleadings, written submissions, and the proofs of witnesses, as well as transcripts and notes of the evidence given in the arbitration." A preliminary injunction to seal an arbitration award in which the movant was found liable for antitrust violations was denied in Group v. Karteria Shipping, Ltd., 2000. Both parties argued that the public has a strong countervailing interest in knowing the results of (ordering the production of documents from a London arbitration). However, on the ground that it is "implicit in the nature of private arbitrations that the proceedings are confidential, and that strangers shall be excluded from the hearing", confidentiality was maintained.

Although there are exceptions to the general duty of confidentiality under English law, the drafters of the English Arbitration Act of 1996 decided against including a provision explicitly addressing confidentiality. For example, English courts will only allow disclosure if the parties agree to it, if the court orders it in a later action, if it is "reasonably necessary" to protect or pursue a legal right, or if it is "in the interests of justice." However, these exceptions are strictly construed. If an expert witness takes a position diametrically opposed to the expert's position in a prior arbitration, for instance, the court may find that "the interests of justice" justify an exception to the general prohibition. Thus, parties to arbitrations governed by English arbitration law run a high risk whenever they make details of the arbitration public. The Ali Shipping decision gained support from many commentators who were concerned about the erosion of arbitral confidentiality. However, French law appears to provide even more stringent protection for the confidentiality of arbitral proceedings and awards. Several of the proceedings are secret, and the decision doesn't even seem to make room for the few exceptions allowed by English law. The duty of arbitral confidentiality has been written into law in one country. In order to avoid the Australian Esso decision being used as a precedent in New Zealand courts, Section 14 of the Arbitration Act of 1996 states that "the parties shall not publish, disclose, or communicate any information relating to arbitral proceedings under the agreement or to an award made in those proceedings"18 unless the parties agree otherwise. Since a dispute over confidentiality may not be heard in the national courts of the arbitration situs, one cannot assume, for example, that English confidentiality standards will apply to all arbitrations held in London. There is a chance that it will come up in an ongoing enforcement action in the country where the information is disclosed. No supranational court exists in our world to settle these kinds of international disputes. Furthermore, as will be shown below, institutional rules alone will not remedy the situation. A simple incorporation of an arbitral institution's rules is unlikely to clear up any questions of privacy. Institutional rules typically state that the arbitrators must keep the proceedings private, but rarely prohibit disclosure by the parties. For instance, Article 25(4) of the UNCITRAL Arbitration Rules states that hearings shall be held "in camera ", but it does not specify what the parties may or may not disclose outside of the hearing. The largest international arbitration institution, the ICC, merely permits the arbitral tribunal to "take measures for protecting trade secrets or confidential information" and excludes "persons not involved in the proceedings" from hearings. However, the ICC Rules are silent on the confidentiality of awards and of materials produced and information divulged in the proceeding. Some arbitral institutions provide greater protection. The London Court of International Arbitration is now known as LCIA Arbitration International (LCIA). According to Rule 9 of the LCIA Rules (which superseded the previous rules from 1985), "the parties undertake as a general principle to keep confidential all awards in their arbitration, together with all materials in the proceedings created for the purpose of the arbitration, and all other documents produced by another party in the proceedings not otherwise in the public domain—save and to the extent that disclosure may be required of a party by legal duty." This discord between national courts and arbitral institutions over the existence and scope of a duty of confidentiality promotes uncertainty, the bane of international business transactions.

The effects of the different kinds of arbitral proceedings and awards, on both parties and their contracting parties and business associates can be noted. Simply recommending that everyone do their homework is not a good enough argument. Firms should not be expected to "do their homework" on a wide variety of confidentiality requirements before entering into a contract or agreeing to arbitrate. It is unreasonable to expect businesspeople or even their attorneys to keep up with the ever-changing body of legal precedents in this area. The courts, arbitration institutions, and arbitrators themselves do not have a quick fix for this problem. Due to the "balkanization" of the rules on issues like confidentiality, businesses must "hire guides to explain the little differences," which is an extremely inefficient use of resources. Precedent and competing interests mean that courts rarely reach a decision that is acceptable to all parties. Whether or not a country is willing to uphold an implied duty of confidentiality is likely to have an impact on whether or not it is attractive as an arbitration venue and whether or not it attracts the business that goes along with arbitrations. A clause in the parties' agreement addressing whether or not the arbitral proceeding and the award are to be kept confidential, and to what extent, could be the answer to this problem. While there are no guarantees, it could be beneficial. One, even years after a contract has been signed, disputes that warrant arbitration may arise. It is difficult to anticipate where one's interest will lie on the spectrum of privacy at such a distant time. Secondly, a clause that would cover all eventualities would need to be very detailed and lengthy, increasing the transactional costs of entering into the agreement at a time when the parties prefer not to focus on potential future disputes. Finally, it is unclear whether a national court would uphold all of the agreements between the parties, including provisions that are contrary to the public policy of the forum country. The parties' inclusion of the rules of an arbitral institution with strong confidentiality protections in their agreement will not be sufficient to avoid the difficulties. This set of rules does not address the issue of what a party can do if there is a breach of confidentiality after the arbitration is over. In order to resolve the dispute, one side would need to file a lawsuit in court, where the particulars of national law would be applied. Consider whether a court in New Zealand or the United States would recognize an agreement to maintain confidentiality if the parties had incorporated the LCIA Arbitration International or CIETAC rules. It's possible, but it's risky to rely on such a supposition because of how little data exists. If for no other reason than to prevent widespread dissatisfaction with the arbitral process, a unified rule has been proposed because the confidentiality issue seems so pressing and intractable that it requires a joint resolution. Due to the lack of clarity surrounding the current scope of confidentiality protections, a uniform rule is urgently required, but no one knows what it should look like or how to get there. A default rule in all arbitrations can be provided. The arbitrators shall require at the threshold that the parties agree on the scope of confidentiality, failing which the above rule shall apply. Default rules save money because they eliminate the need for extensive negotiations or, at the very least, provide a starting point to spur effective negotiations. If a claim alleging a breach of the parties' confidentiality agreement or protective order is brought up during the arbitration, the arbitrators will make a decision on the matter. The parties agree to submit any disputes arising from a violation of the terms of the confidentiality agreement or protective order after termination to arbitration under the terms set forth in the parties' arbitration agreement. Depending on the circumstances, an arbitrator may award monetary damages and other penalties to the victim of a protective order or confidentiality agreement violation. Transaction costs may be factored into the parties' negotiations as they determine initial allocations. The default rule has the advantage that it would not require parties to decide on confidentiality terms at the time of contracting when most parties prefer to leave this issue open (as evidenced by the fact that most contracts are silent on this issue). Furthermore, it would result in an agreement by the parties that courts would likely enforce, even in countries that do not recognize an implied duty of confidentiality. Courts would be avoided except in the rarest of circumstances; however, arbitration of confidentiality disputes would be the norm. With the threat of repercussions for violating the agreement's secrecy, parties would be deterred from doing so even if the potential for actual harm is low, and this would have the added benefit of protecting the privacy of a dispute resolution process.

To improve the chances that the parties will agree on confidentiality terms and to reduce the likelihood that a protective order will be necessary, the arbitrators should provide several "prefabricated" confidentiality clauses that reflect varying levels of confidentiality protection for the parties to choose from. But what should the protective order include if there is no agreement? The arbitrators should tailor the order to the particulars of the case whenever possible, but in most instances, the order should impose a duty of confidentiality analogous to that found in English law. It is suggested (in favour of "floating law clauses" to accommodate the fact that parties often "value open terms in contracts"). Most likely, the parties would go with an option, which conforms to standard practice and the generally held belief that private arbitrations ought to remain private. It is important to include language in the proposed agreement or protective order that outlines the permissible and non-permissible categories of disclosure. Some parties, such as insurers, auditors, banks, and courts, may need to be informed of arbitration proceedings. It may be desirable to restrict disclosure beyond such mandates in order to prevent a claimant from disclosing the respondent's potential liabilities to the respondent's customers, creditors, and contracting partners. While it may be impractical to prevent the prevailing party from announcing to the world, "I won," the terms of the award, including the amount of any damages, should be prohibited from disclosure. No matter how "educational" it might be for the public if the arbitrators' explanations of their award were made public, they should be kept confidential. A "penalty" default rule, one set at what the parties do not want to encourage negotiations and disclosure of all relevant information, is not preferable to a "market-mimicking" default rule, with which it is hard to imagine that any party would agree, should it find itself on the wrong side. The problem here is not improper bargaining due to lack of information or strategic withholding of information, but rather the high cost and often futile effort of obtaining reliable data on the enforceability of confidentiality clauses. In cases of the inverted hierarchy of dispute, making that party is less able to persuasively argue its position. If a party hires outside legal representation but restricts the resources available for case presentation (due to lack of funds, insufficient personnel, or any number of other factors), or if they choose less-experienced but less-expensive counsel, the same thing could happen. In almost all cases of international commercial disputes, businesspeople and/or governmental authorities will make these decisions, weighing the pros and cons of possible actions. In most cases, the parties' own actions result in the existing imbalance of forces.

Whether in a domestic court or international arbitration, the decision to forego legal representation carries real-world consequences. Choosing to represent yourself in arbitration, or having in-house counsel represent you, can save you money in the short run. One advantage of representing oneself in court is the potential for increased agency in the development and presentation of one's case. For these and other reasons, state parties in international and investment arbitration often opt to proceed without external counsel or with limited involvement of external counsel.

On the other hand, hiring outside counsel allows to reap the benefits of having a subject-matter expert represent you. This knowledge and experience are useful in any dispute, but it is especially useful in international disputes, where complicated procedural and judicial issues may arise and where there may be no available appeals.

Without legal representation, parties often submit weaker arguments and commit more procedural errors, making the other party's job and the arbitral tribunal's job more difficult. Lack of presentation, procedural, and related skills on the part of lay parties can also lead to a lack of clarity and misunderstanding of a party's case or evidence. Lawyers in these cases may be expected to present their client's case with greater objectivity or to take a more moderate stance on procedural or other issues than would normally be the case. Moreover, a tribunal may unintentionally or intentionally play a role in elucidating the situation for the unrepresented party.

The work of counsel in such a situation is particularly difficult. A lawyer must vigorously advocate for his or her client without appearing to take advantage of the pro se party and must take advantage of every available procedural opportunity. This calls for exceptional persuasiveness and clarity.

Article 18.2 of the proposed 2014 LCIA Rules, it does not represent a ground breaking change, but rather is similar to provisions in other institutional rules, such as Article 26(4) of the 2012 ICC Rules ("The parties may appear in person or through duly authorized representatives..."), Article 20 of the 2012 China International Economic and Trade Arbitration Commission (CIETAC) Rules ("A Power of Attorney shall be forwarded to the Secretariat of the CIETAC by the party o").

It is common to practice for the parties to voluntarily submit evidence of counsel's authority, such as a power of solicitor. The arbitral tribunal should, as a matter of good practice, ask for written evidence to prove that counsel has the necessary authority to act on their behalf.

In a number of ways, questions of representation can undermine an award's legal standing. As with a party's default, a lack of legal representation is not a basis for challenging or refusing to recognize an award. The lack of representation of a party in a highly complex case where that party's chosen representative is wholly incapable of presenting the party's case may, however, raise issues of enforceability in unusual circumstances.

A party may seek to have an award nullified or not recognized if the party is prevented from using the representative or counsel of their choice. The New York Convention, article V(1)(d), may not recognize an award if it is found that the parties were not given the opportunity to select their own legal counsel, as is the case under many institutional arbitration rules (or comparable grounds for annulment).

To effectively present the cases in the manner they expect when agreeing to arbitration, the parties should be allowed to choose their own representation, a right that has traditionally been recognized as an important aspect of the arbitral process. This autonomy is acknowledged by the majority of institutional arbitration rules and by the laws of most countries that have codified arbitration. Nonetheless, in a few places, lawyers representing parties in locally seated arbitration must be qualified to practice in that location. For instance, in Turkey and Thailand and in Singapore, Japan, and a few other jurisdictions.

However, most legal systems have come to the conclusion that limiting parties' ability to hire legal representation from within their own jurisdiction is both inadvisable and inappropriate in international arbitrations. It is normal, given that restricting the parties' freedom to choose their own legal counsel runs counter to arbitration's intended purpose as a personalized and malleable method of resolving disputes and, as mentioned above, could be grounds for challenging the validity of an award.

Experience and dedication are essential qualities in an international arbitration solicitor. It is not possible to replace either one with anything else. Lawyers must also pay close attention to the arbitrators, following the tribunal's lead on issues of importance and concern. Procedural rules, such as those of any applicable institutional arbitration rules and the directions of the arbitral tribunal, are also very important in arbitration. Counsel must be well-versed in the ethical and responsibilities of professional responsibility rules established by the bar in the respective jurisdiction. Counsel in a locally seated arbitration may also be subject to ethical requirements under the law of the arbitral seat, though this is unusual.

In their current form, the IBA's Guidelines on Party Presentation in International Arbitration are not particularly helpful. Unlike the IBA Guidelines on the 'Taking of Evidence' in International Arbitration, the Guidelines do not provide substantially clear guidance for counsel and are therefore not of long-lasting value.

CONCLUSION

Many of the most influential treaties establishing the rules for International Commercial Arbitration deal with the validity and enforcement of arbitral awards made in international business deals. These include the 1980 CISG and the 1958 New York Convention on the Recognition and Enforcement of Foreign Arbitral Awards (both of which are examples of international treaties). The International Centre for the Settlement of Investment Disputes (ICSID) and the United Nations Conference on Trade and Development are just two examples of the many venues available for international commercial arbitration (UNCTAD). Several awards issued in International Commercial Arbitration have not yet been made public. It is evident that confidentiality in arbitration is either maintained or violated depending of varying circumstances.

REFERENCES

Bennett, D.R. & Hodgson, M.A. (2017). *Confidentiality in Arbitration.* A Principled Approach, Canadian Legal Information Institute. https://www.canlii.org.

Bhagner, H. (2001). *Confidentiality—A Fundamental Principle in International.* Calis. calis.edu.cn http://fulltext.calis.edu.cn

Brown, J. C. P. (2021). *The Protection of Confidentiality in Arbitration.* London Metropolitan University, http://repository.londonmet.ac.uk

Campbell, C. M. (2018). *U.S.A. vs. the World: Right to Public Access of Court Records.* University of South Carolina. https://scholarcommons.sc.edu

Craig, P. (2000). *International Chamber of Commerce Arbitration.* Oxford Press.

Cremades, B. M. (2013). The Principle of Confidentiality in Arbitration: A Necessary Condition. *Korea Science.* https://koreascience.kr

Dessemontet, F. (1996). *Arbitration and Confidentiality.* UNIL. https://www.unil.ch

Egonu, M. I. (2022). *Confidentiality.* Jus Mundi. https://jusmundi.com

Fabian, K. (2021). *Confidentiality in international commercial arbitration.* Central European University. https://www.etd.ceu.edu

Jacob, D. (1979). *Organization of American States.* OAS. http://www.oas.org

Khan, T. (2021). *The who, why and when of confidentiality in Arbitration.* SCC Online. https://www.scconline.com

Poorooye, A. (1958). *Confidentiality and Transparency in International Arbitration*. Harvard Negotiation Law Review. https://www.hnlr.org

Reuben, R. C. (2006). *Confidentiality in Arbitration: Beyond the Myth University of Missouri*. Scholarship Law. https://scholarship.law.missouri.edu

Sarles, J. W. (2022). *Solving the Arbitral Confidentiality Conundrum in International Arbitration*.

Singer, D. C. (2020). *Arbitration Privacy and Confidentiality In the Age*. National Institutes of Health. https://www.ncbi.nlm.nih.gov

Tweeddale, A. (2002). *Confidentiality in Arbitration and the Public Interest Exception*. Corbett. corbett.co.uk, https://corbett.co.uk

Yu, H. L. (2021). *The duty of confidentiality within the global landscape*. University of Stirling. https://dspace.stir.ac.uk

Zamoff, M. (2022). *Safeguarding Confidential Arbitration Awards*. Wiley. https://onlinelibrary.wiley.com

KEY TERMS AND DEFINITIONS

Confidentiality in Arbitration: This refers to the agreement between parties to maintain the confidentiality of the dispute intended to be resolved by arbitration, as well as the information adduced and contentions asserted in any such arbitration. The parties agree to maintain in strict confidence and agree to neither make nor suffer any public disclosure of the fact of, contentions or evidence, discovered, developed or introduced in and the result of any such arbitration.

Good Faith: It is a legal term that describes the intention of the parties in a contract to act honestly and fairly towards each other.

New York Convention and Foreign Arbitral Awards: It is a treaty that was adopted by a United Nations diplomatic conference on June 10, 1958, and entered into force on June 7, 1959. . The Convention seeks to provide common legislative standards for the recognition of arbitration agreements and court recognition and enforcement of foreign and non-domestic arbitral awards . Its principal aim is that foreign and non-domestic arbitral awards will not be discriminated against and it obliges Parties to ensure such awards are recognized and generally capable of enforcement in their jurisdiction in the same way as domestic awards .

Non-Disclosure Clause: This is a legal agreement between parties specifying information that one or both of the parties consider confidential and prohibiting the other party from disclosing it. The party disclosing the information is commonly referred to as the "Disclosing Party" and the party receiving it is referred to as the "Receiving Party."

Pleadings: These are formal written statements submitted by parties in a legal proceeding that set forth or respond to allegations, claims, denials, or defences.

Swedish Law on Arbitration: The Act is applicable to both international and domestic arbitration but deals only with arbitral proceedings seated in Sweden. It allows the parties to design their dispute resolution as per their needs and the mandatory rules are a few only.

Written Submissions: These refer to documents submitted by parties in a legal proceeding that contain arguments, citations, and facts to support their case.

Chapter 9
Policies, Practices, and Protocols for International Commercial Arbitration:
A Review

ABSTRACT

Although the policies, practices, procedures, and protocols governing international commercial arbitration can vary from one country to the other, they all share a common goal: to facilitate the peaceful resolution of disputes between disputing parties without the need for drawn-out, expensive litigation. But policies shift, practices vary, and protocol requirements differ across nations. An effort to provide comprehensible discussions of these in a variety of national contexts is made in this chapter.

BACKGROUND

In the wake of the increasing significance of alternate dispute redressal mechanisms as a cost-effective, efficient, facilitating, and hastening mechanism for conflict resolution, to enable a transparent, justiciable system, the policies, practices, and protocols of the ADR in any country context is expedient. Each of the same viz policies, practices, procedures, and protocols need to be studied closely and analyzed to arrive at appropriate inferences. In this chapter, such an effort is attempted.

DOI: 10.4018/978-1-6684-4040-7.ch009

This chapter is purported to achieve the following objectives:

1. To analyze the arbitration policies, practices, and protocols of some select countries
2. To provide a brief sketch of some scholarly literature
3. To discuss the materials gathered to arrive at appropriate inferences

This chapter is based on the analysis of secondary source materials collated from print and electronic media which are relevant and appropriate for this study.

PREVIOUS RESEARCH LITERATURE

International commercial arbitration is affected by several factors including the policies of the states in which arbitration takes place, the procedures laid down, and the practices that are followed in the context of the arbitration. Several scholarly studies have been carried out examining different aspects of the policies, procedures, and protocols. A brief sketch of such studies is attempted here.

Examining public policy and international commercial arbitration, three levels of public policy are defined as domestic, international, and transnational (Buchanan, MA; 1988). The Law Merchant or Lex Mercatoria has rules which are common to all or most of the states which are engaged in international trade. Such rules have to be ascertainable (Lando, O; 1985). The effect of party autonomy is significant where the rules and practices are mentioned in international commercial arbitration (Lew, JDM et. al., 2003). There are rules which are most controversial. The roles of mandatory rules in international commercial arbitration decide the outcome of the arbitration especially where the corporate citizens are involved (Barraclough, A,& Waincymer; 2003). Prior to 2020, international arbitration included the treatment of annulment, recognition of awards, and counselling on ethics (Born, GB; 2020). The peculiarity of international commercial arbitration is that their entitlement is tailored to their own arbitration proceedings and needs of international action (Fouchard, P & Goldman, B; 1999). The role and power of arbitrators are based on the strategies and depend on the laws, rules, and guidelines which vary from state to state (Moses, ML; 2017). There is a limited application of the public policy exception in international commercial arbitration which is necessitated with respect to both the parties and not just to one party that initiated the proceedings (Garcia de Enterria, J; 1989). It has been attempted to examine the issues on the ICA scene in recent years and summarised the recent developments in the rules (Craig, WL; 1995). The contention of national public policies on the arbitral process focuses primarily on the survival of ICA (Chukwumeriie, O; 1994). The regime of international commercial arbitration in business practices and strategies has become increasingly complex and transnational (Lynch, K & Lynch, KL; 2003). When engaged in international trade and international exchange, some common core procedural rules can be identified which will be different from national public policy to international public policy. (Kurkela, MS & Turunen, S; 2010).

Arbitration on an international scale is an option for settling disagreements that emerge out of international business deals. When disputing a business transaction on a global scale, one may want to consider using international commercial arbitration as an alternative to going to court. This type of arbitration is governed by the terms agreed upon by the parties involved, rather than by any specific country's laws or procedures. Most contracts include a clause stating that the parties agree to submit any dispute arising out of the contract to binding arbitration rather than to court. At the time of the contract, the parties may also choose to define the applicable law and forum for any legal disputes that may arise.

What is meant by "arbitration" is simply the private, amicable, or third-party resolution of a disagreement. During the time of Greek civilization and Roman law (around the sixth century), the arbitral process was the norm. After initially being met with hostility, arbitration has become the preferred method for resolving disputes among businesses. Because there are already too many people trying to get their day in court, arbitration became more feasible. Over ninety crore cases are pending in India's national courts, according to the government's report. Therefore, resolving disputes in court wastes time and money, and the relief that is finally obtained is not worth the wait. There have been numerous attempts by both the legislature and the judiciary to address this issue through the establishment of special courts and forums, but none of these measures have been particularly successful. Because of the overwhelming caseloads, no forum or tribunal is currently capable of delivering relief in a timely manner.

The court finds a novel approach to resolving the disputes in order to get around this obstacle. It's proper to call this approach "Alternative Dispute Resolution" (ADR). Alternative dispute resolution (ADR) takes many forms, including conciliation, arbitration, mediation, negotiation, and so on. Ultimately, arbitration is the most common type of this process. Arbitration is preferable to judicial resolution of a dispute for many reasons, including its speed and lower cost, as well as the fact that it avoids the hyper legalism and complexity of judicial proceedings and subsequent appeals. When a dispute arises between two parties located in different countries, it can be intimidating to go to court in the other party's country. However, arbitration can alleviate this concern by providing a neutral third party to resolve the dispute on their behalf.

When private parties opt for arbitration, they are using a binding alternative dispute resolution process that they have voluntarily chosen. The arbitration process consists of three phases: (1) the pre-arbitration phase (the period before the dispute arises), (2) the arbitration phase, and (3) the arbitral award phase.

It is possible to have an "ad hoc" or "institutional" arbitration. The arbitration procedure is established by the terms of the contract. The term "ad hoc arbitration" is used to describe situations in which the parties to a contract have devised their own arbitration rules. Ad hoc arbitration is a form of private dispute resolution in which the disputing parties determine all aspects of the arbitration on their own, including the number of forums, the number of arbitrators, the rules and procedures to be followed, and any other matters that may arise. Institutional arbitration occurs when the parties to a contract have agreed to have the institution in question handle the dispute. The International Chamber of Commerce in Paris stands as the preeminent international organization or institution offering services for arbitration between parties of different nationalities. The Chamber of Commerce in Zurich, Stockholm, etc., is another example, as is the London Court of Arbitration, the American Arbitration Institution, and so on.

The UNCITRAL Model Law on International Commercial Arbitration serves as a guide for states to help them update and reform their arbitral laws to meet the demands of international commercial arbitration. This model controls the entire arbitration procedure, including the scope of judicial involvement, the arbitral tribunal's composition and jurisdiction, the arbitration agreement, and the enforcement of the arbitral award. This framework is also reflective of the main international arbitration practices that are followed in the various legal or economic systems around the world.

AGREEMENTS AND TREATIES

It has been noted that awards are easier to enforce in jurisdictions that adhere to multilateral conventions and treaties, as opposed to jurisdictions that follow transnational laws that make the public policy a ground to set aside an award. The situation is hindered by the fact that the laws and procedures for enforcement of the award vary widely and are often quite complex from one country to another country, which is not ideal for the development of international commercial arbitration.

As a result, numerous attempts have been made in various forums to achieve unification and certainty in the enforcement of the award in the interest of improved global trade. Occasionally, positive signals have been shown by multilateral conventions and treaties, and regional arrangements towards the elimination of all the contentious problems. Some of the most important conventions are:

The award made in the territory of the state other than the state where recognition and enforcement of the award arising out of the difference between the contracting parties shall be recognized and enforced shall be subject to the New York Convention on the Recognition and Enforcement of the Foreign Arbitral Award (1958).

The European Convention of 1961 governs the recognition and enforcement of domestic arbitration awards made between European Union members. While trying to nullify an award, the European Convention is a step up from the New York Convention.

For the implementation of the Arbitral Award under Articles 31–37 of the United Nations Commission on International Trade Law (UNCITRAL), Arbitration Rules, 1976 are followed. Although the Arbitration Rules of the International Chamber of Commerce (article 19 rules) recognize and give effect to a different system of jurisdiction, it is preferred to maintain majority rules rather than giving an award by the arbitrator alone if no majority can be reached.

Other conventions and treaties include the "I.B.R.D. Convention, 1996," the "Moscow Convention, 1972," the "Montevideo Treaty, 1889," the "ESCAP Arbitration Rules, 1996," the "Arbitration Rules of Un/EC, 1996," and "The UNCITRAL Model Law on International Commercial Arbitration, 1985," among others.

Objections to Arbitration Decisions

The grounds for challenging an arbitral award vary by jurisdiction. These proceedings must be initiated in the countries where the award was issued and must not be illegal there. The challenge to the arbitration award was denied under Article 34 of the UNCITRAL Model Law (1985) and Article V of the New York Convention. It is important to give an arbitration sufficient time to look into why an award was vacated before deciding where to hold the proceedings. Once the inquiry is complete, the award is treated with the same degree of finality as a court order.

The incompetence of a party, non-applicability of the subject matter under the law of arbitration, the invalidity of the agreement, compositional defects of the arbitral tribunal, and conflicts with the public policy of the country are all grounds for setting aside an award.

Public Administration

The parties frequently seek to have the arbitral award nullified on the basis that it is contrary to public policy. Moreover, article V (2)(b) of the convention gives the contracting states a "safety valve" that allows them to prevent the enforcement of the award if it is contrary to their legal system. Since the national courts approach public policy in international arbitration from a variety of perspectives, the issue continues to be hotly contested, controversial, and complex. The national courts' perspective makes it impossible to implement the public policy for the benefit of the parties. This mentality predominates in India, where judicial obstruction has stymied the development of internationally recognized public policy.

Almost every country, though some more than others, has acknowledged the undeniable role of national courts in international arbitration. This is due to the fact that arbitration is generally administered in accordance with national laws and has a close relationship with national courts. As soon as the award has been made, the jurisdiction of the national court becomes more central to the arbitration procedure. This holds true during the enforcement phase when an arbitral award must meet certain statutory conditions before being upheld. Article V of the Convention on the Recognition and Enforcement of Foreign Arbitral Awards 1958 (also known as the New York Convention) specifies situations in which a national court may refuse to enforce an arbitral award. The New York Convention does not provide any guidance to national courts regarding the interpretation of the public policy defense. Thus, domestic courts give the public policy provision their own interpretation. The International Law Association (ILA) attempted to create a unified definition of "International Public Policy" to address this issue, but they were unable to do so due to disagreements over what exactly should be included in this category.

Though the term "public policy" has a different meaning in each jurisdiction, it is generally agreed that a court may vacate an award if it is found to be in violation of the most basic standards of fairness, honesty, and justice. That's why a shady process can lead to the nullification of a prize.

Setting an award on the basis of corruption is a valid ground in most modern law jurisdictions. In this regard, the U.S. Federal Arbitration Act (FAA) is also crystal clear. In accordance with the FAA, if it is determined that the arbitrator who rendered the award is corrupt, that the award was obtained through fraud, corruption, or undue influences, or that the arbitrator was otherwise guilty of misconduct, then the award will not be enforceable. If there was a major irregularity with the tribunal, the proceeding, or the award, it is possible to have the award nullified under the English Arbitration Act.

National Policy and International Public Administration

Since there is only one nation involved in domestic arbitration, the national courts are only required to apply domestic public policy. There is no other factor other than national public policy. When discussing international public policy, however, the situation changes because of the fact that more than one national public policy may be at play. Therefore, in this case, national courts must apply public policy while considering international implications. The rules of a nation's domestic public policy that are also applied in an international context make up what is known as international public policy.

Public Policy, Both Substantive, and Procedural

The arbitrator is limited to one's interpretation of applicable law. It's possible that the award violates public policy for both substantive and procedural reasons. The matter for the award is subject to substantive public policy, while the award's adjudication process is subject to public policy concerning the manner in which the matter was decided. Therefore, moral and just principles would be a matter of substantive public policy. Additionally, rules serving the state's political, social, or economic interests are also examples of principles that violate the state's substantive public policy.

Expenditures and Expanding Scope

International commercial arbitration with a public policy provision has been shown to affect economic growth and investment. When the other side challenges the award on the basis of a violation of public policy, it is clear that the foreign party will likely lose the case.

The majority of cases of this type in India involve a domestic party losing a case to a foreign party and then filing a case in national courts to challenge the award. Foreign businesses cannot understand why this is happening and are therefore cautious about conducting business in India. This ultimately hinders foreign companies' ability to conduct business with their Indian counterparts.

Public policy can be used effectively through a number of different approaches. To begin, there is a pressing need for the creation and effective implementation of similar initiatives to the International Law Association (ILA). To increase the number of nations that can work together to agree on basic public policy principles. Further, the arbitrator should receive training in arbitration from institutions like the Institute of Chamber of Commerce and other organizations. The concept and complexities of arbitration can only be grasped by examining the case in detail. Similarly, the parties and the arbitrators must be aware of the consequences of relying on public policy in a case.

Commercial Arbitration on a Global Scale

Commercial disputes between private parties that arise out of international business transactions can be arbitrated internationally as an alternative to litigation in national courts.

The best resources for locating treaties, national legislation, procedural rules, and arbitral awards pertaining to international commercial arbitration are available. The secondary sources are crucial to the serious investigation, which can also be accessed.

Arbitration in International Business: Essential Materials

The Global Arbitration Review (GAR) is an authoritative publication that tracks trends in international commercial arbitration. Also releases annual surveys and guides for working professionals.

The International Chamber of Commerce's (ICC) Dispute Resolution Library includes excerpts from arbitral awards issued in disputes heard by the ICC's International Court of Arbitration.

Primary legal materials (treaties, national laws, arbitral awards, and judicial decisions) and secondary sources (law reviews, commentaries, and scholarly articles) are both available in the searchable database. Both primary legal materials and peer-reviewed articles from TDM's online-only journal are available to users of Transnational Dispute Management (TDM).

This Westlaw database offers primary legal materials from some countries, secondary sources, and drafting tools for international arbitration.

Arbitration Rules for International Business Transactions: Standards and Procedures

Protocols and guidelines for conflict prevention and resolution are developed for use in mediation, arbitration, and other forms of ADR. They are created by people who are actually using dispute resolution services and are written by the CPR Institute, the organization's think tank.

Analysis of Issues

Commercial disputes between private parties that arise out of international business transactions can be arbitrated internationally as an alternative to litigation in national courts.

International arbitration provides a more definitive resolution than court proceedings ever could. One of the drawbacks of the judicial system is that judgments are sometimes appealed, and it can take years for these to be resolved.

Generally speaking, American Arbitration Association (AAA)offers better value for claims which are below the value of $5,000,000, while the International Institute of Conflict Prevention and Resolution (CPR) offers better value for claims whose values are above $5,000,000. The arbitrators of Judicial Arbitration and Mediation Services (JAMS) and the American Arbitration Association (AAA) are not permitted to issue an award based solely on the default or absence of a party.

According to the 2021 Queen Mary University of London and White & Case International Arbitration Survey, which was published on May 6th,

Singapore and London were chosen as joint first and second most preferred places for arbitration worldwide.

Due to their overwhelming caseloads, many courts across the country are not the best places to seek justice. International arbitration, when compared to domestic courts, also produces higher-quality decisions. When compared to litigation, arbitration saves both time and money.

While JAMS is most well-known for being an industry-leading mediation service, more than 30% of our revenue comes from 3,500 arbitration cases filed both domestically and internationally.

JAMS's internal training programs and the extensive experience of its panellists have contributed to the organization's standing as a leading arbitrator provider.

i. A barrister is not required to represent either party in an arbitration.

There is no need for a barrister during the arbitration process. One may like to hire a lawyer to help prepare and present the case in a dispute resolution proceeding because such proceedings are adversarial in nature and the outcome is often final and affects one's rights.

ii. Arbitration dispute resolution procedure

Arbitration is a dispute resolution procedure that can be used instead of going to court. It is held in a separate location from the courtroom, most frequently a conference room. The arbitrator acts as a judge in place of the traditional judicial system.

Arbitration is favored because it is more informal and cheaper than litigation, though the exact savings will depend on who is chosen as the arbitrator. However, some of them can cost a bit. The parties to a dispute do not have to wait for their day in court, so this method is seen as a faster alternative to litigation.

iii. The methodology of Arbitration

The parties submit their dispute to an impartial arbitrator, who acts as a judge informally, during the arbitration process. Following a hearing at which both parties present their cases, the arbitrator will render a decision and issue an award.

While there are rules for arbitration, there are no established procedures for the presentation of evidence or the filing of motions in arbitration. In other words, unlike in court, a party does not have to know the rules for gathering and submitting evidence, nor will have to spend time writing detailed explanations of what transpired.

However, one may be able to conduct informal discovery (research your case and collect evidence) if necessary. It is also possible to conduct depositions (interview witnesses). Like in court, witnesses give testimony under oath during arbitration proceedings.

iv. Binding Arbitration

When people sign contracts, they frequently agree to binding arbitration as a means of resolving disputes. In order to avoid legal entanglements, one party may include an arbitration clause in the small print. In the event of a dispute, the parties hereto agree to forego litigation in favour of arbitration.

In other words, parties agreeing to arbitration are waiving their right to file suit in court. Moreover, they acknowledge that the arbitrator's decision will be final and that they will have no recourse against it.

All proceedings in arbitration are confidential and cannot be viewed by the general public. The arbitrator's decision is also private unless one of the parties seeks court intervention to enforce it.

v. Legal Representation in Arbitration

Legal representation in arbitration can be useful in different situations

vi. Legal Protections

The fact that arbitration is a judicial proceeding with potential implications for legal rights is probably the most compelling argument in favor of having legal counsel present during the process. Because the arbitral award cannot be changed, the proceedings have to be watched carefully.

2. A Solicitor Can Make the Case Easy for Argument

Without proper legal counsel, presenting one's case effectively can be more challenging than one might expect. This is especially true if a statute or law governs your situation, as in a claim for racial, age, or national origin discrimination in the workplace. A solicitor can help construct an argument that is grounded in the law and the facts.

3. Normally, Arbitration Rules Are in Favour of Employers and Large Businesses

Arbitration clauses are common in legal contracts. Banks and credit card companies are notorious for including mandatory arbitration clauses in their customer contracts, compelling customers to use arbitration rather than litigation in the event of a dispute.

Arbitration, unfortunately, usually rules in favor of the more powerful party, which is typically the larger company or employer. Having a solicitor can help even the playing pitch, which is another reason why many people find them useful.

4. Experience the Superiority of the Parties

It's possible that the other side is so used to arbitration that they already know who will be presiding over their case. A large company, for instance, may employ arbitration lawyers and maintain a list of arbitrators who favor businesses over individuals. One may want an equally experienced corporate lawyer on your side if you're going up against one.

5. Influence of Choice

The potential impact of the arbitration decision on one's life is an important factor to think about when choosing a solicitor to represent the party. One probably doesn't need a solicitor if one isn't overly worried about what could go wrong. However, the American Arbitration Association suggests at least consulting with a solicitor if the outcome will significantly impact your life, such as whether one gets to keep one's job or whether one might lose a significant amount of money.

6. Arbitrator Selection

Whether arbitration is proceeding because the parties are required to do so by a clause in the contract or because the parties have mutually agreed to use arbitration as a means of resolving the dispute.

In most cases, arbitration clauses will outline who will act as the arbitrator or how the arbitrator will be selected. The American Arbitration Association's National Roster of Arbitrators and Mediators is one place to start looking for a qualified arbitrator if one decides to go through the arbitration process on one's own. One should always look for an arbitrator who has experience with cases that are similar to the case that arose.

Find an impartial and competent arbitrator with the assistance of a solicitor. This is yet another argument in favor of seeking legal counsel.

Most arbitrators have prior experience working as lawyers or judges, and some jurisdictions even mandate that arbitrators be licensed attorneys or members of the state bar. However, the licensing, registration, or certification of arbitrators is not mandated in all jurisdictions.

CONCLUSION

The regulations, customs, and norms could be different from one country to another country. All of these factors must be taken into account before entering into a contract that includes provisions for International Commercial Arbitration in order to mitigate losses, increase the likelihood of obtaining awards that are justifiable, and serve the interests of both parties.

REFERENCES

Baniassadi, M.R. (1992). Do mandatory rules of public law limit choice of law in international commercial arbitration. *International Tax & Business Law*, HeinOnline.

Barraclough, A. & Waincymer, J. (2005). *Melbourne Journal of international Arbitration*. search.informit.org.

Born, G. B. (2020). *International Commercial arbitration* books.google.com

Buchanan, M. A. (1988). *Public policy and international commercial arbitration*. American Business Law Journal, Hein Online. doi:10.1111/j.1744-1714.1988.tb01153.x

Chukwumerije, O. (1994). *Choice of law in international commercial*. eLibrary. arbitration.elibrary.ru

Craig, W. L. (1995). *Some trends and developments in the laws and practice of international commercial arbitration.* Texas International Law Journal, HeinOnline.

Croff, C. (1982). *The Applicable Law in an International Commercial Arbitration: Is It Still a Conflict of Laws Problem? The International Lawyer.* JSTOR.

Donovan, D.U. (1994). International commercial arbitration and public policy. *New York University Journal of International Law & Policy*

Fouchard, P. & Goldman, B. (1999). *On International Commercial Arbitration.*

Garcia de Enterria, J, (1989). The Role of Public Policy in International Commercial Arbitration. *Law & Policy International Business*, Hein Online.

Kurkela, M.S. & Turunen, S. (2010). *Due process in international commercial arbitration.* Research Gate.

Lando, O. (1985). The lex mercatoria in international commercial arbitration. *International & Comparative Law Quarterly.*

Lynch, K. & Lynch, K.L. (2003). *The forces of economic globalization: Challenges to the regime of international commercial arbitration.*

Mistelis, L.A. (2003). Comparative international commercial arbitration. *JDM Law.*

books.google.com

Moses, M. L. (2017). *The principles and practice of international commercial arbitration.* Research Gate. books.google.com

Redfern, A & Hunter, M (2004). *Law and practice of international commercial arbitration.*

KEY TERMS AND DEFINITIONS

Binding Arbitration: This is a private method of resolving disputes between two or more parties. The parties agree to let a neutral third party, called an arbitrator, make a final and binding decision on the matter. The arbitrator will review the evidence and listen to the arguments of both sides.

Legal Protection in Arbitration: This refers to the protection provided by law to parties involved in an arbitration process. In the US, this protection is provided by the Federal Arbitration Act, and every state will have various laws that govern the arbitration process.

National Policy: This refers to a broad course of action or statements of guidance adopted by the government at the national level in pursuit of national objectives.

Public Administration: This is both an academic discipline and a field of practice. It refers to the implementation of government policies, administration of government establishment (public governance), management of non-profit establishment (nonprofit governance), and also a subfield of political science taught in public policy schools that studies this implementation and prepares people, especially civil servants in administrative positions for working in the public sector.

Public Policy: This refers to a set of actions the government takes to address issues within society. For example, public policy addresses problems over the long-term, such as issues with healthcare or gun control, and as such, it can take years to develop. Public policy addresses issues that affect a wider swath of society, rather than those pertaining to smaller groups.

Suggestions for Settlement: In arbitration law, parties may submit suggestions for the settlement of the dispute to the conciliator. This can be done on their own initiative or at the invitation of the conciliator. The conciliator will then consider these suggestions while trying to facilitate a settlement between the parties.

Westlaw: This is an online legal research service and proprietary database for lawyers and legal professionals available in over 60 countries. Information resources on Westlaw include more than 40,000 databases of case law, state and federal statutes, administrative codes, newspaper and magazine articles, public records, law journals, law reviews, treatises, legal forms and other information resources.

Chapter 10
Sample Arbitration Forms:
A Brief Analysis

ABSTRACT

Various arbitration treaties have been established amongst different countries. Reading the arbitration agreements will help one to understand the importance given to different factors during the implementation of arbitration procedures. Some sample contracts from the Netherlands, the United Kingdom, Singapore, Hong Kong, the United States of America, India, and Japan have been briefly analyzed in general in this chapter. Furthermore, some attempts at making comparisons are made, with the resulting insights being highlighted.

BACKGROUND

To address the concerns of conflicts during commercial transactions, international commercial arbitration has been resorted to in several countries. To achieve the goals, it is essential that the procedures and processes should be carried out in a manner that the parties involved should not only meet with the ends of justice but also that justice should seem to have been done. Therefore, greater transparency should be ensured rather than indulging in the alternative dispute redressal mechanism in an open-ended form, it is now mandated in many countries that the arbitration agreement should also contain a format with appropriate clauses to be displayed for the parties to the dispute as being able to understand the processes and their obligations. This will enable ease in the enforcement of the arbitral awards also. The various

DOI: 10.4018/978-1-6684-4040-7.ch010

sample contracts from different countries are analyzed here with a view to achieving the goals of drawing appropriate inferences from the analysis.

This chapter envisages achieving the following objectives:

1. To understand the necessity for standardized forms of arbitration agreements
2. To get a picture of the previous scholarly research studies and the issues identified by the research investigation
3. To present the sample forms of contracts from some countries
4. To gain a comparative view from the analysis

For achieving the goals, the methodology used is content analysis as also analysis of secondary data as accessed from published books, journals, and web resources.

PREVIOUS RESEARCH LITERATURE

As is evident, the arbitration agreements are prepared based on the national laws, legal systems prevalent in the states, judicial requirements relating to the standard formats to be maintained, and the ease and convenience of conducting the arbitral procedures. Accordingly, different countries have designed and streamlined their arbitral agreement forms. They provide a clear picture of the commitments and also standards set by the states of the arbitration centers. Some of the previous studies on arbitration systems point out the methods used by different countries emphasizing varying aspects of arbitral agreements. The scope of arbitration is reshaping its form and the line of demarcation between private and public adjudication is blurred. This can be seen in the USA viewed from all three domains like international arbitration agreements within the country, international arbitration agreements per se, and the international arbitration awards themselves (Hensler, DR, & Khatam; 2017). It is reported that the average consumer experience is the use of pre-dispute arbitration clauses and the parties volunteer to use the agreement format designed before the dispute (Demaines, LJ & Hensler, DR, 2004). The judicial enforcement of the agreements has to be provided for in the agreement format and the filings of Form 8-K in the USA by the corporations are made effective (Stipanovich, TJ; 2010). In employment arbitration, personnel manuals are used. In repeat situations, the imposition of arbitration through an adhesive employment contract is allowed. (Bingham,

LB; 1997). An empirical study of the arbitration clauses as stated in the agreement forms was studied concerning the consumers and non-consumers when entering into a contract (Eisenberg, T, et al ; 2007). The small prints in the arbitration agreements are meant for protecting the big business claims from the employee and consumer rights associations (Schwartz, DS; 1997). In the agreement forms of the parties, most standard clauses of arbitration forms are covered (Paulsson, J, et al ; 2011). Arbitration clauses are present in many forms in the contracts through which consumers try to resolve disputes. There are complications arising out of such formats. However, these complications are not present in the context of adhesion arbitration agreements (Ware, SJ; 2006). In publications of books through print or electronic media, a condition is placed in the format of arbitration that no part of the publication may be reproduced in any form (Rubino-Sammartano, M; 2014) About half a million **contracts** filed with **arbitration clauses** are less frequently adopted than clauses referring parties to the domestic system (Nyarko, J; 2019). It is generally criticized that individual lack both the information and economic incentive to evaluate the pre-dispute arbitration agreement forms of contract (Drahozal, CR; 2001). In the law and practice of international arbitration agreements, most standard forms contain significant clauses of arbitration agreements (J Paulsson,J, et al ; 2011). There are some other forms of dispute resolution where the clauses are not important and are not printed in the forms (Bom, GB, 2021). In the USA, the federal and state courts typically have enforced arbitration clauses in the standard forms of consumer agreements unless they contain specific provisions that violate state policy. (Eisenberg,T, et al 2007).

ARBITRATION FORMS OF SOME COUNTRIES

Hague Conventions on Arbitration

Professionals typically consider arbitration and court litigation when thinking about how to handle international business disputes. However, it is not necessarily a case of either/or. In the event that litigation is necessary before, during, or after the arbitration proceedings, the parties to the dispute may choose the NCC District Court or NCC Court of Appeal, as the case may be. Because of this, they will be able to do things like filing a setting-aside claim with the NCC Court of Appeal in English.

There are several provisions in the Dutch Code of Civil Procedure that allow for court intervention and handling of issues arising from arbitration, so there is an entire chapter devoted to the subject in the code. The options given are detailed below.

The usual NCC requirements (detailed further below) must be met, and the arbitration must take place in Amsterdam before the NCC District Court or NCC Court of Appeal will hear the case. The "place of arbitration" is only a theoretical location, and the actual proceedings may be held anywhere. Moreover, the parties must agree that the NCC District Court or the NCC Court of Appeal will have jurisdiction over the case. Standard terms and conditions may contain such a clause so long as it is accepted by the parties either in the agreement itself or in some other document. There are two issues specified. i. Structured clause

The NCC Encourages a Particular Vocabulary

Binding arbitration administered by [arbitration institute] shall be used to resolve any disputes arising out of or in connection with the Agreement or any agreements entered into as a result thereof. Disputes are to be arbitrated in Amsterdam (the Netherlands). In front of the International Commercial Chambers, all proceedings must be conducted in English. Before, during, or after an arbitration proceeding in the Netherlands, all judicial proceedings shall be conducted exclusively before the Amsterdam District Court or the Amsterdam Court of Appeal, as applicable (Netherlands Commercial Court, which consists of the NCC District Court, the NCC Court in Summary Proceedings and the NCC Court of Appeal). In this case, the NCC Rules of Procedure will be applied. A possible appeal to the Supreme Court is not intended to be precluded by this provision.

Examining the NAI Arbitration and NCC Court Litigation Clause as a Real-World Example

If the Netherlands' pre-eminent commercial dispute resolution institution, Rechtspraak.nl (NAI), and the NCC see value in giving parties the option to use both NAI arbitration and NCC court litigation, both of which will be conducted in English. As a result of this data, the involved parties can speed up the procedure and cut costs. The NCC Court of Appeal may hear a setting-aside claim in English from the parties after an award has been made. This saves the parties the trouble and expense of having to learn Dutch in order to settle legal disputes.

After an NAI arbitration award has been made, the parties may choose to take their case to court in either the NCC District Court or the NCC Court of Appeal, depending on the circumstances. If the NCC is to take the case seriously, it has to be ensured that the general NCC requirements are met (detailed below) and that the arbitration takes place in Amsterdam. Based on Article 1037(3) of the Dutch Code of Civil Procedure (DCCP), "place of arbitration" is merely a legal concept and hearings can be held wherever the parties agree.

The following language should be included in the arbitration clause between the parties, as recommended by the NAI and the NCC:

All disputes arising under or in connection with this Agreement or any agreements entered into pursuant hereto shall be resolved by binding arbitration in accordance with the rules of the Netherlands Arbitration Institute (NAI). Disputes are to be arbitrated in Amsterdam (the Netherlands). All proceedings shall be conducted in the English language.

To the extent permitted by law, any court proceedings in the Netherlands before, during, or after the arbitration, following proceedings in English before the Chambers for International Commercial Matters, shall be exclusively before the Amsterdam District Court or the Amsterdam Court of Appeal, whichever has jurisdiction (Netherlands Commercial Court, which consists of the NCC District Court, the NCC Court in Summary Proceedings and the NCC Court of Appeal). In such cases, the NCC Rules of Procedure will be applied. A possible appeal to the Supreme Court is not intended to be precluded by this provision.

As the phrase "to the extent allowed by law" suggests, NCC is subject to certain legal restraints.

Under Amsterdam's judicial system's binding legal force, cases involving international civil or commercial disputes between unrelated third parties consensus among the parties that the NCC should hear their case in English. Standard terms and conditions may contain such a clause so long as it is accepted by the parties either in the agreement itself or in some related document. For cases like these, the Amsterdam District Court can intervene. Because of the Arbitration Chapter of the DCCP, the location has been chosen. Jurisdiction is vested in the Court pursuant to the Rules of Court (e.g., domicile of the defendant).

Options for Out-of-Court Settlement

The DCCP's Arbitration Chapter provides guidance for a wide variety of arbitration-related scenarios. On the NAI website, one can find the chapter in English as well.

There are different courts within the NCC and the types of cases they can hear.

The law acknowledges that in some cases, parties may mutually agree to have a neutral third party handle a dispute instead of going to court. This means that one should read the NCC's arbitration rules thoroughly before filing any arbitration-related proceedings with the NCC. In the NCC Summary Proceedings Court:

Temporary and protective measures, such as reviewing a copy or an extract from specific documents, may be sought by the parties if the desired decision cannot be obtained in arbitration or cannot be obtained in a timely manner (Articles 1022c and 1074d DCCP),

Provision for The Number of Arbitrators (Articles 1026(2) and 1072 DCCP)

The appointment of arbitrators (DCCP Articles 1026(4), 1027(3), 1028(1), and 1072), removal of an arbitrator or arbitral tribunal (Articles 1029 (2)(4)(5) and 1072 DCCP), a challenge to an arbitrator or the third party overseeing an appeal of an arbitrator's decision (Articles 1035(1)(7) and 1072 DCCP), the DC Code of Criminal Procedure allows for the appointment of a judge to hear a case involving a hostile witness in Articles 1041a(1), 1074c, and 1072. Currently being heard by various Dutch courts, arbitration cases are being consolidated (Article 1046 DCCP), neutralization, postponement, or mitigation of an arbitrator-imposed penalty (Article 1056 DCCP). The District Court of the NCC is where one will meet with appropriate regulations.

Articles 187, 1022b, and 1074b of the Dutch Code of Criminal Procedure require a preliminary evidentiary hearing to be held in Amsterdam if either the court expected to have jurisdiction over the case is in Amsterdam or if the witnesses, or the majority of the witnesses, have their domicile or habitual residence in Amsterdam, requesting a site inspection or expert testimony before going to trial, with the Amsterdam District Court as the most likely venue (Articles 203, 1022b and 1074b DCCP). A critical analysis of selected (full or partial) documents can be noted in (Article 1022b). The NCC (CSP) has no jurisdiction over matters that are not directly related to the independence of the parties. The following issue might fit this description:

i. acceptance of a Dutch arbitration award (Article 1062 DCCP).
ii. A Petition Filed with the NCC Court

When the parties agree (Article 1064a (1) DCCP) and the arbitration takes place within the Amsterdam appellate district, the NCCA Court of Appeal can hear an appeal seeking to vacate the award. Suspension of the award pending the outcome of an appeal or reversal (Article 1066 DCCP), invalidation of the arbitral decision because of new evidence, or proof of fraud (Article 1068 DCCP). The NCC Court of Appeal has no jurisdiction over questions that the parties themselves cannot resolve. There are some potential issues: i. a decision affirming an arbitration award made outside of the Netherlands (Article 1075 DCCP), ii. a request for review of a denial of permission to enforce a Dutch arbitral award (under Article 1063(4) of the Dutch Civil Procedure Act).

Agreement to Arbitrate Forms for the United Kingdom

Alterations to the Agreement that should be made. They Were at the Top of Their Game for Conflicts Settlement. The following clause should be included in any contract between parties who want to have any future disputes arbitrated using the LCIA Rules. The information between the square brackets can be ignored or completed as appropriate: Any controversy or claim arising out of or relating to this Agreement, including any question regarding its existence, validity, or termination, shall be submitted to and finally resolved by arbitration in accordance with the LCIA Rules, which Rules are deemed to be incorporated by reference into this clause. The arbitrators will consist of [one/three]. The arbitration shall take place in [City and/or C], as the case may be.

The venue for the arbitration hearings shall be determined. This Agreement is governed by the internal substantive law of the country.

Conflicts already at hand: The following clause is recommended if a dispute has arisen but an arbitration agreement has not been reached between the parties, or if the parties wish to modify an existing dispute resolution clause to provide for LCIA arbitration. The text enclosed by square brackets needs to be edited by omitting or filling in the appropriate words. Please contact the LCIA Secretariat if you would like to make any modifications to the suggested clauses, such as allowing parties to nominate arbitrators or instituting accelerated procedures. The LCIA also provides recommended clauses and procedures for Mediation, Expert Determination, Adjudication, and other forms of ADR that it will administer or in which it will act as appointing authority.

A. Singapore-Style Arbitration Clauses

Any and all controversies or claims arising out of or in connection with this Contract, including any question regarding its existence, validity, or termination, shall be submitted to and finally resolved by arbitration administered by the Singapore International Arbitration Centre ("SIAC") in accordance with the Arbitration Rules of the Singapore International Arbitration Centre.

B. U.S. Arbitration Contract Templates
C. Agreements to Arbitrate as Examples in India
D. Arbitration Clause Examples in Japan

Common Phrases

Domestic Arbitration Agreement Forms

Without a well-written arbitration clause, a contract is incomplete.

E. HKIAC recommends that the party should consult a lawyer before using any of the following model clauses, even though it is encouraged to use them where they make sense.

Hong Kong International Arbitration Centre-administered arbitration

HKIAC arbitration with UNCITRAL membership

Ad hoc arbitration under the rules of the UN Commission on International Trade Law

The HKIAC's Domestic Arbitration Rules Will Be Applied at the Venue.

Arbitration by the Hong Kong International Arbitration Centre will be conducted in private and will be binding.

To submit any future disputes to arbitration under the HKIAC Administered Arbitration Rules, the parties may include an arbitration clause in their contract.

Any and all controversies, differences, claims, or disputes arising out of or in connection with this Agreement, or the existence, validity, interpretation, performance, breach, or termination thereof, or any dispute regarding non-contractual obligations arising out of or in connection with it, shall be submitted by the parties to binding arbitration administered by the Hong Kong International Arbitration Centre (HKIAC) in accordance with the HKIAC Administered Arbitration Rules.

This arbitration clause shall be governed by Hong Kong regulations.

The site of the arbitration hearings will be Hong Kong.

There will be three arbitrators in this case. (Either 1 or 3). The location of the arbitration hearing is specified and the language is also filled in the format.

Issues such as the identity of the parties to the arbitration clause and its formation, existence, scope, validity, legality, interpretation, termination, effects, and enforceability may be governed by the law of the arbitration clause, but this does not pre-empt the law governing the substantive contract.

The parties may agree to submit any pending or future disputes between them to arbitration under the HKIAC Administered Arbitration Rules under the following conditions:

The undersigned agrees to submit to binding arbitration any and all disputes, controversies, differences, or claims (including those involving non-contractual obligations) arising out of or relating to: "We, the undersigned, agree to refer to arbitration administered by the Hong Kong International Arbitration Centre (HKIAC) in accordance with the HKIAC Administered Arbitration Rules.

(It has to be mentioned that the key clauses of the contract from which the dispute or claim stems, including whether or not they are applicable).

Hong Kong law shall govern this arbitration agreement.

The site of the arbitration hearings is Hong Kong.

There will be three arbitrators in this case. (Either 1 or 3). The location of the arbitration hearing is in Hong Kong.

Verified by: (Claimant)

Proof from: (Respondent)

Date: _________"

Issues such as the formation, existence, scope, validity, legality, interpretation, termination, effects, and enforceability of the arbitration clause and the identities of the parties to the arbitration clause may be governed by the law of the arbitration clause rather than the law of the substantive contract or the law of the seat.

HKIAC arbitration with UNCITRAL membership

The parties may agree to submit any future disputes to arbitration before the HKIAC in accordance with the UNCITRAL Rules by including an arbitration clause similar to the one shown below in any applicable contract.

"Any dispute, controversy, difference or claim arising out of or relating to this Contract, including the existence, validity, interpretation, performance, breach or termination thereof, or any dispute regarding non-contractual obligations arising out of or relating to it, shall be referred to and finally resolved by arbitration administered by the Hong Kong International Arbitration Centre (HKIAC) under the UNCITRAL Arbitration Rules in force when the Notice of Arbitration is given."

For purposes of this arbitration agreement, the laws of Hong Kong (Regulations applicable in Hong Kong).

The venue for the arbitration shall be in Hong Kong.

There will be three arbitrators in this case (Either 1 or 3). The location of the arbitration hearing is in Hong Kong.

Issues such as the identity of the parties to the arbitration clause and its formation, existence, scope, validity, legality, interpretation, termination, effects, and enforceability may be governed by the law of the arbitration clause, but this does not pre-empt the law governing the substantive contract.

Ad hoc arbitration under the rules of the UN Commission on International Trade Law

If the parties to a contract want to resolve any potential legal conflicts through arbitration under the UNCITRAL Rules, they can do so by including the following clause in their agreement.

"Any controversy, difference, or claim concerning the existence, validity, interpretation, performance, breach, or termination of this Contract, or concerning non-contractual obligations arising out of or relating to it, shall be referred to and finally resolved by arbitration in accordance with the UNCITRAL Arbitration Rules in force at the time the Notice of Arbitration is submitted.

Laws of shall apply to this arbitration agreement (Regulations applicable in Hong Kong).

The ones who get to make these choices will (Hong Kong International Arbitration Centre).

In Hong Kong, all arbitration hearings must be held.

Three arbitrators will be appointed in this case (Either one, two, or three). When it comes time for arbitration, it will be held in Hong Kong (Complete this sentence in one's own words)

All questions concerning the existence, scope, validity, legality, interpretation, termination, effects, and enforceability of the arbitration clause, as well as the identities of the parties to the arbitration clause, shall be governed by the law of the arbitration clause; provided, however, that such law shall not be deemed to supersede the law of the substantive contract.

Models of Arbitration Provisions

Sample Agreements Regarding Arbitration

The inclusion of a model arbitration clause drafted by an arbitral institution is usually all that is required to transfer a commercial dispute from a domestic court system to arbitration. There have been thousands of arbitrations using this type of clause because it includes wording that avoids the possibility of jurisdictional disputes.

In the past, including fast-track arbitration rules in contracts was the only way to streamline arbitration proceedings for smaller disputes. Over the past decade, however, many major arbitral institutions like the ICC, SCC, SIAC, HKIAC, and ICDR have incorporated opt-out expedited arbitration proceedings into their arbitration rules, making this provision automatic.

Any dispute or claim arising out of or in connection with this Agreement or the breach thereof shall be settled by arbitration conducted by the AAA International's Centre for Dispute Resolution (ICDR) in accordance with its International Arbitration Rules (the "Model Clause").

Any controversy, claim, or dispute concerning or relating to this Contract or the breach, termination, or invalidity thereof shall be settled by arbitration in accordance with the Arbitration Rules of the Arbitration Institute of the Stockholm Chamber of Commerce (SCC).

In the event of a dispute or disagreement arising out of or in connection with this contract, the parties agree to submit the matter to arbitration under the rules of the Association Française d'Arbitrage (AFA).

This contract, as well as any controversy, claim, or dispute arising out of, relating to, or in connection with it, shall be resolved by arbitration in accordance with the ACICA Arbitration Rules, regardless of whether the controversy, claim, or dispute arises during or after the term of this contract.

In accordance with the rules of the Beijing Arbitration Commission / Beijing International Arbitration Centre, any and all disputes arising out of or in connection with this Contract shall be resolved through arbitration in Beijing. Any decision made by the arbitrator shall be final and binding on all parties.

Reference is made to the model arbitration provision published by the Cairo Regional Centre for International Commercial Arbitration (CRCICA): It states that "any dispute, controversy, or claim arising out of or relating to this Contract or the interpretation, execution, termination, or invalidity thereof shall be settled by arbitration in accordance with the Rules of Arbitration of the Cairo Regional Centre for International Commercial Arbitration."

The rules of the Mexican arbitration centre Centro de Arbitraje (CAM) state that "all disputes arising in connection with the present contract shall be finally settled by one or more arbitrators appointed in accordance with said Rules."

Noncontractual disputes that arise out of, in connection with, or related to this Agreement shall be resolved through binding arbitration before a single arbitrator or a panel of three arbitrators selected in accordance with the Rules of the Milan Chamber of Arbitration (the Rules), which are hereby incorporated by reference.

Chinese Institute of Economic and Trade Arbitration (CIETAC) "Any controversy or claim arising out of or in connection with this Contract shall be submitted to CIETAC for arbitration, which shall be conducted in accordance with the CIETAC's arbitration rules in effect at the time of application for arbitration. All rulings by the arbitrator shall be final and binding upon the parties.

It states, "Any disputes arising out of or related to this agreement shall be finally settled by an arbitrator or arbitrators appointed in accordance with the Arbitration Rules of the Court of Arbitration at the Polish Chamber of Commerce in force on the date of commencement of the proceeding."

To resolve any controversy or claim arising out of or relating to this Contract, its formation, invalidity, interpretation, performance, or termination, the parties agree to submit their dispute to binding arbitration before the Court of International Commercial Arbitration of the Chamber of Commerce and Industry of Romania (CICA) in accordance with the CICA's Arbitration Rules. A final and binding decision will be made.

Any and all controversies arising out of or in connection with this Agreement shall be finally settled by one or more arbitrators appointed in accordance with the provisions of Title IV of the Treaty on the Harmonization of the Law of Business Throughout Africa and the Rules Governing Arbitration Before the Court of Common Justice and the Arbitration Board of the Organization for the Harmonization of Business Law in Africa (CCJA/OHADA).

This contract provides that "any dispute arising out of the formation, performance, interpretation, nullification, termination or invalidity of this contract or arising therefrom or related in any manner whatsoever shall be settled by arbitration in accordance with the provisions set forth under the DIAC Arbitration Rules ("the Rules"), by one or more arbitrators appointed in accordance with the Rules."

Any and all disputes concerning the interpretation, performance, or breach of this Contract shall be resolved exclusively through binding arbitration conducted by the German Arbitration Institute (DIS) in accordance with its Arbitration Rules, rather than through the courts. The arbitral tribunal shall consist of [insert "a single arbitrator" or "three members"]. The location of the arbitration hearing, including city and country, must be specified. In paragraph 4, one will have the opportunity to designate the language to be used during the arbitration. In the fifth paragraph, you can specify the body of law or set of rules that will apply to the merits of the case.

"Any controversy, difference, or claim concerning the existence, validity, interpretation, performance, breach, or termination of this Contract, as well as any controversy, difference, or claim concerning non-contractual obligations arising out of or relating to it, shall be referred to and finally resolved by arbitration administered by the Hong Kong International Arbitration Centre (HKIAC) under the HKIAC Administer. For the purposes of this arbitration clause, [law] shall apply. Disputes are to be arbitrated in [City]. Arbitrators can be selected at random in numbers of one to three. The language to be used during the arbitration is [language].

"The [Government]/[name of constituent subdivision or agency] of the name of Contracting State (hereinafter the "Host State") and name of investor (hereinafter the "Investor") hereby consent to submit to the International Centre for Settlement of Investment Disputes (hereinafter the "Centre") for resolution of any disputes which may arise between them." ") [conciliation]/[arbitration]/[conciliation] at the Centre to settle any dispute arising out of or relating to this Agreement.

Any and all controversies or claims arising out of or relating to this Agreement shall be resolved exclusively through binding arbitration conducted by the International Chamber of Commerce before one or more arbitrators are chosen in accordance with the ICC's Rules of Arbitration.

Any dispute, controversy, or claim arising out of or in connection with this Contract, including any question regarding its existence, validity, or termination, shall be submitted to and finally resolved by arbitration in accordance with the Rules of the London Court of International Arbitration (LCIA), which Rules are deemed to be incorporated by reference into this clause. It has been decided that [one/three] arbitrators will hear this case. In the event of an arbitration, the proceedings shall be held in [City and/ or Country]. Language to be used during arbitration proceedings shall be [that of the city]. This Agreement shall be construed in accordance with the substantive laws of (city).

The parties agree that any and all controversies, disputes, or claims arising out of or in connection with this Agreement or the breach, termination, or invalidity thereof shall be resolved through binding arbitration administered by the Permanent Court of Arbitration in accordance with its Arbitration Rules as in effect as of the date hereof.

The existence, validity, and/or termination of this Contract, as well as any dispute arising out of or in connection with it, shall be submitted to and finally resolved by arbitration administered by the Singapore International Arbitration Centre ("SIAC") in accordance with the Arbitration Rules of the Singapore International Arbitration Centre ("SIAC Rules") for the time being in force, which rules shall be deemed to be in accordance with the United Nations Convention on the Law of the Sea.

"Any controversy, claim, or dispute arising out of or relating to this Contract, including the validity, invalidity, breach, or termination thereof, shall be settled by arbitration in accordance with the Swiss Rules of International Arbitration of the Swiss Chambers' Arbitration Institution in effect on the date the Notice of Arbitration is submitted in accordance with these Rules. The parties agree to appoint ["one," "three," "one or three"] arbitrator (s. Unless both parties agree otherwise, the arbitration will take place in [insert name of Swiss city here]. Location-specific language here Arbitration hearings will be held in.

Any controversy, claim, or dispute between the parties relating to or arising out of this Contract or the breach, termination, or invalidity thereof shall be settled by arbitration in accordance with the UNCITRAL Arbitration Rules.

All claims and disputes arising out of or in connection with this Contract, including those concerning its validity, breach, termination, or nullity, shall be finally settled by one or three arbitrators appointed in accordance with the Rules of Arbitration (Vienna Rules) of the Vienna International Arbitration Centre (VIAC) of the Austrian Federal Economic Chamber.

WIPO's Centre for Arbitration and Mediation in Intellectual Property Disputes

"All questions and disagreements, whether contractual or extracontractual in nature, concerning the formation, validity, binding effect, interpretation, performance, breach, or termination of this Contract or any subsequent amendments to this Contract shall be submitted to and finally resolved by arbitration in accordance with the WIPO Arbitration Rul. The arbitral tribunal shall consist of a [individual arbitrator] [panel of three arbitrators]. Any arbitration hearings must take place in [your preferred jurisdiction]. Both parties must agree on a language or languages to be used during the arbitration. To settle this dispute, controversy, or claim, [insert applicable jurisdiction] law shall apply.

Agreement Comparisons: Some Remarks

It is the responsibility of the arbitration boards and the contracts with arbitration agreements to be detailed and specific to avoid further litigations despite the commercial arbitration in the international context. This is because all commercial arbitration agreements contain appropriate provisions to refer controversies or other disputes in the claim of arbitration awards to the laws of the respective countries.

CONCLUSION

Commercial arbitration agreements look different in every country. In order to better illustrate the points made above, several sample agreements from the Hague, the UK, Singapore, the US, India, and Japan can be perused. However, it is noticed that all sample agreements have some key features which are common to all the agreements.

REFERENCES

Bingham, L. B. (1997). *On repeat players, adhesive contracts, and the use of statistics in judicial review of employment arbitration awards*. McGeorge Law Review, HeinOnline.

Born, G. B. (2021). *International Arbitration: Law and Practice*. Research Gate. books.google.com

Demaine, L.J. & Hensler, D.R. (2004). *Volunteering to Arbitrate Through Pre-dispute Arbitration Clauses: The Average Consumer's Experience, Law & contemporary practices*. Hein Online.

Drahozal, C. R. (2001). *Unfair Arbitration Clauses*. University of Illinois Law Review, Hein Online.

Eisenberg, T. (2007). Arbitration's Summer Soldiers: An Empirical Study of Arbitration Clauses in Consumer and Non-consumer Contracts. *University of Michigan Journal of Law Reform*. Hein Online.

Hensler, DR & D Khatam, D, (2017). Re-inventing arbitration: how expanding the scope of arbitration is re-shaping its form and blurring the line between private and public adjudication. *Nevada Law Journal*, Hein Online.

Nyarko, J. (2019). We'll See You in the Court! The lack of arbitration clauses in international commercial contracts. *International Review of Law and Economics*, Elsevier.

Paulsson, J. (2011). The Freshfields guide to arbitration clauses in international contracts. Research Gate.

Paulsson, J. (2011). *The Freshfields Guide to Arbitration Clauses in International Contracts*. Research Gate.

Rubino-Sammartano, M, (2014). *International Arbitration Law and Practice*. Research Gate.

Schmitz, A. J. (2010). *Legislating in the Light: Considering Empirical Data in Crafting Arbitration Reforms; Harvard*. Negotiation Law Review, Hein Online.

Schwartz, D. S. (1997). *Enforcing small print to protect big business: employee and consumer rights claims in an age of compelled arbitration*. Wisconsin Law Review, Hein Online.

Stipanowich, T.J. (2010). Arbitration: The new litigation. *University of Illinois, Law Review*. Hein Online.

Ware, S. J. (2006); The Case for Enforcing Adhesive Arbitration Agreements-With Particular Consideration of Class Actions and Arbitration Fees. *Journal of American Arbitration*. papers.ssrn.com

KEY TERMS AND DEFINITIONS

Hague Convention on Arbitration: I couldn't find any information on a Hague Convention specifically related to arbitration. However, there is a Hague Convention on Choice of Court Agreements that may be relevant.

Place of Arbitration: The place of arbitration refers to the legal seat or location where the arbitration proceedings are conducted

Standardized Form for Arbitration: A standardized form for arbitration is a pre-made template with terms of agreement that removes the requirement of drafting a new contract from scratch . For example, the International Chamber of Commerce (ICC) provides a standard ICC Arbitration Clause .

Structured clause: A structured clause in arbitration refers to a model dispute resolution clause that assists contracting parties in drafting alternative dispute resolution (ADR) clauses

The Hague Convention on Choice of Court: It is an international treaty concluded within the Hague Conference on Private International Law. It was concluded in 2005 and entered into force on 1 October 2015. The Convention aims to promote international legal certainty and predictability in cross-border commercial disputes by providing rules and procedures for honoring exclusive choice of court agreements between parties involved in international contracts. It provides a framework for the recognition and enforcement of such agreements.

Venue for Arbitration: The venue for arbitration determines the physical location where the proceedings are conducted for the convenience of the parties. This means that the invalidity of the substantive commercial contract does not affect the validity of the arbitration agreement, except if the arbitration agreement itself is directly impeached as void ab initio. Kompetenz-Kompetenz is a jurisdictional principle that empowers an adjudicating body to rule on issues related to its own jurisdiction.

Chapter 11
Conclusion:
Future of International Commercial Arbitration

ABSTRACT

The world of business has become small, interconnected, and driven by a desire for growth and profits. In all parts of the world, human desires and consumer appetites are demanding that the economy produce, distribute, and sell. The net result has been a rapid increase in commercial transactions: more negotiations, more contracts, more business obligations and, consequently, more disputes to be resolved. Most business disagreements, domestic or transnational, are resolved over the phone. Sometimes, a face-to-face meeting may be required; but negotiations are the main method of dispute resolution. Some intractable controversies survive. Whatever such methods may be called conciliation, mediation, med/arb, mini-trial, etc., they have created a new terminology for advocates and neutrals. From the foregoing discussions on identified issues, a concluding chapter attempts to provide the future of international commercial arbitration, the lessons from experiences, challenges to address and the summary and inferences.

DOI: 10.4018/978-1-6684-4040-7.ch011

BACKGROUND

The entire research investigation and discussions of the various chapters in this work have been to understand the procedures, practices and protocols of international commercial arbitration in view of the emerging popularity of the alternate dispute redressal mechanism, the world over. It is argued that arbitration has a great future, considering the hassles in the judicial court procedures and the pending litigations which would take years before cleared up fully, and unfortunately, newer litigations are flowing in speedily thereby the heaped-up files are continuing in the court cupboards. Therefore, greater thrust should be given to the settlement of commercial conflicts by adopting arbitrations. It is in this background that the previous narrations were attempted in this work and the present conclusion is presented.

This chapter aims to provide the following:

1. To describe the nature of business emerging and trending
2. To foresee the future of arbitration as an ADR
3. To wrap up the various discussions made in the context of the sketch of previous literature

The methodology used is descriptive narration and drawing inferences from the material collated from the secondary sources which are from the print media as well as website resources.

After discussing several of the issues relating to International Commercial Arbitration, a wrap-up is well within the context. Before the write-up is concluded a few studies are worth mentioning which have examined the recent trends in international commercial arbitration, the prospects for the global ethics in arbitration counselling, the business dispute settlement, the crisis in an international arbitration settlement, the conflicts in arbitration regulation, the future of arbitration as such and the perceptions of the status of commercial arbitration about two decades from now.

PREVIOUS RESEARCH LITERATURE

A survey of the special relationship between international commercial arbitration and soft law instruments was carried out (DiMatteo, LA; 2013). There are two most argued theories relating to international commercial arbitration in India. They are the delocalization theory and the seat theory which have been analysed (Pareek, NS; 2013). In the China International commercial court, the parties are expected to apply to the CICC for a court ruling on the preservation of property, evidence or conduct before or after the arbitration (Fei, L; 2020). There are regulations for ICA in the European Union for the relevant and applicable laws governing recognition and enforcement of the award and other applicable rules (Yuksel, B; 2011). In the Russian Federation, article 16 of the ICA Act provides for the validity of an arbitration agreement (Volkova, NG; 1999). The ICA has been successively adopted in nine jurisdictions in Asia, making the practice of ICA(Ali, SF & Ginsburg; 2013). It is reported that ICA is a very attractive field of alternate dispute resolution and more and more aspiring arbitrators and practitioners are showing significant interest (Strong, SL; 2012). The arbitration practitioners are confirming that the Covid-19 pandemic had a great impact on arbitration as a profession which is beyond the specific circumstances of the confinement (Huang, A; 2023). The ICA Convention has gone beyond the regional framework (Axmetovna, MA & Sherzod, o'gli'; 2023). There is a question of probing or otherwise of the corruption in ICA (Igbokwe, EO; 2023). There is a foreign community which is involved in the development of ICA with newer horizons for ICA and beyond (Berg, AJ; 2005). Cases of ICA have been analysed for corruption in international trade and international commercial arbitration (Syed, A; 2004). There are several business entities in international trade and the practice is such that the principles of procedure go beyond equal treatment (Trunk, A; 2023). In a discussion of the future of ICA, it is reported that by aligning well with institutional or ad hoc rules, ICA has a good future (Bermann, GA; 2021). Some predictability, even if not consensus, is expected for the future award to be treated as "stateless" (Paulsson, J; 1983). In the context of the African countries, it is reported that the business conflicts will increase in the future and the African law practitioners have a role to play in shaping and refining the applicable laws. (Sempasa, SL; 1992). The approach of publicising the arbitration rules will help in the degree of transparency for ICA in the future (Legum, B; 2005). In the future, the ICA cases will be subjected to more and more empirical research based on the focus and analysis of empirical data (Drahzal, CR; 2006). If the disputes are resolved in advance, it will help to create a "neutral playing field" increasing the comfort level of the parties to the conflict and will promote the future involvement of international commercial transactions (Gelander, JL; 1996). The dynamics of ICA practices have to be widened to make future research beneficial quickly (Bhatia, VK, et al ; 2012). The ability to create a legal environment has to be borne in mind by those involved in drafting any future convention (Strong, SI; 2014). Thus, umpteen studies have been carried out that provide insights into the past, present and future of commercial arbitration.

THE PROSPECTS FOR GLOBAL BUSINESS DISPUTES SETTLEMENT

The rapid dissolution of the Soviet bloc and the rejection of centralised economic planning; the willingness of the United States and its allies to enforce national boundaries with the backing of overwhelming and sophisticated military power; and the ever-increasing economic connectedness made possible by rapid communications. Travel, and currency transfers are just a few examples of the dramatic changes that have occurred in the world in recent years. A hunger for expansion and financial gain has shrunk the business world and made it more interdependent than ever. Production, distribution, and retailing are required everywhere due to rising demand from satisfied consumers. With more business happening all the time, there are more opportunities for disagreements to arise and more disputes to settle. Telephone conflict resolution is the norm in international and domestic business. Even though in-person meetings can be helpful, negotiations are typically the best way to settle a disagreement. There continues to be some irresolvable debates yet. With regard to the former, the emerging field of Alternative Dispute Resolution ("ADR") has seen some success, at least in the States. Whatever one wants to call them (conciliation, mediation, med/arb, mini-trial, etc.), the fact is that these processes have spawned a whole new vocabulary for lawyers and arbitrators. This is encouraging news because large organisations like governments, corporations, and the like need all the help they can get to keep out of court. They make the same kind of clumsy beginnings as other hierarchies do when trying to figure out how to conduct negotiations for resolving a dispute. Huge corporations have a hard time making decisions. Internal conflicts can be resolved using the same alternative dispute resolution (ADR) methods as external conflicts between businesses. The CEO, a designated government official, or the general in charge are more likely than a judge to resolve an internal dispute, in contrast to an inter-organizational dispute, which must be settled by a judge. If not, the arguments can be very heated. Legal disputes between parties have three possible avenues for resolution: going to court, submitting the dispute to arbitration, or severing ties altogether. There is now a more widespread agreement with the view that ADRs are more preferable to courts than such views in the past. The popularity of arbitration clauses in business contracts has grown as the courts have become even slower in their efforts to provide timely and reasonable decisions. Over ninety per cent of civil cases are dismissed or settled by attorneys, but only after protracted and costly legal wrangling. Businesses are getting poor service. The United States isn't the only country with a clumsy system for handling commercial disputes. Delays in delivering court determinations are increasing in Germany, Japan, and most other developed countries. When it comes to resolving international commercial disputes in a timely and objective manner, the transnational business community is well aware that national courts, especially those of a "foreign" party, are not desirable tribunals. Without a reliable international court system, international commercial arbitration is the best option. The following components should be present in any perfect model of international arbitration. Availability of (1) unbiased, expert administrative firms in all principal economic hubs. The arbitrators and national arbitration laws for each country would be shared between these organisations, which would work together in a cooperative fashion. In some situations, they would also offer secretarial services. (2) Relatively uniform, up-to-date rules of procedure would be issued and made public so that parties could make an educated choice of forum when drafting arbitral clauses and deciding on the location and administrative sponsors for their arbitration. It would be possible to select arbitrators based on their specific areas of expertise thanks to (3) a global pool of qualified and impartial arbitrators who have been educated in arbitral procedure and the applicable law and who have a wide range of professional experiences, (4) another major factor would be the ability of the parties to choose their own arbitrators. Arbitrators would be required to follow strict ethical guidelines and would be required to maintain their objectivity and independence, with limited exceptions. (5) In order for arbitrators and attorneys to do their jobs ethically, they would receive training from organisations dedicated to the field of arbitration and legal advocacy. (6) The most important economic hubs would have in place the New York Convention and cutting-edge national laws pertaining to international commercial arbitration. The various arbitral institutions could provide information on these laws and on any inconsistent practises. When a dispute arises between two parties who both agree to have it resolved through arbitration, the law in their home country must respect that decision. (7) The local business community or the national Voluntary Organizations Commission would provide sufficient funding for arbitration agencies. This is the pinnacle of international dispute resolution. Professor Bernardo Cremades criticised the current practise, highlighting an "increasing concern as to the complexity, the cost, and the delay of international arbitration." This concern was also voiced at the 1990 Congress of the International Council for Commercial Arbitration in Stockholm. The following are some examples of problems with the current system. A common problem with arbitration clauses is that (1) they don't automatically take effect. In order to have issues that could be decided by an administrative agency under institutional procedures (such as the appointment of arbitrators, whether a dispute is arbitrable, or whether an arbitrator should be challenged) decided, a party seeking arbitration must first go to a local court. Unfortunately, not all major urban centres have access to a governmental body willing to take such decisive action. The policies and procedures of some government organisations are hopelessly out dated. Most others receive insufficient funding. Even more people are held hostage by anti-modern regimes. (2) The party appointed arbitrator system, which is largely perpetuated by the 1978 UNCITRAL rules, creates a wide range of procedural problems, including numerous opportunities to stall or delay the arbitration, compounded by ambiguity as to whether either party's designated arbitrator will serve as an advocate or as an impartial arbitrator. (3) Not all organisations offer education and communication between themselves regarding competent arbitrators. When arbitrators hold sway over an organisation, training can become an end in itself, generating revenue for its own sake.. According to the American Arbitration Association, parties should have complete independence, and arbitrators should be made available on a non-exclusive basis whenever possible. There are businesses that only want to work with private, invitation-only panels of experts. (4) The right of a foreign party to obtain a speedy, fair arbitration in a country's jurisdiction can be unnecessarily hampered by the fact that some countries, such as Japan and Singapore, limit the participation of foreign counsel. Some countries don't allow foreigners to serve as arbitrators or bring in evidence and witnesses freely. We need to find these kinds of constraints and break them down. (5) Not all nations have adopted the New York Convention regulations or passed contemporary laws governing international commercial arbitration. The UNCITRAL model law is a helpful tool for some of these jurisdictions, as noted in the Canada-United States Law Journal. For international commercial arbitration to serve its purpose of resolving commercial disputes expeditiously and in accordance with the expectations of the parties, it is crucial that lawyers and business executives continue to receive training on the arbitral process. This will be easier to accomplish if and when such practices become more standardised. Training should emphasise advocacy and arbitrating within a standard framework rather than the nuances of specific procedures and national laws. Investment in bolstering such a system would be a no-brainer for the world's business community. In terms of institutional arbitration, the United States is currently far ahead of other countries. It's estimated that in 1990, the American Arbitration Association (AAA) presided over 68,000 arbitration proceedings. As far as it is known, the American Bar Association (ABA), still have a long way to go in terms of case volume arbitrated in other countries. Agencies need to make significant shifts, shifting their focus from development towards service. Numerous foreign arbitration organisations now have access to the AAA's International Arbitration Rules. These methods are cutting-edge with regard to global commercial arbitration and could be replicated elsewhere. Because of these inherent difficulties, judicial reform proceeds at a glacial pace. Due to its private, contract-based nature, international commercial arbitration should be more adaptable and capable of rapid self-reform, especially if parties are creative and willing to break free from the entrenched interests of arbitrators and international lawyers. The parties who agree to arbitrate can decide how the process will work. The procedures can still be innovated and updated.

Unlike investor-State arbitration, international commercial arbitration is not as heavily scrutinised, but it will still face difficulties in the future. These obstacles are numerous. Some of them have to deal with the past concerns about global settlements. The neutrality of the arbitrator is another important factor, along with the costs, delays, and unnecessary formality of the process. Although not new, issues of arbitration ethics, diversity, and transparency are gaining prominence. Other examples simply illustrate novel developments that are more or less extraneous to international arbitration but with which it must nonetheless contend. The data protection movement, the proliferation of settlement agreements, and the emergence of international commercial courts are just a few examples of the ways in which international arbitration has evolved over the past few decades.

REFLECTIONS ON PAST EVENTS

Mediation in international business deals has traditionally been studied in two ways: first, in terms of the procedure involved in settling specific disputes; and second, in comparison to other possible resolutions, such as transnational litigation or international commercial arbitration. Even though experts in dispute system design recommend thorough academic investigations of the international mediation regime as a whole, there are surprisingly few of these Disputes Systems Design (DSD). DSD is distinct from other fields of study in that it does not aim to promote or analyse any particular method or process for the purpose of improving dispute resolution, but rather it focuses on larger structural issues. The parties, policymakers, and academics involved in the resolution of cross-border business disputes can only gain a full understanding of the factors at play through the adoption of such a broad analytical framework. Despite the fact that a comprehensive Dispute Systems Design analysis is not intended here, extensive empirical research in this area of law, addresses crucial design issues in international commercial mediation. This chapter applies a default theoretic analysis to the field of international dispute resolution, specifically looking at how different moves influence individual and institutional choices in the context of international commercial mediation. As such, the discussion not only offers a fresh structural take on the relationship between litigation, arbitration, and mediation in the international commercial context, but also provides suggestions for improving the current system to better resolve disputes between companies based in different countries.

From Gary Born's optimistic and encouraging opening remarks, the entire workshop gained a positive and productive momentum (Wilmer Hale; 2023). International arbitration has been under fire recently, but as Gary Born pointed out, these complaints have been around for over two centuries. The practise of international arbitration, however, lives on and has even expanded. According to Born, international arbitration has been so effective because it is an expression of rights such as the freedom to enter into contracts and the freedom to associate with others, which are cornerstones of any functional society. States have not come up with a viable replacement for international arbitration, leading him to the conclusion that it is hard to picture a world without it.

Challenges to international arbitration's legitimacy, highlighting problems with decision-makers, counsel behaviour, the effectiveness of the proceedings, and domestic court oversight, among others were also issues that gained attention. Amidst these concerns, the current criticisms show that international arbitration is in crisis and offer some conclusions.

Decision-Makers

Parties to an international arbitration are often given the option to select the arbitrators who will ultimately render a ruling. Despite its prominence as a selling point for international arbitration, this feature has also been criticised. Particularly, sceptics have questioned the reliability of an award made by arbitrators who were privately appointed.

The option to choose the arbitrators involved greatly strengthens the process's credibility. In particular, it is the responsibility of the arbitrators appointed by the parties to ensure that the tribunal gives due weight to the evidence and arguments presented by those parties. This improves the likelihood that the losing party will accept and comply with the award, in addition to ensuring that the award accurately takes into consideration the views of the parties. Many countries as well as private parties have concurrence over this view.

To prevent parties from abusing their right to nominate arbitrators (by, for example, appointing unqualified individuals or coercing a nominee into resigning to delay proceedings), it was agreed that strict conflict rules, procedural controls on appointments, and rules of ethics are all essential. When asked how the legitimacy of arbitrators chosen by the parties themselves could be bolstered, it was suggested that the parties first agree on the President of the tribunal and then nominate the other two arbitrators with the consent of the President.

Ethics in Counselling

Counsel for the parties play a crucial role in international arbitration, but they may not always share the same values or ethical principles due to differences in legal traditions and cultural norms. However, the regulation of counsel conduct is difficult in practise, and the legitimacy of international arbitration is called into question, because there is no globally binding uniform code and no authority to enforce it.

Recently, there has been a growing consensus about the need to regulate and sanction unethical conduct by a counsel, a topic that has been the subject of much discussion in recent years. It is argued that the standards should centre on non-subjective concerns, such as the filing of frivolous challenges to arbitrators and arbitrator conflicts caused by the appointment of new counsel during the proceedings. Indeed, this is the stance taken by the two most well-known sets of guidelines, the International Bar Association's

Guidelines on Party Representation in International Arbitration and the London Court of International Arbitration's General Guidelines for the Parties' Legal Representatives.

The issue of who should regulate arbitration, was not agreed upon. Possible candidates include state or federal courts near the arbitration's seat, state or federal bar associations, arbitral institutions, or a global ethics counsel. It is accepted that the idea of arbitral institutions taking on the responsibility of standard-setting is beneficial. This strategy makes sense because it would promote experimentation and lead to improved standards in the long run. By approving its Guidelines in 2014, the LCIA was an early adopter of this strategy. Article 18.6 of the LCIA rules specifies that international tribunals are responsible for applying the standards. As the LCIA suggests, the "counsel conduct is a due process issue," and therefore, the courts have to ensure compliance with the rules.

The Proceedings Were Efficient

Critics say that international arbitration is too time-consuming and expensive. Sixty-eight per cent of respondents in the 2015 Queen Mary/White & Case International Arbitration Survey cited the high cost of arbitration as a major drawback, while 39 per cent said they lacked transparency into the effectiveness of the arbitrators, and 36 per cent complained about the slow pace of proceedings.

Using bifurcation and summary judgement motions was one strategy considered. When the issue at hand is narrow enough that it can be resolved quickly and on its own, it can be agreed that these procedures have the scope for improving efficiency. The inefficiencies of bifurcation and motions for summary judgement become more apparent when the issue is intertwined with other parts of the case and requires the same evidence and witnesses to be presented more than once. The most important factor in ensuring that bifurcation and motions increase efficiency is the discussion and establishment of clear ground rules at the outset of the proceedings by the parties and the tribunal. It was mentioned that Rule 41(5) of the ICSID Arbitration Rules is a successful summary judgement procedure.

A solution to the problem of arbitral tribunals taking too long to provide their awards is another issue. If an arbitral tribunal fails to submit a draft award within three months of the last substantive hearing or the last substantive post-hearing submission, the ICC will reduce the fees it pays to the tribunal.

This was announced in 2016. The discounts can range from 5% to 20% or higher, depending on how long the delay is. It is also possible for instituting a reporting mechanism requiring arbitrators to report to the parties on their progress periodically after a certain amount of time has passed, as well as asking arbitrators more questions about the amount of time they have available for the drafting of the award before appointing or confirming their appointment. The possibility of public disgrace serving as an incentive for the arbitrators to quickly issue their decision is significant.

Local Legal Supervision

The arbitration process has been criticised for allegedly being too divorced from the authority of domestic courts and laws. Because of this, the merits of having the courts monitor the arbitration process more closely is also considered and in vogue now in some countries. The New York Convention, the ICSID Convention, and national laws have all been cited as examples of instruments through which states have defined the functions of national courts and arbitral tribunals. Thus, if a more active role for the courts is deemed appropriate, it is for States to change the existing balance through legislation or treaties. But the flip side to this is that most national courts lack the time, resources, and technical expertise to adequately perform better monitoring. This is in fact a key factor contributing to arbitration's rise in favour and acceptance in many states.

When courts become more involved in the arbitration process, the line of demarcation becomes too thin. This runs counter to the very purpose of using arbitration as a means of resolving legal disputes. It would also run counter to the expectations of those who use international arbitration. It is viewed that in the 2015 Queen Mary/White & Case International Arbitration Survey, the "avoiding specific legal systems/national courts" was one of the most valuable characteristics of international arbitration.

A CRISIS IN INTERNATIONAL ARBITRATION

Though international arbitration has been criticised, especially in relation to the investor-state system, this does not mean it is in crisis or on the verge of extinction.

The International Court of Justice (ICC) and the International Centre for Settlement of Investment Disputes (ICSID) both report either stable or record-breaking levels of arbitration applications. The ICSID Convention has been signed by 153 states, while the New York Convention has 157. Even though some countries, like Ecuador, Bolivia, India, South Africa, and Indonesia, have backed out of Bilateral Investment Treaties that included investor-state arbitration provisions, the vast majority of countries, including vocal opponents of the practise like Venezuela, have not done so. Contracts between states and private parties and investment laws increasingly include arbitration provisions. Notable sceptics of investor-state arbitration include Brazil and a few other states.

The system is stronger for the criticisms that have been levelled at it. In order to make the arbitration process more effective and equitable, arbitral institutions have updated their rules and procedures. Among these are the LCIA (2014), ICC (2015), ICDR (2014), and SIAC (2016). Even the fifth revision of ICSID's Arbitration Rules has taken place. Concerning issues like conflicts of interest and counsel conduct, professional organisations like the International Bar Association have updated and adopted guidelines. These developments highlight the vitality of international arbitration. Arbitrators can prevent international arbitration from becoming obsolete by remaining open to constructive criticism. It will always be a respectable option for settling international disagreements, and often the best one.

Potential Problems and Benefits

There were difficulties within the framework of international arbitration. Despite this, the time was ripe for international arbitration to reach its full potential. Numerous young lawyers are making their mark in the field, and the groups they belong to are thriving.

There had never been so many arbitral centres across the world, and that there was "a thirst for knowledge" about arbitration that was being satisfied by specialised publications.

The international trade would expand, creating more potential for legal disputes and thus more work for arbitration practitioners. However, the importance of addressing the issues that plague international trade needs to be realised.

There is criticism of international commercial and investor-state arbitration that must be addressed, and that in order to overcome these obstacles, arbitrators and lawyers must return to basics and make effective use of established procedures.

The need for the parties to lock down the arbitral schedule for a case early on, the need to deal with jurisdictional issues equally promptly, and a series of helpful suggestions as to how to manage arbitrators are just some of the issues that gain attention, besides the costs and time. An award date as early as possible and feasible has to be announced and it has to be complied with for the credibility.

Investor-state Dispute Settlement (ISDS) is a complex topic. The arbitration community should be involved to have its influence on matters concerning them.

While the international arbitration system had its own problems, it also had some advantages due to the diversity of its participants and beneficiaries.

Many research investigations have shown that diverse teams make better decisions, and it' is encouraging to see data which reveal that the institutions are making progress on diversity issues.

Transnational Arbitration Patterns by Region

Given the global nature of arbitration, an overview of recent developments in Asia, Africa, the Americas, Europe, and Russia, is helpful and cross-institutional consolidation of international arbitration proceedings put forth by the Singapore International Arbitration Centre (SIAC) is significant.

There are developments taking place in the arbitration scenario of Asia. There are reforms carried out to the Swedish Arbitration Act by bringing changes to the system of arbitrator appointments that would make Swedish arbitration more attractive to international parties. Swedish efforts to make arbitration more accessible as also efforts to make choice-of-law provisions in contracts between parties clearer. The new rules became effective from 2019. Finland would adopt similar changes.

It needs to be noted that the European Union has dealt with BITs since the Achmea litigation. The trend towards a more permissive stance in intra-EU BITs had already begun before the decision was made. The decision that intra-EU BITs are in conflict with EU law raised more questions than it answered. After Achmea, courts around the world can be swamped with cases asking which law tribunals should be used in award disputes.

Hungary had previously challenged an award on Achmea grounds, and the decision will be useful to arbitration lawyers whether they choose to consult on the decision or use it in their own cases.

The arbitration in Latin America, on topics such as Argentina, Mexico, the latest developments with NAFTA, and the growth of investment courts in response to EU trade proposals, using the Canadian experience as an example is a development worth focusing on. The United States is the only state that does not use an investment court in any potential EU-US deal.

Some recent reforms to arbitration in Russia have taken place. The elimination of "pocket" arbitration centres had mitigated some potential dangers, and the reforms had led to unintended consequences. Conversely, it had not always been easy to get a licence for a new, reformed centre.

Due to the lengthy and tedious nature of the approval process, few foreign institutions sought permission to host arbitrations. Russia already had four arbitral institutions, and the country would not be getting any more centres, anytime soon. However, in terms of arbitration, both Hong Kong and Singapore are examples of cities that will be increasingly connected to Russia in the future..

Further, the recent changes made to the rules used by the Hong Kong International Arbitration Centre (HKIAC), as well as the HKIAC's extensive outreach efforts in both Russia and London were also gained centre stage after the follow up of attention on the changes in Asia. SIAC's proposed consolidation of arbitrations, wherein all institutions would share the same seat of arbitration was also focussed. Singapore being the seat of arbitration in the vast majority of SIAC arbitrations, similar situation existed in Hong Kong and other Asian cities also.

However, the litigants might use this as a strategic ploy and enforcement may not be easy always. There are concerns that the protocol developed is not executable as the ICC realised.

A lack of prescription on confidentiality gave all parties a choice on how to address confidentiality issues, which helped to make arbitral bodies more distinctive, based on different approaches to transparency in other jurisdictions, while also emphasising the need for comparative evidence from other jurisdictions to test any proposals for change.

There are increasing convergence of the two forms of dispute resolution, as well as the trends in courts competing with arbitration and the similarities between the two in addressing issues like joinder and consolidation. In order to illustrate the importance of the institutions selected, the judicial backing, and the administrative decisions made, there are several examples. Yet, in the Halliburton decision, an appellate ruling that centred on the arbitrator's obligation to disclose appointments in overlapping cases and how the resulting disclosure issues triggered the issue of bias, real or apparent. There is a need to consider the apparent bias in the arbitral awards and a question of what constitutes apparent bias, and whether it should be disclosed or not is also an issue. There are relative merits of objective and subjective tests for bias, but the English courts selects the subjective bias as an issue to be dealt with.

Conflicts in Regulations

There are conflicts in regulations which vary from country to country. In the case of Russia, there are shell companies which create difficulties in the realities of award enforcement. In Russia, there are difficulties in dealing with shell companies and special purpose vehicles (SPVs), as well as the enduring problem of piercing the corporate veil. In another country like Luxembourg, it can be noted as an ideal location for the enforcement of awards because of the country's status as a major financial centre, making it highly likely that the subject assets would be located there.

There are questions of including judicial insight into its deployment and how to get receivers appointed, by providing a focused exposition on the innovative use of receivership in enforcement proceedings. In some cases, insolvency powers, combined with litigation funding and insurance, can strengthen the enforcement process. At times, the asset recovery is the best way for enforcement. For utilizing this possibility, it is necessary to identify the assets, their locations, the ownership, the method of holding the assets etc.

What augurs well is the availability and use of the electronic tools for enforcement. The use of artificial intelligence helps in the analysis and review of documentation in the enforcement of the award.

Consequences

Facilitating greater trade and long-term economic growth and development among Commonwealth countries is a top priority for the organisation. The expansion and improvement of the economy is largely due to international trade. Nonetheless, disagreements are inevitable in any kind of commercial transaction. For small and medium-sized enterprises (SMEs), which would rather self-hedge than take the risk associated with cross-border trade, the lack of clarity surrounding how to manage the dispute resolution risk has been identified as a trade barrier. Foreign direct investment necessitates a dispute resolution regime that is fair, quick, and inexpensive. One option for resolving disagreements that may arise in international trade is international commercial arbitration. International commercial arbitration has a number of benefits, including the ability for disputing parties to select impartial arbitrators, the enforceability of the resulting arbitral awards (thanks to the 1958 Convention on the Recognition and Enforcement of Foreign Arbitral Awards (New York Convention), which has been signed by 161 countries), and the protection of the parties' privacy.

It is interesting to note some of the insights from a research on International Commercial Arbitration. A research was commissioned at a meeting of senior officials of Commonwealth Law Ministries in October 2018 to assess the state of international commercial arbitration and to survey the contemporary landscape of commercial arbitration across all Commonwealth member countries. The terms of reference for the investigation were to examine the socio-economic benefits of international commercial arbitration. Thus the study of International Commercial Arbitration in the Commonwealth jurisdictions, attempted to determine what obstacles may be preventing local businesses from using international commercial arbitration as a dispute resolution mechanism, and to suggest ways to overcome these obstacles while respecting diversity and taking into account the unique requirements of small, developing Commonwealth nations. As can be seen in research results, the Black letter law, law in context, and comparative law analysis, as well as the compilation of national country reports covering all Commonwealth jurisdictions, as well as stakeholder surveys and interviews, were used in this study to evaluate the difficulties of international commercial arbitration. Ten barriers to the expansion of international commercial arbitration within the Commonwealth have been identified by the researchers. The overall effectiveness of the applicable arbitration framework is one of the primary obstacles to the widespread use of international commercial arbitration in the Commonwealth. Many Commonwealth nations' approaches to international commercial arbitration fall short of current standards of practise. In particular, the high costs associated with such proceedings can discourage their use. 58% of Commonwealth countries do not have an international arbitration framework that is up to date with current best practises. Just a handful of nations lack any kind of comprehensive arbitration law. Thirty per cent of Commonwealth countries have also yet to ratify the New York Convention. Foreign direct investment (FDI) and trade revenue could be lost if a country's business community didn't have access to a modern dispute resolution regime, such as an effective international arbitration framework. The rising costs of international commercial arbitration have been identified as one of the foremost challenge in stakeholder surveys, interviews, other international arbitration surveys, and the literature. The judiciary, the business community and users, and the legal profession have been identified as the three key stakeholder groups most in need of gaining a deeper understanding of international commercial arbitration. Businesses, especially small and medium-sized enterprises (SMEs), in general lack familiarity with international commercial arbitration. The legal profession lacks understanding and expertise in international commercial arbitration, which discourages foreign direct investment and the use of international commercial arbitration by businesses. This is due to the fact that the study of international commercial arbitration is still a novel topic on (Commonwealth) university curricula. Consequently, many lawyers are unlikely to have learned about international commercial arbitration in school. It has been noted that the quality and diversity of arbitrators are problems for international commercial arbitration in the Commonwealth. Furthermore, many international arbitration practitioners do not have a sufficient caseload to acquire the necessary in-depth expertise regarding international commercial arbitration. Stakeholder interviews and survey responses from this research show that there is some apprehension about the quality of arbitrators used in international commercial arbitration. The lack of arbitrators with specialised industry knowledge contributes to the quality concern, among other things. The lack of diversity within the international commercial arbitration community has been identified as an issue hindering the development and widespread use of international commercial arbitration by the international commercial arbitration community itself. The inability of the international arbitration system to perceive and give full weight to geographical or cultural factors that might have informed the dealings of the disputing parties is hampered by the lack of diversity in the international commercial arbitration community, particularly among arbitrators. Today's dispute resolution relies heavily on the use of technology. The use of video conferencing and hearing room technology, AI, and cloud storage can all aid in the smooth running of arbitration. Important issues to consider in this context include users' technological literacy, ease of access to technology, and online safety. However, the impact of arbitration on the evolution of the law may be seen as a challenge, and so stakeholders are not yet making full use of technology to aid in international commercial arbitration. The secretive nature of arbitration may impede the effective application and interpretation of the law, which in turn may slow down the process of law reform. As a result, the study proposed seven solutions to the problems that have been identified. First and foremost, every country in the Commonwealth ought to have a cutting-edge, internationally commercial arbitration framework, updated to include best practise and improve efficiency at a reasonable cost. Cost-effectiveness can be improved in a number of ways, as outlined in the study. These include making sure that legal aid is available for businesses and for international commercial arbitration, which can reduce costs. The business community, especially small and medium-sized enterprises (SMEs), the legal profession, government officials (in particular policy and legal advisers), and the Commonwealth Secretariat should all be made more familiar with international commercial arbitration. Commonwealth member jurisdictions should collaborate with all stakeholders to develop and promote such a strategy. Capacity-building calls for a multifaceted response; in particular: Commonwealth jurisdictions should send a clear signal to and collaborate with their universities, law societies, bar councils, and business communities about their expected respective roles regarding capacity building in the international commercial arbitration space and the use of technology to facilitate international dispute resolution. The study emphasised the significance of diversity within the international commercial arbitration community and laid out a number of possible actions which actively foster diversity, such as diversity reporting, a Commonwealth diversity initiative, and the availability of scholarships to gain proficiency in international dispute resolution, and in particular international commercial arbitration. Modifications to existing regulations, as well as the introduction of new mechanisms and initiatives, could improve the environment for international commercial arbitration in the Commonwealth. Common Wealth Members should ease restrictions on the participation of foreign counsel in arbitration, tightening up on visas and taxes, and informing stakeholders about the effects of the European Union's General Data Protection Regulation (GDPR). Other mechanisms and initiatives include the promotion of online dispute resolution platforms, the formation of a Commonwealth cross-border dispute resolution regime, and the establishment of an association of Commonwealth arbitral institutions.

FUTURE AREAS OF RESEARCH

International Commercial Arbitration is currently facing several challenges as it moves ahead. Some of these challenges relate to the concerns that have been with this field for a long time like the duration for settlement, costs of the processes and procedures, unwarranted formalities, impartiality of the arbitrators, and judicial supervision being invited. There are also other issues like the ethics of arbitrators, the diversity of disputes, and the dynamics of transparency and confidentiality. These issues have been in existence over time but emerged with greater urgency. International Commercial Arbitration has to cope with these problems in a newer context and environment. The current landscape has other issues arising from technological developments and movements like data protection. The questions of settlement agreements and international commercial courts are also very relevant.

International Commercial Arbitration depends more on advocacy in written form. But litigation is done more based on oral arguments. Therefore, it is often observed that very few practitioners and arbitrators have received any formal training in how to research and present written arguments in this unique area of law. Newcomers to the field of arbitration are disadvantaged as the authorities of law used in international commercial arbitration are unique. Novices often do not know how to source materials even when they are knowledgeable that materials are available and found out. Therefore, researchers have to focus on addressing the concerns by investigating the different aspects of this phenomenon.

The questions that spring up from the above scenario are worth researching and making insights available to all stakeholders. There are resources available that can help in practical guidance on how to conduct research in international commercial arbitration. Even non-specialists can also gather insight into this difficult and unique area of law. Such resources combine a "how-to" guide with bibliographic information providing an explicit and practical guide to research methods rather than listing the sources of arbitration law.

A complete study of the previous research and the findings delineated can help to frame many new researchable questions for the future. For future endeavours of research, adequate time has to be devoted to scanning the detailed review of the literature available in the field of the different aspects of International Commercial Arbitration.

CONCLUSION

A growing awareness is being felt everywhere to launch the ADR as commercial transactions skyrocket around the world, in response to the growing number of disputes in various countries and the judicial system's inability to deliver justice. Increased trade and long-term economic growth and development are high on the agendas of the Commonwealth nations. The importance of international trade and business activities to economic growth and development is also recognised. However, it is well-known that disputes can arise from business transactions. For small and medium-sized enterprises (SMEs), which would rather self-hedge than take the risk associated with cross-border trade, the lack of clarity surrounding how to manage the dispute resolution risk has been identified as a trade barrier. Foreign direct investment necessitates a dispute resolution regime that is fair, quick, and inexpensive. While the future of arbitration in international commercial activities is bright, there is a greater need to learn from past experiences. Multiple obstacles in international commercial arbitration's systems, procedures, and protocols necessitate a contextual review.

REFERENCES

Ali, S. F., & Ginsburg, T. (2013). *International commercial arbitration in Asia*. SSRN. papers.ssrn.com

Axmetovna, MA & Sherzod, O. (2023). Arbitration (Multilateral and Bilateral Agreements in the field of Commercial Arbitration. *World Bulletin*.

Berg, A.J. (2005). *New Horizons for International Commercial Arbitration and Beyond*. torrossa.com

Bermann, G. B. (2021). *The Future of International Commercial Arbitration*. Columbia University. scholarship.law.columbia.edu

Bhatia, V. K. (2012). *Discourse and practice in international commercial arbitration*. Research Gate.

DiMatteo, L. A. (2013). Soft law and the principle of fair and equitable decision making in international contract arbitration. *The Chinese Journal of Comparative Law*. academic.oup.com

Drahozal, C. R. (2006). *Arbitration by the Numbers: The State of Empirical Research on International Commercial Arbitration*. Research Gate. academic.oup.com

Fei, L. (2020). Innovation and Development of the China international commercial court. *The Chinese Journal of Comparative Law*. academic.oup.com

Gelander, J. L. (1996). *Judicial review of international arbitral awards: Preserving independence in international commercial arbitrations, Marq.* Law Review, Hein Online.

Huang, A. (2023). *Development of International Commercial Arbitration in Virtual Reality During the COVID-19 Pandemic, International Law and Development in the Global.* Springer.

Igbokwe, E. O. (2023). *Dealing with Bribery and Corruption in International Commercial Arbitration: To Probe or Not to Probe.* Research Gate. books.google.com

Legum, B. (2005). *Investment Treaty Arbitration's Contribution to International Commercial Arbitration.* search.proquest.com

Pareek, N. S. (2013). International commercial arbitration in India: governing law issues. *Uniform Law Review.* academic.oup.com

Paulsson, J. (1983). Delocalisation of international commercial arbitration: when and why it matters. *International & Comparative Law Quarterly*

Sayed, A. (2004). *Corruption in international trade and commercial arbitration.* Torrossa. torrossa.com

Sempasa, S.L. (1992). Obstacles to international commercial arbitration in African countries. *International & Comparative Law Quarterly.*

Strong, S.I. (2012). Navigating the Borders Between International Commercial Arbitration and US Federal Courts: A Jurisprudential GPS. *Journal of Dispute Resolution,* Hein Online

Strong, S. I. (2014). *Beyond international commercial arbitration-the promise of international commercial mediation.* Washington University Journal of Law & Policy, Hein Online.

Trunk, A, (2023). *Some Remarks on International Commercial Arbitration in the Region of the Caucasus and Central Asia.* Brill.

Vilkova, N. G. (1999). *Practice of the International Commercial Arbitration Court at the Chamber of Commerce and Industry of the Russian Federation.* academic.oup.com

Yuksel, B, (2011). The Relevance of the Rome I Regulation to International Commercial Arbitration in the European Union. *Journal of Private International Law.* Taylor & Francis.

KEY TERMS AND DEFINITIONS

Conflict Management and Conflict Resolution: These are two different approaches to dealing with conflicts. Conflict management refers to the way we identify and handle conflicts fairly and efficiently. The goal is to minimize the potential negative impacts that can arise from disagreements and increase the odds of a positive outcome. Conflict management does not imply conflict resolution. Conflict management minimizes the negative outcomes of conflict and promotes the positive outcomes of conflict with the goal of improving learning in an organization. On the other hand, conflict resolution is defined as the reduction, termination, or elimination of conflict. Conflict management helps the parties to create an open-mindedness within their relationship, which can often lead to resolution as the parties learn to listen to each other and be more open to other experiences. Conflict management doesn't resolve conflicts, terminate, or reduce them – at least it isn't directly meant to.

Dispute System Design Analysis: ADR system design helps to match the appropriate dispute resolution process with the type of dispute and the culture of an organization. The analysis produces a dispute resolution structure that is both appropriate for the organization and cost-effective.

Ethics in Counselling: It refers to the standards of conduct based on professional values that help safeguard both the client and the therapist. These values almost certainly influence how a counsellor approaches their work. Following these values might feel natural and even intuitive, and it might feel as though they don't warrant closer examination. However, when practicing counselling or psychotherapy, working without a defined counselling code of ethics is a bit like sailing a ship without using a compass. There are a variety of professional organizations that have published frameworks to help counsellors navigate the challenging and disorienting landscape of ethics. Members of these organizations are often recommended or required to adhere to a framework, so if you belong to one of them and you're not familiar with their respective code of ethics, this should be your first port of call. However, these ethical frameworks are also often available online for anyone to read, and so you don't need to join an organization to adhere to its principles. Some personal moral qualities that are a part of counselling include empathy, which refers to the ability to understand the client's feelings from the client's viewpoint, and integrity, which refers to being honest and having strong moral values.

Legal Supervision: It refers to the supervisory power of the courts. It is one of the legal principles in most legal systems in the world. Supervision features in contemporary legal profession regulatory frameworks as a component of both legal education and lawyers' professional responsibility obligations. The supervision aspects of contemporary legal education frameworks are markedly different in Australia, the United Kingdom, and the United States.

Med-Arb: Med-Arb is a hybrid mediation-arbitration approach that combines the benefits of both techniques. In this process, parties first attempt to collaborate on an agreement with the help of a mediator. If the mediation ends in impasse, or if issues remain unresolved, the parties can then move on to arbitration. The mediator can assume the role of arbitrator (if qualified) and render a binding decision quickly, or an arbitrator can take over the case after consulting with the mediator.

Mini-Trial: A mini-trial is not so much a trial as it is a settlement process. Each party presents their highly summarized case. At the end of the mini-trial, the representatives attempt to settle the issue.

Telephone Conflict Resolution: It is the process of resolving conflicts or disputes between customers and companies over the phone. It is essential for people who communicate predominantly on the telephone, as communicating in this way is very different from face-to-face interactions. The training will build a structured approach to managing challenging calls, help de-escalate and develop resolution skills. Conflict resolution means solving the problem at hand and deciding on an outcome or action that both parties agree to. In some cases, conflict resolution involves the two parties agreeing to disagree. Companies with effective strategies for handling these situations and skilled customer service agents capable of diffusing tension can turn difficult customer interactions into opportunities to exceed expectations, influence the customer's perception of their business, and improve the customer experience to boost customer retention.

Compilation of References

Ademowo, J. (2015). Conflict Management in Traditional African Society. Research Gate.

Ademowo, J. (2015). *Conflict Management in Traditional African Society*. Research Gate.

Agarwal, A. (2022). *A brief history of commercial arbitrations*. Linkedin. Akram, W. (2016). *Arbitration as an alternative method of settling international business disputes*. United States Documents. ; https://documents.pub/document/arbitration-as-an-alternative-method-of

Al Dalaien, M. N. (2021). Problems of Proving the Electronic Arbitration Agreement. Taylor & Francis. https://www.tandfonline.com

Alford, R. P. (2003). *The American Influence on International Arbitration*. Ohio State Journal on Dispute Resolution, Hein Online.

Ali, S. F., & Ginsburg, T. (2013). *International commercial arbitration in Asia*. SSRN. papers.ssrn.com

Anusornsena, A, (2012). *Arbitrability and Public Policy in Regard to the Recognition and Enforcement of Arbitral Award in International Arbitration: the United States, Europe, Africa, Middle East*. Digital Commons. digitalcommons.law.ggu.edu.

Arrowsmith, S, (2004). *Public procurement: An appraisal of the UNCITRAL model law as a global standard*. International & Comparative Law Quarterly, cambridge.org

Axmetovna, MA & Sherzod, O. (2023). Arbitration (Multilateral and Bilateral Agreements in the field of Commercial Arbitration. *World Bulletin*.

Ayittey, G. (2014). *African Solutions, African Problems, Real Meaning*. Research Gate.

Baboolal, R. (2022). *A Review of Judicial Enforcement of Arbitral Awards in South Africa, Conflict Resolution Quarterly*. Wiley Online Library.

Bachand, F, & Gélinas, F, (2013). *The UNCITRAL model law after twenty-five years: Global perspectives on international Commercial Arbitration*. UN.

Bambach, L.A. (2009). The Enforceability of Arbitration Decisions Made by Muslim Religious Tribunals: Examining the Beth Din Precedent. *Journal of Law and Religion*, cambridge.org

Bandle, AL, & Theurich, S, (2011). Alternative Dispute Resolution and Art-Law-A New Research Project of the Geneva Art-Law Centre. *Journal of International Commercial Law & Technology,* Hein Online.

Baniassadi, M.R. (1992). Do mandatory rules of public law limit choice of law in international commercial arbitration. *International Tax & Business Law*, HeinOnline.

Bantekas, I. (2015). *An introduction to international arbitration, Books*. Google. Com. doi:10.1017/CBO9781316275696

Barraclough, A. & Waincymer, J. (2005). *Melbourne Journal of international Arbitration.* search.informit.org.

Bennett, D.R. & Hodgson, M.A. (2017). *Confidentiality in Arbitration.* A Principled Approach, Canadian Legal Information Institute. https://www.canlii.org.

Berends, A. J. (1998). *The UNCITRAL Model Law on cross-border insolvency: a comprehensive overview*. Tulsa Journal of International & Comparative Law, Hein Online.

Berg, A.J. (2005). *New Horizons for International Commercial Arbitration and Beyond*. torrossa.com

Bermann, G. B. (2021). *The Future of International Commercial Arbitration*. Columbia University. scholarship.law.columbia.edu

Bersani, M. D. (1993). *The Enforcement of Arbitration Awards in China*. Journal International Arbitration, HeinOnline. doi:10.54648/JOIA1993013

Bhagner, H. (2001). *Confidentiality—A Fundamental Principle in International*. Calis. calis.edu.cn http://fulltext.calis.edu.cn

Bhatia, V. K. (2012). *Discourse and practice in international commercial arbitration*. Research Gate.

Binder, P. (2019). *International commercial arbitration and mediation in UNCITRAL Model Law jurisdictions*. UN. books.google.com

Bingham, L. B. (1997). *On repeat players, adhesive contracts, and the use of statistics in judicial review of employment arbitration awards*. McGeorge Law Review, HeinOnline.

Böckstiegel, K. H. (1998). *An introduction to the new German arbitration act based on the UNCITRAL model law*. Arbitration International.

books.google.com

Born, G. B. (2020). *International Commercial arbitration* books.google.com

Born, G. B. (2021). *International Arbitration: Law and Practice*. Research Gate. books.google.com

Born, G. B. (2014). *The law governing international arbitration agreements: An international perspective*. Hein Online.

Born, G. B. (2015). *International arbitration: cases and materials, Books*. Google. Com.

Born, G. B. (2021). *International arbitration: law and practice, Books*. Google. Com.

Brill. (2021); *Arbitrary Judicial Interference in Human Rights Guaranteed*. Brill. https://brill.com

Brody, R. (1991). *The United Nations Creates a Working Group on Arbitrary*. Cambridge University Press & Assessment. https://www.cambridge.org

Brown, J. C. P. (2021). *The Protection of Confidentiality in Arbitration*. London Metropolitan University, http://repository.londonmet.ac.uk

Brunet, E. (1987). *Questioning the quality of alternate dispute resolution*. Tulsa Law Review, Hein Online.

Buchanan, M. A. (1988). *Public policy and international commercial arbitration*. American Business Law Journal, Hein Online. doi:10.1111/j.1744-1714.1988.tb01153.x

Bucy, D. R. (2010). *How to best protect party rights: the future of interim relief in international commercial arbitration under the amended UNCLTRAL model law American University International Law Review*. Hein Online.

Cabral, H. (2018); 'Law and Practice of Commercial Arbitration in Sri Lanka https://ft.lk/opinion/-Law-and-Practice-of-Commercial-Arbitration-in.ln

Caldwell, C. A. (2012). *Cultural Evolution and Perpetuation of Arbitrary*. PLOS. https://journals.plos.org

Cambridge University Press. (2021). *Ruler of Qatar v. International Marine Oil Company, Ltd., International Arbitrations*. Cambridge University Press.

Campbell, C. M. (2018). *U.S.A. vs. the World: Right to Public Access of Court Records*. University of South Carolina. https://scholarcommons.sc.edu

Campbell, M. (2021). *How to determine the law governing an arbitration agreement*. Research Information. bris.ac.uk https://research-information

Carbonneau, T.E. (2003). The Exercise of Contract Freedom in the Making of Arbitration Agreement. *Vanderbilt Journal of Transnational Law*, Hein Online..

Chendil, K. (2021). *The Governing Law of Arbitration Agreement: Settling the Unsettled*. SCC Online. https://www.scconline.com

Cheung, S.O. (1999). Critical factors affecting the use of alternative dispute resolution processes in construction. *International Journal of Project Management*, Elsevier.

Chiatoh, D. (2003). on the Afo-a-Kom Yahoo Chat. *Group*.

Choi, S. (1995). Judicial enforcement of arbitration awards under the International Centre for Settlement of Investment Disputes and New York Conventions. Online *New York University Journal of International Law and Politics*.

Chua-Rubenfeld, S, (2019). Religious Arbitration of Federal Rights. *The Yale Law Journal.*

Chukwumerije, O. (1994). *Choice of law in international commercial.* eLibrary. arbitration. elibrary.ru

Cliff, J. (2004). UNCITRAL Model Law on Cross-Border Insolvency-A Legislative Framework to Facilitate Coordination and Cooperation in Cross-Border Insolvency. *eHein Online.*

Cole, S. R. (1995). *Incentives and Arbitration: The Case Against Enforcement of Executory Arbitration Agreements Between Employers and Employees.* UMKC Law Review, Hein Online.

Collins v. Collins, (1858); 28 LJ Ch 184; 53 ER 916

Cona, F. A. (1997). *Application of Online Systems in Alternative Dispute Resolution.* Buffalo Law Review, Hein Online.

Craig, P. (2000). *International Chamber of Commerce Arbitration.* Oxford Press.

Craig, W. L. (1995). *Some trends and developments in the laws and practice of international commercial arbitration.* Texas International Law Journal, HeinOnline.

Cremades, B. M. (2013). The Principle of Confidentiality in Arbitration: A Necessary Condition. *Korea Science.* https://koreascience.kr

Croff, C. (1982). *The Applicable Law in an International Commercial Arbitration: Is It Still a Conflict of Laws Problem? The International Lawyer.* JSTOR.

Cullinan, T. (1998). *Contracting for an Expanded Scope of Judicial Review in Arbitration Agreements, Vanderbilt Law.* Review, Hein Online.

Day, W. (2021). *Applicable Law and Arbitration Agreements.* Cambridge.

Delgado, R. (1985). Fairness and formality: Minimizing the risk of prejudice in alternative dispute resolution. *Wisconsin Law Review*, Hein Online.

Demaine, L.J. & Hensler, D.R. (2004). *Volunteering to Arbitrate Through Pre-dispute Arbitration Clauses: The Average Consumer's Experience, Law & contemporary practices.* Hein Online.

Dessemontet, F. (1996). *Arbitration and Confidentiality.* UNIL. https://www.unil.ch

Diamant, N. J. (2000). Conflict and Conflict Resolution in China Beyond Mediation-Centered Approaches. *The Journal of Conflict Resolution*, *44*(4), 523–546. doi:10.1177/0022002700044004006

DiMatteo, L. A. (2013). Soft law and the principle of fair and equitable decision making in international contract arbitration. *The Chinese Journal of Comparative Law.* academic.oup.com

Dindjer, H. (2021). *What Makes an Administrative Decision Unreasonable.* Wiley. https://onlinelibrary.wiley.com

Domke, M. (2023);Commercial arbitration law |Britannicahttps://www.britannica.com/topic/commercial-arbitration

Donovan, D.U. (1994). International commercial arbitration and public policy. *New York University Journal of International Law & Policy*

Drahozal, C. R. (2006). *Arbitration by the Numbers: The State of Empirical Research on International Commercial Arbitration*. Research Gate. academic.oup.com

Drahozal, C. R. (2001). *Unfair Arbitration Clauses*. University of Illinois Law Review, Hein Online.

Edwards, H.T. (1985). Alternative dispute resolution: Panacea or anathema. *Harvard Law Review*. Hein Online.

Egonu, M. I. (2022). *Confidentiality*. Jus Mundi. https://jusmundi.com

Eisenberg, T. (2007). Arbitration's Summer Soldiers: An Empirical Study of Arbitration Clauses in Consumer and Non-consumer Contracts. *University of Michigan Journal of Law Reform*. Hein Online.

Fabian, K. (2021). *Confidentiality in international commercial arbitration*. Central European University. https://www.etd.ceu.edu

Fei, L. (2020). Innovation and Development of the China international commercial court. *The Chinese Journal of Comparative Law*. academic.oup.com

Flecke-Giammarco, G, (2015). CISG and Arbitration Agreements. *Korea Science*.

Fouchard, P. & Goldman, B. (1999). *On International Commercial Arbitration*.

Gabriel, H. D. (2019). *Uniform Law Review*. The UNCITRAL Model Law on Electronic Transferable Records. academic.oup.com

Gaillard, (2010), Legal theory of international arbitration

Garcia de Enterria, J, (1989). The Role of Public Policy in International Commercial Arbitration. *Law & Policy International Business*, Hein Online.

Gelander, J. L. (1996). *Judicial review of international arbitral awards: Preserving independence in international commercial arbitrations, Marq*. Law Review, Hein Online.

Gharavi, H & Liebscher, C, (2002). *The International Effectiveness of the Annulment of an Arbitral Award: Challenge in International Commercial Arbitration*. books.google.com.

Gisbergen, D. (1992). *Assignment of Rights and Agreement to Arbitrate*. Oxford University Press. https://academic.oup.com

Glover, J. M. (2006). *Beyond Unconscionability: Class Action Waivers and Mandatory Arbitration Agreements*. Vanderbilt Law Review, Hein Online.

Goel, S. (2015); International Commercial Arbitration, https://www.researchgate.net

Goss. (1995). *An introduction to alternative dispute resolution*. Alberta Law Review, Hein Online.

Gowak, S.M. (2008). *Alternative dispute resolution in Ethiopia-a legal framework.* African Research Review.

Hensler, DR & D Khatam, D, (2017). Re-inventing arbitration: how expanding the scope of arbitration is re-shaping its form and blurring the line between private and public adjudication. *Nevada Law Journal*, Hein Online.

Hensler, D. R. (2003). *Our courts, ourselves: how the alternative dispute resolution movement is re-shaping our legal system.* Penn State Law Review, Hein Online.

Herrmann, G. (1985). *The UNCITRAL Model Law–its background, salient features and purposes.* Arbitration international. academic.oup.com

Holbrook, J.R., & Gray, L.M., (1995). *Annexed Alternative Dispute Resolution Contemporary Law.* Hein Online.

Hollering, M. F. (1986). *The uncitral model law on international commercial arbitration, The International Lawyer.* JSTOR.

Huang, A. (2023). *Development of International Commercial Arbitration in Virtual Reality During the COVID-19 Pandemic, International Law and Development in the Global.* Springer.

Hunter, J. M. H. (1985). *The UNCITRAL Model Law*. International Business Law, Hein Online.

Igbokwe, E. O. (2023). *Dealing with Bribery and Corruption in International Commercial Arbitration: To Probe or Not to Probe.* Research Gate. books.google.com

Illankoon, I. (2022). Causes of disputes, factors affecting dispute resolution and effective alternative dispute resolution for Sri Lankan construction industry. *International Journal, Taylor & Francis.*

Islam, M.Z. (2012). Provision of Alternative Dispute Resolution Process in Islam. *Journal of Business and Management.*

Jacob, D. (1979). *Organization of American States.* OAS. http://www.oas.org

Jossey-Bass. (2005). Arbitration. The Handbook of Dispute Resolution. Research Gate.

Jye, I. B. (2022). *How are arbitrary and deliberate decisions similar and different?* Oxford University Press., https://academic.oup.com

Kaufman, I. R. (1990). *Reform for a system in crisis: alternative dispute resolution in the federal courts.* Fordham Law Review, Hein Online.

Khan, T. (2021). *The who, why and when of confidentiality in Arbitration.* SCC Online. https://www.scconline.com

Kimani, E. (2021). *A Critique of The Law Governing Capacity of Parties to Arbitrate.* Social Science Research Network. https://papers.ssrn.com

Kleinheisterkamp, J. (2009). *The impact of internationally mandatory laws on the enforceability of arbitration agreements.* World Arbitration & Mediation Review. papers.ssrn.com

Kojovic, T. (2001). Court Enforcement of Arbitral Decisions on Provisional Relief How Final is Provisional? *Journal of International Arbitration.*

Kurkela, M.S. & Turunen, S. (2010). *Due process in international commercial arbitration.* Research Gate.

Lando, O. (1985). The lex mercatoria in international commercial arbitration. *International & Comparative Law Quarterly.*

Legum, B. (2005). *Investment Treaty Arbitration's Contribution to International Commercial Arbitration.* search.proquest.com

Liang, B.A. (1998). Understanding and applying alternative dispute resolution methods in modern medical conflicts. *Journal of Legal Medicine.*

Lide, E. C. (1996). ADR and cyberspace: the role of alternative dispute resolution in online commerce, intellectual property and defamation. Ohio State Journal on Dispute Resolution.

Lieberman, J.K. & Henry, J.F. (1986). Lessons from the alternative dispute resolution movement. *The University of Chicago Law Review.*

Lim, C. (2022). International Commercial Arbitration. *LibGuides.* https://libguides.nus.edu.sg/commercialarbitration/books

Lord, E.L. (1892). *International Arbitration.* Sage.

Lynch, K. & Lynch, K.L. (2003). *The forces of economic globalization: Challenges to the regime of international commercial arbitration.*

Mann, F. A. (1967). *British Year Book of International Law, 1967, State contracts and international arbitration.* Hein Online.

Maoz, U. (2019). *Neural precursors of decisions that matter—an ERP study.* eLife Sciences. https://elifesciences.org

Mayer, P. (1986). *Mandatory rules of law in international arbitration.* Arbitration International. academic.oup.com

McCormack, G & Wai Yee, W (2018). The UNCITRAL model law on cross-border insolvency comes of age: new times or new paradigms. *Texas International Law Journal*, Hein Online.

McNerney. (1986). ME & and CA Esplugues. International Commercial Arbitration: the UNCITRAL Model Law, Boston College of International and Comparative Law. Hein Online.

Meghas. (2021). *International Commercial Arbitration - Legal Services India.* Legal Services in India. https://www.legalservicesindia.com/article/2196/International

Menkel-Meadow, C. (2016) *Is ODR ADR? Reflections of an ADR Founder.* From 15th ODR Conference, The Hague, The Netherlands.

Menkel-Meadow, C. (2018). Ethics in alternative dispute resolution: New issues, no answers from the adversary conception of lawyers' responsibilities, Mediation, taylorfrancis.com.

Metzloff, T. B. (1992). *Alternative dispute resolution strategies in medical malpractice.* Alaska Law Review, HeinOnline.

Mevorach, I. (2011). On the road to universalism: a comparative and empirical study of the UNCITRAL Model Law on Cross-Border Insolvency. *European Business Organization Law Review (EBOR).*

Miles, T. J. (1983). *Neither Arbitrary nor Capricious.* International Budget Partnership. https://internationalbudget.org

Mistelis, L. A. (2013). Award as an investment: The value of an arbitral award or the cost of non-enforcement. *International Centre for Settlement of Investment Disputes Review*. academic.oup.com

Mistelis, L.A. (2003). Comparative international commercial arbitration. *JDM Law.*

Mnookin, R. H. (1998). *Alternative dispute resolution.* CORE. core.ac.uk

Mohan, S. C. (2012). Cross-border Insolvency Problems: Is the UNCITRAL Model Law the Answer? [- Wiley Online Library]. *INSOL International Insolvency Review, 21*(3), 2012. doi:10.1002/iir.1203

Mondaq. (2016). *India: Evolution Of Arbitration In India.* MONDAQ. https://www.mondaq.com/india/arbitration-dispute-resolution

Moses, M. L. (2017). *The principles and practice of international commercial arbitration.* Research Gate. books.google.com

Nazzini, R. (2016). *The Law Applicable to the Arbitration.* Cambridge University Press & Assessment. https://www.cambridge.org

Nazzini, R. (2016). *The Law Applicable to the Arbitration.* JSTOR. https://www.jstor.org › stable

Nevisandeh, M. (2016). *The Nature of Arbitration Agreement.* Science Direct. https://www.sciencedirect.com

Nkwi, P. (1987). *Traditional Diplomacy: A Study of Inter-Chiefdom Relationships in the Western Grassfields, North West Province of Cameroon.* Yaoundé, Cameroon: Publication of the Department of Sociology, University of Yaoundé.

Nkwi, P., & Warnier, J.-P. (1982). *Elements for a History of the Western Grassfields.* SOPECAM.

Nyarko, J. (2019). We'll See You in the Court! The lack of arbitration clauses in international commercial contracts. *International Review of Law and Economics*, Elsevier.

Org, U. N. (2023). *Rule of Law and Democracy: Addressing the Gap.* UN. https://www.un.org

Overby, A. B. (1999). *Will Cyberlaw be uniform—an introduction to the uncitral model law on electronic commerce.* Tulsa Journal of International & Comparative Law, Hein Online.

Pareek, N. S. (2013). International commercial arbitration in India: governing law issues. *Uniform Law Review*. academic.oup.com

Paterson, R. K. (1993). *International Arbitration: Implementing the UNCITRAL Model Law*. Hein Online.

Paulsson, J. (1983). Delocalisation of international commercial arbitration: when and why it matters. *International & Comparative Law Quarterly*

Paulsson, J. (2011). The Freshfields guide to arbitration clauses in international contracts. Research Gate.

Paulsson, J. (2011). *The Freshfields Guide to Arbitration Clauses in International Contracts*. Research Gate.

Peerenboom, R. (2001). Seek truth from facts: An empirical study of enforcement of arbitral awards in the PRC. *The American Journal of Comparative Law*. academic.oup.com

Phua, M. (2020). *Distinctive status of international arbitration agreements*. Academic. https://academic.oup.com

Poorooye, A. (1958). *Confidentiality and Transparency in International Arbitration*. Harvard Negotiation Law Review. https://www.hnlr.org

Poudrette, & Besson, S, (2007). *Comparative law of international arbitration*.

Pryles, M. (1976). Comparative Aspects of Prorogation and Arbitration Agreements. *International & Comparative Law*. Cambridge Press.

Redfern, A & Hunter, M (2004). *Law and practice of international commercial arbitration*.

Reuben, R. C. (2006). *Confidentiality in Arbitration: Beyond the Myth University of Missouri*. Scholarship Law. https://scholarship.law.missouri.edu

Ridley-Duff, R, & Bennet, A, (2011). Towards mediation: developing a theoretical framework to understand alternative dispute resolution. *Industrial Relations Journal*.

Rigby, K. J. (1983). *Alternate Dispute Resolution, Los Angelas Law Review*. Hein Online.

Rivkin, D. W. (1993). *Enforceability of Arbitral Awards Based on Lex Mercatoria*, Arbitration International. academic.oup.com

Rolph, E. (1997). *Arbitration Agreements in Health Care: Myths and Reality*. Law and Contemporary Problems, Hein Online.

Rubino-Sammartano, M, (2014). *International Arbitration Law and Practice*. Research Gate.

Sabatino, J. M. (1998). *ADR as Litigation Lite: Procedural and Evidentiary Norms Embedded within Alternative Dispute Resolution*. Emory Law Journal, HeinOnline.

Sandrock, O. (1993). *Arbitration Agreements in Groups of Companies*. International Law, Hein Online.

Sarles, J. W. (2022). *Solving the Arbitral Confidentiality Conundrum in International Arbitration.*

Sayed, A. (2004). *Corruption in international trade and commercial arbitration.* Torrossa. torrossa.com

Schachter, O, (1960). The Enforcement of International Judicial and Arbitral Decisions. *American Journal of International Law*

Schmitz, A. J. (2010). *Legislating in the Light: Considering Empirical Data in Crafting Arbitration Reforms; Harvard.* Negotiation Law Review, Hein Online.

Schroeder, P. A. (2015). *Arbitrary numbers counter fair decisions.* National Institutes of Health. https://www.ncbi.nlm.nih.gov

Schwartz, D. S. (1997). *Enforcing small print to protect big business: employee and consumer rights claims in an age of compelled arbitration.* Wisconsin Law Review, Hein Online.

Sempasa, S.L. (1992). Obstacles to international commercial arbitration in African countries. *International & Comparative Law Quarterly.*

Shavell, S. (1995). Alternative dispute resolution: an economic analysis. *The Journal of Legal Studies*. journals.uchicago.edu

Sherman, E.F., (1992). Court-Mandated Alternative Dispute Resolution: What Form of Participation Should Be Required. *SMUL Review.*

Singer, D. C. (2020). *Arbitration Privacy and Confidentiality In the Age.* National Institutes of Health. https://www.ncbi.nlm.nih.gov

Somarajah, M, (1989). *Journal of International Arbitration.* Hein Online.

Sovern, J. (2015). *Whimsy little contracts with unexpected consequences: An empirical analysis of consumer understanding of arbitration agreements.* Maryland Law Review, Hein Online.

Steyn, J. (1994). *England's Response to the UNCITRAL Model Law of Arbitration.* Arbitration International. academic.oup.com

Stipanovich, TJ, (2004). ADR and the "Vanishing Trial": the growth and impact of "Alternative Dispute Resolution." *Journal of Empirical Legal Studies.*

Stipanowich, T.J. (2010). Arbitration: The new litigation. *University of Illinois, Law Review.* Hein Online.

Stone, K. V. W. (2004). *Alternative Dispute Resolution.* SSRN. papers.ssrn.com

Strazisar, B. (2018), Alternative Dispute Resolution, https://www.researchgate.net

Strong, S.I. (2012). Navigating the Borders Between International Commercial Arbitration and US Federal Courts: A Jurisprudential GPS. *Journal of Dispute Resolution,* Hein Online

Strong, S. I. (2014). *Beyond international commercial arbitration-the promise of international commercial mediation.* Washington University Journal of Law & Policy, Hein Online.

Teo, EAL, & Aibinu, AA, (2007). Legal framework for alternative dispute resolution: Examination of the Singapore national legal system for arbitration. *Journal of Professional Issues in Engineering.*

The History of International Commercial Arbitration - A Sketch. (2020). Abitraion Law. https://arbitrationlaw.com/library/history-international-commercial.

The Kom Heritage Foundation. (2014). *A Short Cultural History of the Kom People.* Bamenda: Destiny Prints.

Thilakarathna, K.A.A.N. (2021). *A Utopia or Reality: Possibility of Using the Proper Law.* Scientific Research Publishing.

Trunk, A, (2023). *Some Remarks on International Commercial Arbitration in the Region of the Caucasus and Central Asia.* Brill.

Tweeddale, A. (2002). *Confidentiality in Arbitration and the Public Interest Exception.* Corbett. corbett.co.uk, https://corbett.co.uk

Ugarte, R. (2010). *Journal of International Arbitration.* Winston & Strawn LLP, https://www.winston.com

Van den Berg, AJ, (2014). *Should the setting aside of the arbitral award be abolished?* International Centre for Settlement of Investment Disputes Review.

Van Ginkel, E. (2004). *Journal of International Arbitration.* Hein Online.

Vedantam, J. (2015). Four steps to conflict resolution from Ancient India. *Cloud Data Management, Analytics & Monetization.* Research Gate.

Vermeule, A. (2015). *Rationally Arbitrary Decisions in Administrative Law.* JSTOR. https://www.jstor.org

Vilkova, N. G. (1999). *Practice of the International Commercial Arbitration Court at the Chamber of Commerce and Industry of the Russian Federation.* academic.oup.com

Villiers, L. (2011). Breaking in the 'unruly horse': The status of mandatory rules of law as a public policy basis for the non-enforcement of Arbitral awards. *Australian International Law Journal*, search.informit.org

Vlahna, K, (2008). *Arbitration and the Importance of the Arbitration Agreement.* Dergi Park. dergipark.org.tr https://dergipark.org.tr

Ware, S. J. (2006). The Case for Enforcing Adhesive Arbitration Agreements-With Particular Consideration of Class Actions and Arbitration Fees. *Journal of American Arbitration*. papers.ssrn.com

Ware, S. J. (2006); The Case for Enforcing Adhesive Arbitration Agreements-With Particular Consideration of Class Actions and Arbitration Fees. *Journal of American Arbitration*. papers.ssrn.com

Ware, S.J. (2001). Paying the Price of Process: Judicial Regulation of Consumer Arbitration Agreements. *Journal of Dispute Resolution*, Hein Online.

Warner. (2022). Arbitrary grounding. Springer. https://link.springer.com

Westermann, W. L. (1907). Interstate Arbitration in Antiquity. The Classical Journal, 2(5). The Classical Association of the Middle West and South, Inc. (CAMWS)

Wolaver, E. S. (1934). *The Historical Background of Commercial Arbitration*. UPenn.

Xu, S. (2008). *Are decisions "Arbitrary" in our International Business*. Research Gate. https://www.researchgate.net

Yang, T. J. (2020). Ascertaining the Proper Law of an Arbitration Agreement. *Kluwer Law Online*. https://kluwerlawonline.com › JOIA2020030

Yoshida, I. (2009, September 1). History of International Commercial Arbitration and its Related System in Russia. *Arbitration International*, *25*(3), 365–402. doi:10.1093/arbitration/25.3.365

Yu, H. L. (2021). *The duty of confidentiality within the global landscape*. University of Stirling. https://dspace.stir.ac.uk

Yuksel, B, (2011). The Relevance of the Rome I Regulation to International Commercial Arbitration in the European Union. *Journal of Private International Law*. Taylor & Francis.

Zafarovich, T.S. (2022). Different Approaches in Enforcement of Arbitral Award Annulled at the Place of Arbitration. Miasto Przyszłości;.

Zamoff, M. (2022). *Safeguarding Confidential Arbitration Awards*. Wiley. https://onlinelibrary.wiley.com

Zhang, T. (2013). *Enforceability of ad hoc arbitration agreements in China: China's incomplete ad hoc arbitration system*. Cornell International Law Journal, Hein Online.

About the Authors

Khan Basheer Ahmed Mohammed, Supreme Court of India Bar Association, New Delhi, India, holds his Ph.D. and D.Litt. degrees besides MBA and Law Degrees and has been teaching for over five decades in different Universities in India like Pune, Pondicherry, Dumka, and Middle East. He has graduated over 54 doctorates from various universities in India and abroad. He is currently a litigating lawyer in different Indian Courts.

Kaushal Kishore holds an MBA and Law degrees and has been litigating for nearly a decade in the different courts of law in India. He is currently a member of the Supreme Court of India Bar Association, New Delhi, India.

Index

A

B

C

D

E

F

G

H

I

J

L

M

N

P

S

www.ingramcontent.com/pod-product-compliance
Lightning Source LLC
LaVergne TN
LVHW081329300926
849161LV00008B/1923